D1283346

The New York Times

LITTLE LUXE BOOK OF CROSSWORDS

The New York Times

LITTLE LUXE BOOK OF CROSSWORDS

Edited by Will Shortz

ST. MARTIN'S GRIFFIN ❧ NEW YORK

THE NEW YORK TIMES LITTLE LUXE BOOK OF CROSSWORDS.
Copyright © 2008 by The New York Times Company. All rights
reserved.
Printed in China. For information, address St. Martin's Press,
175 Fifth Avenue, New York, N.Y. 10010.

www.stmartins.com

All of the puzzles that appear in this work were originally published
in *The New York Times* from April 25, 2007, to November 30, 2007.
Copyright © 2007 by The New York Times Company.
All rights reserved. Reprinted by permission.

ISBN-13: 978-0-312-38622-1
ISBN-10: 0-312-38622-2

First Edition: October 2008

10   9   8   7   6   5   4

DIFFICULTY KEY

Easy: ★

Moderate: ★ ★

Hard: ★ ★ ★

The New York Times

LITTLE LUXE BOOK OF CROSSWORDS

1

ACROSS

1 Clothing
5 It's arched above the eye
9 iPhone maker
14 Creme-filled cookie
15 Wine: Prefix
16 Burger side order
17 Bean-filled bag moved with the foot
19 Expire, as a subscription
20 Honor bestowed by Queen Eliz.
21 Farm unit
22 Bowling alley divisions
23 Postcard sentiment
25 Comedy club razzer
27 Simple
28 Electric cord's end
30 Where dirty dishes pile up
31 Say "Do this," "Do that" . . . blah, blah, blah

34 Border on
36 Prefix with classical
37 Like some hams
41 Fishing pole
42 Loads
43 Id's counterpart
44 Beverages in barrels
46 Fall
48 Statutes
52 Pop artist David
54 Bucharest's land
57 Gather, as information
58 Opposite of fall
59 Auto gizmo that talks, for short
60 Scarecrow's wish in "The Wizard of Oz"
61 2004 film "I ♥ ___"
63 ___ living
64 On the briny
65 Like a first-place ribbon
66 "What ___!" ("It's so dirty!")

67 Dakota ___ (old geog. designation)
68 Depletes, as strength

DOWN

1 "Get out of here!"
2 Where Saudis live
3 Nook
4 ___ choy (Chinese green)
5 Chocolate syrup brand
6 Stand on the hind legs, as a horse
7 "___ upon a time . . ."
8 Chinese cooking vessel
9 Insurance co. with a "spokesduck"
10 Throwing cream pies and such
11 Oil conveyor
12 Abated
13 180° from WNW
18 "That's great news!"
22 Peanut, e.g.

24 Out of ___ (not harmonizing)
25 Parts of cars with caps
26 Early MGM rival
29 ___ rest (bury)
32 Letters before an alias
33 Flax-colored
35 Dress (up)
37 3-D picture
38 "You don't say!," after "Well"
39 Actor Calhoun
40 Kind of nut
41 Stadium cry
45 Balls of yarn
47 Person comparing costs
49 Actress Lansbury
50 Use a paper towel
51 Gives some lip
53 Grandmas
55 Schindler of "Schindler's List"

by Andrea Carla Michaels

56 ___ culpa
58 Subterfuge
60 Actress
Arthur
61 Sombrero,
e.g.
62 Kids' ammo

2

ACROSS
1 Bit of smoke
5 "Jeepers!"
11 Burton who produced "The Nightmare Before Christmas"
14 Popular plant gel
15 Native name for Mount McKinley
16 Long-distance number starter
17 Subversive group
19 Buddy
20 Four: Prefix
21 QB Manning
22 Repulsive
23 Soap or lotion, say
27 Searched
29 Gardner of Hollywood
30 Debtor's promise
31 Wise ones
34 Suspect's excuse
38 ___ Ness monster

40 Where you may find the ends of 17-, 23-, 52- and 63-Across
42 Social slight
43 Actor Hawke
45 Sirius or XM medium
47 Three: Prefix
48 No ___, ands or buts
50 Furry burrowers
52 Notorious stigma
57 Umpteen
58 Fish eggs
59 Mullah's teaching
62 Traveler's stopover
63 Coveted film honor
66 Stocking's tip
67 Hardly hip
68 Drooling dog in "Garfield"
69 Evil spell
70 Freshman's topper
71 Spiffy

DOWN
1 Blow gently
2 Tennis champ Nastase
3 One who'll easily lend money for a hard-luck story
4 Fuel by the litre
5 U.S. health promoter: Abbr.
6 Auto last made in the 1930s
7 Shoreline opening
8 Newswoman Zahn
9 New York city where Mark Twain is buried
10 What it is "to tell a lie"
11 Subject of discussion
12 With everything counted
13 Fracas
18 Flags down, as a taxi

22 Pharmacy containers
24 Vault
25 Ventriloquist Bergen
26 Big electrical project inits.
27 Mah-jongg piece
28 Underlying cause
32 Fed. air quality monitor
33 Marsh plant
35 Period between
36 Jefferson's first vice president
37 Curve-billed wader
39 Hirsute
41 Real sidesplitter
44 Org. for Colts and Broncos
46 Eye-related
49 Calm
51 Charlton of "The Ten Commandments"
52 Suffix with black or silver

by Lynn Lempel

53 It gets a
paddling
54 Building
add-on
55 Puccini
opera
56 Pretend

60 Met highlight
61 Assemble
63 Fella
64 Hawaiian
dish
65 ___ du Diable

3

ACROSS

1 Pear variety
5 Filthy place
11 Mardi ___
15 Paul who sang "Puppy Love"
16 Win over
17 Bringing up the rear
18 "Floral" film that was the Best Picture of 1989
21 Ran into
22 Some ales
23 Wilderness photographer Adams
24 Quit, with "out"
25 Glossy alternative
26 "Again!"
27 Gave utterance to
29 Customers
30 Celtic dialect
31 Regional dialect
34 "Floral" film of 2006 with Josh Hartnett and Scarlett Johansson
40 Cowboy contests
41 "SportsCenter" channel
43 Feudal workers
47 Traveling group of actors
49 Motown's Franklin
50 Newspapers, TV, radio, etc.
53 Teacher's favorite
54 "Get lost!"
55 System of government
56 La ___, Bolivia
57 "Floral" film of 1986 based on an Umberto Eco novel
60 Swedish soprano Jenny
61 Like some inspections
62 ___-friendly
63 "For" votes
64 Shorthand takers
65 Fictional detective Wolfe

DOWN

1 "You'll regret that!"
2 Written up, as to a superior
3 Easily startled
4 Cleveland cager, for short
5 Group of five
6 Bar of gold
7 Entire range
8 Slug, old-style
9 ___ and turn
10 1812, 2001, etc.: Abbr.
11 Quick look
12 ___ d'être
13 State with conviction
14 Shag, beehive, updo, etc.
19 "Woe ___!"
20 From Copenhagen, e.g.
26 Kazan who directed "On the Waterfront"
28 Grade between bee and dee
29 Atlantic swimmers
31 Cushions
32 Hole-in-one
33 W.B.A. decision
35 The Creator, to Hindus
36 Name repeated in "Whatever ___ wants, ___ gets"
37 Virgo's predecessor
38 Noncommittal agreement
39 One who's making nice
42 EarthLink alternative
43 To a huge degree
44 Jughead's pal
45 One of tennis's Williams sisters
46 Bleachers
47 Gives 10% to the church
48 Funnywoman Martha

by Harvey Estes

50 Bullwinkle,
   e.g.
51 Spritelike
52 "Me, too"
55 Shut (up)
58 Calendar
   pgs.
59 Hurry

ACROSS

1 "Lady Marmalade" singer ___ LaBelle
6 Musical phrase
10 On the briny
14 Birdlike
15 Poet ___ Khayyám
16 Butter slices
17 T. S. Eliot title character who measures out his life with coffee spoons
20 Not just recent
21 Muck
22 "The Simpsons" bartender
23 Light throw
26 Studio sign
29 Actress MacDowell of "Groundhog Day"
32 Really impressed
34 Geller with a spoon-bending act
35 Light golden lager
38 ___ Bator, Mongolia
39 Editor out to smear Spider-Man
42 Parti-colored
43 Dance class outfit
44 Quantity: Abbr.
45 Sheep cries
46 Rapids transits
50 A goose egg
52 Phobia
55 Unfortunate sound when you bend over
56 Hay storage locale
58 Saw-toothed
61 Vice president who once famously mashed "potato"
65 Come to shore
66 Baby bassoon?
67 War horse
68 Lyric poems
69 Puppy bites
70 Sexy nightwear

DOWN

1 ___ party (sleepover)
2 Frankie of "Beach Blanket Bingo"
3 Cultivated the soil
4 President who later served as chief justice
5 Initials on a cross
6 Where you might hear "Ride 'em, cowboy!"
7 Little devil
8 Distant
9 Lively '60s dance
10 Kitchen spill catcher
11 Brazil's largest city
12 And so on: Abbr.
13 "___ and ye shall receive"
18 CPR pro
19 Grocery offering
24 California city in a 1968 Dionne Warwick hit
25 Accumulation on the brow
27 Persia, today
28 ___ Tin Tin
30 Its first ad touted "1,000 songs in your pocket"
31 German article
33 Humorist Bombeck
36 Singsong syllables
37 Grain bundle
38 Beef quality graders: Abbr.
39 Guitarist Hendrix
40 747, e.g.
41 Be mistaken
42 La ___, Bolivia
45 Hit, as on the noggin
47 Worn at the edges
48 Like the Marquis de Sade or the Duke of Earl
49 Rapid
51 Unilever skin cream brand
53 Fireplace remnants

by Jeremy Horwitz

54 Necessary: Abbr.

57 Roger Rabbit or Donald Duck

59 Corrosion sign

60 Appraise

61 Female singer's 2001 album that debuted at #1

62 "Dear old" guy

63 Slugger's stat

64 Blouse or shirt

5

ACROSS
1 Started a cigarette
6 Sail supporter
10 Rooters
14 Left one's seat
15 Gumbo vegetable
16 Track shape
17 Allotment of heredity units?
19 Parks who pioneered in civil rights
20 Our language: Abbr.
21 Took the blue ribbon
22 Room to maneuver
24 Nuclear power apparatus
27 Top 10 tunes
28 Hole-punching tool
29 Slender cigar
33 Prefix with -hedron
36 Is false to the world
37 Get from ___ (progress slightly)
38 Battle of the ___ (men vs. women)
39 Stadium section
40 Studied primarily, at college
42 Holder of 88 keys
43 Caveman's era
44 Vintage automotive inits.
45 Tennis great Arthur
46 Mediums' meetings
50 Stewed to the gills
53 King Kong, e.g.
54 Lacto-___-vegetarian
55 Sitarist Shankar
56 Preacher's sky-high feeling?
60 Twistable cookie
61 Turn at roulette
62 Decaf brand
63 Give an alert
64 Direction of sunup
65 Sticky problem

DOWN
1 Hearty brew
2 Jim Carrey comedy "Me, Myself & ___"
3 Kingdom east of Fiji
4 Milk for all its worth
5 Pay-___-view
6 Travel by car
7 Closely related (to)
8 Sign at a sellout
9 Bikini wearers' markings
10 TV channel for golfers?
11 State frankly
12 Shuttle-launching org.
13 Murder
18 Delinquent G.I.
23 Greek H's
25 Pasta-and-potato-loving country?
26 Former rival of Pan Am
27 Safe place
29 Mischievous sprite
30 Director Kazan
31 Claim on property
32 Prefix with dynamic
33 Scots' caps
34 Coup d'___
35 Japanese P.M. during W.W. II
36 Mantel
38 Equine-looking fish
41 Take a siesta
42 Split ___ soup
44 Fishing line winder
46 Paid out
47 Nickels and dimes
48 Call to mind
49 Sunken ship finder
50 Furrowed part of the head
51 Dr. Zhivago's love
52 1964 Dave Clark Five song "Glad All ___"

by Fred Piscop

53 Hertz rival
57 Mileage rating org.
58 Cleopatra's biter
59 Eastern "way"

6

ACROSS

1 Does sums
5 Pillow filler
9 Flapper hairdos
13 Scuttlebutt
14 Like a manly man
15 Escapade
16 Part of the eye that holds the iris
17 ___ and pains
18 What "thumbs up" means
19 Bandleader in the Polka Music Hall of Fame
22 Explosive initials
23 Pinocchio, famously
24 Mock
28 Dance with a wiggle
30 Lord
31 Card that's taken only by a trump
32 Mail carriers' assignments: Abbr.
34 Creamy soup
38 City where van Gogh painted sunflowers
40 Suffix with sucr- and lact-
41 Pacific republic
42 Substantial portion
45 Pile
46 Component of bronze
47 Permit
48 Washington's Capitol ___
50 Precipitates at about 32°F
52 Left hurriedly
54 New Deal program inits.
57 One who lost what's hidden in 19-, 34- and 42-Across
60 Hawaiian isle
63 More than perturbed
64 "Unfortunately . . ."
65 Give a hard time
66 Nobodies
67 Small field size
68 Branch of Islam
69 Plow pullers
70 Jean who wrote "Wide Sargasso Sea"

DOWN

1 No longer a minor
2 Couch
3 Made a stand and would go no further
4 Polaris, e.g.
5 Bangladesh's capital, old-style
6 Color of fall leaves
7 "Thank goodness!"
8 Rhinoplasty
9 Chap
10 Tree loved by squirrels
11 Maidenform product
12 Cloud's site
14 Psycho
20 90° turn
21 Ushered
25 "Fantastic Voyage" actress
26 Honda division
27 Get ready to drive, in golf
29 ___-friendly
30 Agents under J. Edgar Hoover, informally
32 Balsa transports
33 Path
35 Booty
36 Tempe sch.
37 Comedian Mort
39 1972 U.S./ U.S.S.R. missile pact
43 Latin American with mixed ancestry
44 Oedipus' realm
49 Wedding vow
51 Doolittle of "My Fair Lady"
52 Distress signal shot into the air
53 Divulge
55 Explorer who proved that Greenland is an island
56 Basilica recesses
58 Fearsome dino
59 Jack of early late-night TV
60 ___ Butterworth's

by Lynn Lempel

61 What a
doctor
might
ask you
to say
62 Israeli gun

ACROSS

1 Indifferent to pleasure or pain
6 Close
10 Jacket
14 Toyota rival
15 Impulse
16 ___ of office
17 Taking back one's words in humiliation
19 "Oh, that's what you mean"
20 Excitement
21 ___-de-sac
22 Receiver of a legal transfer
24 Actress Zellweger
26 Anger
27 Negotiating in a no-nonsense way
32 Baby kangaroos
34 Joel who directed "Raising Arizona"
35 "These ___ the times that . . ."
36 One-named Art Deco designer
37 Vehicles in airplane aisles
39 "Love ___ the air"
40 Big elephant feature
41 Theater award
42 Prayers' ends
43 Pretending to be dead
47 The "et" of et cetera
48 Lock of hair
49 Rip off
53 Moo goo ___ pan
54 Ewe's call
57 Supervising
58 Raising a false alarm
61 Roman statesman ___ the Elder
62 Daylight saving, e.g.
63 ___ Rae (Sally Field title role)
64 Didn't just guess
65 Locales of mineral waters
66 Say with one's hand on the Bible

DOWN

1 New York stadium
2 Relative of a frog
3 Seeing through the deception of
4 Dictator Amin
5 Calls off
6 Cell centers
7 Misplay, e.g.
8 Slack-jawed
9 Edits
10 Neologist
11 Kiln
12 Suit to ___
13 Biblical pronoun
18 Sticky matter
23 Give ___ for one's money
24 Comedic actress Martha
25 Put into cipher
27 Four: Prefix
28 "___ Milk?"
29 Casey with a radio countdown
30 Land o' blarney
31 Achings
32 Army transport
33 Spoken
37 Leads, as an orchestra
38 "Hulk" director Lee
39 Don with a big mouth
41 One of the Sinatras
42 Hands out, as duties
44 Peter of Peter, Paul & Mary
45 Unrestrained revelries
46 Actor Penn
49 Marina fixture
50 "___ Almighty," 2007 film
51 Honor with a roast, say
52 What icicles do
54 Drill

by Andrea Carla Michaels

55 ___ mater
56 Many
miles
away
59 Singer
Sumac
60 "Man alive!"

8

ACROSS
1 Witty sorts
5 Make sense
10 Choice word
14 Think tank nugget
15 On the lam
16 Gerund, e.g.
17 Bond villain
19 Saw red?
20 Ph.D. thesis: Abbr.
21 Gets corroded
22 Bemoan
25 "Beats me" gesture
28 Rub out
29 Certain trout
33 Basis of a suit
34 Endless, poetically
35 Fraternity P
36 "Survivor" shelter
37 Some red wines
38 Obey the coxswain
39 Cheroot residue
40 Wings it
41 Place for a hoedown
42 Classic blues musician
44 Intuit
45 The "35" in John 11:35
46 Prodded
47 Woods or Irons
50 Flair
51 Laugh heartily
52 Patriarchal gorilla
58 Pond organism
59 Primp
60 Natural soother
61 Lounge in the sun
62 Feel nostalgia, e.g.
63 Crips or Bloods

DOWN
1 Faux 'fro?
2 Brouhaha
3 Goo in a do
4 Most mournful
5 Most-wanted group for a party
6 Puts on
7 Follow everywhere
8 Put to work
9 Part of r.p.m.
10 "Stop!"
11 Wall Street minimums
12 Fatty treat for birds
13 Pulls the plug on
18 Ticket cost?
21 Game sheet
22 Deadly
23 Work up
24 First first lady
25 Germ-free
26 As a result of this
27 Patronizes U-Haul, e.g.
29 Plays for time
30 Gofer's job
31 When repeated, cry by Shakespeare's Richard III
32 Consumed heartily
34 Octogenarian, for one
37 Pole tossed by Scots
41 Nontraditional chair style
43 Czech composer Antonin
44 Go up, up, up
46 Filmdom's Close
47 Omani, e.g.
48 Fast-food drink
49 Makes "it"
50 ". . . ___ after"
52 U-2 pilot, e.g.
53 Ill temper
54 Grazing ground
55 Carte start
56 Bamboozle
57 Fraternity party setup

by Steve Kahn

9

ACROSS

1 Wager
4 Gush
10 Willie of the 1950s–'60s Giants
14 Israeli submachine gun
15 Last words of the Pledge of Allegiance
16 ___ vera
17 Atomic energy org.
18 *Popular Sunshine State vacation destination
20 Prepare to shoot
22 Docs
23 Stop for the night, as soldiers
25 Daughter's counterpart
26 Dartboard, for one
28 The "I" of I.M.F.: Abbr.
30 Austrian affirmatives
33 "The Thin Man" pooch
34 Rim
36 Put (down), as money
38 Theater focal point
40 Select, with "for"
41 Language akin to Urdu
42 Serious drinker
43 Arnaz of "I Love Lucy"
45 Depression-era migrant
46 "But I heard him exclaim, ___ he drove . . ."
47 Take too much of, briefly
49 Objected to
51 Brouhaha
52 Keep just below a boil
54 Not deceitful
58 Deck covering to keep out moisture
61 *Like players below the B team
63 "This means ___!"
64 Sets of points, in math
65 "Relax, soldier!"
66 U.K. record label
67 Newspaper essay
68 Mascara goes on them
69 King, in old Rome

DOWN

1 Part of a suicide squeeze
2 Poet Pound
3 *Material for an old-fashioned parade
4 Wipe off
5 Decorate with leaves
6 Erich who wrote "The Art of Loving"
7 Bygone Mideast inits.
8 Slender
9 Firstborn
10 "___ Whoopee!" (1920s hit)
11 One of the Baldwin brothers
12 Toy that might go "around the world"
13 Period in Cong.
19 Coach Rupp of college basketball
21 Take on
24 *Sties
26 One of the five senses
27 Fur trader John Jacob ___
29 Basketball rim attachments
30 Location for the ends of the answers to the four starred clues
31 Actress MacDowell
32 Schussed, e.g.
35 Dumbbell
37 Hampton of jazz fame
39 Wore away
44 Really, really big
48 ___ fin
50 Represen-tations
51 Pungent
53 N.B.A. coach Thomas
54 Normandy town

by Allan E. Parrish

55 Breakfast
   restaurant
   letters
56 "Good shot!"
57 Kett of
   old comics

59 Designate
60 Cereal whose
   ads feature a
   "silly rabbit"
62 ___ ipsa
   loquitur

ACROSS

1 Put out, as a fire
6 Furry TV extraterrestrial
9 Arouse, as interest
14 "In my opinion . . ."
15 Place for sheep to graze
16 Mrs. Bush
17 Utensil used with flour
18 Perry Mason's field
19 Out of kilter
20 Old "Tonight Show" intro
23 Fork over
24 Word after show or know
25 Bygone Rambler mfr.
27 Classic arcade game
31 Set free
36 Pungent-smelling
37 Expensive tooth filling material
38 Sport with beefy grapplers
39 Admonition to a showboating athlete
42 Notes after do
43 Doll's cry
44 Almost any doo-wop tune
45 What a driver's license shows proof of
47 Makes tough
48 Understood
49 By way of
50 "Cheers" bartender
53 Kid's book with a hidden character
60 Atlantic or Pacific
62 Buddhist sect
63 Squirrel away
64 Suspect's story
65 Stephen of "The Crying Game"
66 Out of favor, informally
67 Derby prize
68 The whole shebang
69 Activities in 57-Down

DOWN

1 Satellite TV receiver
2 Garfield's pal, in the funnies
3 ___-friendly (simple to operate)
4 Put money in the bank
5 Poker player's headgear
6 Give the O.K.
7 Wife of Jacob
8 Young Bambi
9 Bench-warmer's plea
10 The Beatles' "___ the Walrus"
11 Wit's remark
12 Celestial bear
13 "Piece of cake!"
21 Rock's Bon Jovi
22 Nita of silent films
26 Windsor, notably
27 Father: Prefix
28 Felt sore
29 Oreo's filling
30 Sinking in mud
31 Hardly cramped
32 Director Kazan
33 Napped leather
34 Cyber-messages
35 Stadium toppers
37 Pesky swarmer
40 Most common U.S. surname
41 Zero
46 Local noncollegian, to a collegian
47 Bro's sibling
49 Open to bribery
50 Suds maker
51 Rights org.
52 Golda of Israel
54 Poet Pound

by Fred Piscop

11

ACROSS

1 With 68-Across, bell ringer
5 Doing nothing
9 Speechify
14 Fashion designer Rabanne
15 Vehicle on tracks
16 Pugilist
17 No. on a bank statement
18 Grotto
19 Material for Elvis's blue shoes
20 Bell ringer
23 "California, ___ Come"
24 Spouse's meek agreement
28 See 52-Across
29 Cy Young Award winner Blue
33 Home that may have a live-in butler
34 Less certain
36 Archaeological site
37 Bell ringer
41 Go backpacking
42 Inside info for an investor, maybe
43 Sheep's cries
46 Unskilled laborer
47 Ordinal suffix
50 Kids' game involving an unwanted card
52 With 28-Across, winner of golf's 1997 U.S. Open
54 Bell ringer
58 Org.
61 Club that's not a wood
62 Al or Tipper
63 Book after Jonah
64 Emperor who reputedly fiddled while Rome burned
65 God of love
66 "Lord, ___?" (biblical query)
67 Pop music's Bee ___
68 See 1-Across

DOWN

1 Geronimo's tribe
2 Poet Lindsay
3 Happens
4 ___ Dame
5 Poison ivy symptom
6 Sketch
7 ___ lamp (1960s novelty)
8 Manicurist's item
9 Dwell (on)
10 Point A to point B and back
11 Firefighter's tool
12 Slugger Williams
13 "Able was I ___ I saw Elba"
21 Honda model
22 Joey with the Starliters
25 Waters, informally
26 Going ___ (fighting)
27 Stimpy's cartoon pal
30 Post-op spot, for short
31 One running away with a spoon, in a children's rhyme
32 Greek fabulist
34 Heartthrob
35 Baptism or bar mitzvah
37 Bit of medicine
38 Squeezed (out)
39 Palindromic tribe name
40 Forty-___ (gold rush participant)
41 "Curb Your Enthusiasm" airer
44 Chinese martial art
45 "___ 'em!"
47 "Bewitched" witch
48 Steering system component
49 Religious dissent
51 Faulkner's "As I Lay ___"
53 Star in Orion
55 Native Canadian

by Sarah Keller

56 Stories passed down through generations

57 1961 space chimp

58 Pal in Paris

59 ___ boom bah

60 Lab field: Abbr.

12

ACROSS
1 Nightfall
5 Sonnet and sestina
10 The Beatles' "Back in the ___"
14 Korea's continent
15 Kind of ink
16 Artsy N.Y.C. locale
17 Many a Westminster show exhibitor
19 Aliens' craft, for short
20 Parrot
21 Makes a cartoon of
23 Robin or swallow
25 Swiss peak
26 Shepherd's domain
29 Mathematician John von ___
33 Play part
36 ___ Remus
38 Predestination
39 Cabbage salad

40 Features found in 17- and 64-Across and 11- and 28-Down
43 Hydrochloric ___
44 ___ noire
45 Sir or madam
46 The "r" in Aristotle
47 It is golden, it's said
49 Superlative ending
50 Louse-to-be
52 Ayatollah's predecessor
54 Walked unsteadily
59 "Lose Yourself" rapper
63 Sailor's greeting
64 Longtime Wal-Mart symbol
66 Grain grinder
67 Tarzan's transports
68 Fox TV's "American ___"
69 Gallup sampling

70 Shareholder's substitute
71 Beach composition

DOWN
1 Miami-___ County, Fla.
2 Quadrennial games org.
3 Sound of relief
4 Skewered lamb, e.g.
5 South Dakota's capital
6 Word before "ignition . . . liftoff!"
7 Icelandic epic
8 Demeanor
9 Wrap for Indira Gandhi
10 Everyday
11 Rear of the roof of the mouth
12 Home for an "old woman" in a nursery rhyme
13 Seamstress Betsy
18 Queens of France

22 Homo sapiens
24 Camper's bag
26 Kind of eclipse
27 Cain's eldest son
28 G.I. Joe, for one
30 Dull photo finish
31 Parthenon's home
32 Born: Fr.
34 Charges on a telephone bill
35 Little bird's sound
37 Ushered
39 Biol. or chem.
41 Geisha's sash
42 Like a sauna room
47 Jeanne d'Arc, e.g.: Abbr.
48 Shabby
51 Pastoral composition
53 Old 45 players
54 Wettish
55 Birthplace of seven U.S. presidents

by Edward M. Sessa

13

ACROSS

1 Exercises sometimes done cross-legged
5 Basement's opposite
10 Place for a ship to come in
14 Rightmost bridge position
15 Grand Canyon transport
16 Western native
17 Base for turkey stuffing, often
19 Wagering parlors, for short
20 Madison Square Garden is one
21 On ___ (when challenged)
22 J. R. of "Dallas"
25 Leave furtively
28 Taoism founder
30 New Balance competitor
31 Opposed to
32 They're seen at marble tournaments
35 What the easiest path offers
41 Waiting to be mailed
42 "O.G. Original Gangster" rapper
43 Items in a "bank"
46 Off course
48 Long-lasting housetop
51 Thrill
52 Appointed
53 Native of Tehran
55 "___ cost you!"
56 Sob stories
61 Orange throwaway
62 Miserable weather
63 Cash drawer
64 This, to Tomás
65 Pal
66 Cherry throwaway

DOWN

1 "Sure thing!"
2 Morsel for Dobbin
3 Overseer of govt. office bldgs.
4 Legendary sunken island
5 French cleric
6 Blinkers signal them
7 "My ___" (dinner host's offer)
8 Levin who wrote "Rosemary's Baby"
9 Fish-and-chips fish
10 Thingamajig
11 Canada's capital
12 Snake charmers' snakes
13 "One Flew Over the Cuckoo's Nest" author Ken
18 Work units
21 Preferred invitees
22 Carrier to Tel Aviv
23 Decrease gradually
24 Greek "I"
26 Have a home-cooked meal, say
27 "___ Fideles"
29 Salary recipient
33 Painting surface
34 Enzyme ending
36 Like a good-sounding piano
37 Emergency military transports
38 Annual hoops championship organizer, for short
39 Penny
40 Suffix with marion
43 Stack in a kitchen cabinet
44 "To be or not to be" speaker
45 Verdi opera
47 City near Lake Tahoe

by Sarah Keller

14

ACROSS
1 It's rounded up in a roundup
5 Propel a bicycle
10 Pinnacle
14 Hawaii's "Valley Isle"
15 "__ Get Your Gun"
16 Linen fiber
17 Operation for a new liver or kidney
20 Home (in on)
21 Mao __-tung
22 That woman
23 "The Sweetheart of Sigma __"
26 Refuses to
28 Encourages
30 Jane who wrote "Sense and Sensibility"
32 Take home a trophy
34 Beer component
35 Swains
36 Cry after a bad swing
37 Decorates, as a cake

38 Beneficial substance in fruits, vegetables and tea
41 Feature of many a wedding dress
43 Picking __ with
44 Alto or soprano
47 Letter-shaped building support
48 Small number
49 Yuletide songs
50 Mortarboard addition
52 Face-to-face test
54 Puppy's bite
55 Inventor Whitney
56 Grain in Cheerios
58 Great-great-great-great-great grandfather of Noah
60 Literary genre popular with women

66 Shortly
67 Message from a BlackBerry, maybe
68 Tiny critters found twice each in 17-, 38- and 60-Across
69 Impose, as a tax
70 Car dings
71 Yuletide

DOWN
1 Insurance grp.
2 Where a phone is held
3 Oriental __
4 Actress Cameron
5 Sponsor
6 Company with a spectacular 2001 bankruptcy
7 Reproductive material
8 "__ it the truth!"
9 Made smaller
10 C.I.O.'s partner
11 Kind of suit

12 Street opening for a utility worker
13 Spreads
18 Most recent
19 Place to hang one's hat
23 Taxi
24 Shade
25 "I, Robot" author
27 Four
29 Key of Saint-Saëns's "Danse macabre"
31 Radio receiver parts
33 Eye part
36 __ gras
39 Puffed up
40 King Arthur's burial place
41 Without metaphor
42 Mother-of-pearl source
45 151, in old Rome
46 Telepathy, e.g.
49 "Streets" of Venice
51 Period in history
53 Size again

by Steven Ginzburg

57 It heals all wounds, in a saying
59 ___ Lee of Marvel Comics
61 One or more
62 Soup container
63 Year, in Spain
64 Sault ___ Marie
65 Fashion inits.

15

ACROSS
1 Town known for witch trials
6 __-friendly
10 Jane Austen heroine
14 Politician who wrote "The Audacity of Hope"
15 Senate errand runner
16 Authentic
17 Fortune-seeking trio
19 Formerly
20 Hrs. in a Yankee schedule
21 Mimicked
22 Feels sorry for
24 Hits the roof
26 Brought to ruin
27 Barely make, with "out"
28 Peru-Bolivia border lake
31 Mosey along
34 Walnut or willow
35 Oozy roofing material
36 Grass-eating trio
40 One of the Manning quarterbacks
41 Giant birds of lore
42 Brain sections
43 Pedestrian's intersection warning
46 Soccer Hall of Famer Hamm
47 Exclamations of annoyance
48 Took a load off one's feet
52 Respectful tribute
54 War on drugs fighter
55 China's Chairman __
56 Enthusiastic
57 Gift-giver's trio
60 Frilly material
61 Pint, inch or second
62 Bird on the Great Seal of the United States
63 Ran away from
64 Turner of "Peyton Place," 1957
65 Sticks around

DOWN
1 They're always underfoot
2 Put up with
3 Coffee concoction
4 Aid provider to the critically injured, briefly
5 "Nonsense!"
6 Increased
7 Uttered
8 Omelet ingredient
9 Peaceful interludes
10 Titillating
11 Trio at sea
12 Riot-control spray
13 Draft picks in pubs
18 Fencing sword
23 Amin of Africa
25 Peddle
26 Food regimens
28 Racecourse
29 Casual eatery
30 Obedience school sounds
31 In the sack
32 Venus de __
33 Trio on the run
34 Hammers and hoes
37 Appreciative
38 Minor hang-ups
39 Highway or byway
44 Sent to another team
45 Jokester
46 Painter Chagall
48 December list keeper
49 Alpha's opposite
50 In a weak manner
51 Sniffers
52 50%
53 Football-shaped
54 Dresden denial

by Lynn Lempel

58 Cell's
protein
producer
59 Item with a
brim or
crown

16

ACROSS
1 "Woe is me!"
5 With 72-Across, the end of 20-, 37-, 44- or 59-Across
10 Scribbles
14 Hiker's snack
15 Els of the links
16 Stuntmaster Knievel
17 Et ___ (and others)
18 Prices
19 Like a Playmate of the Month
20 1951 Montgomery Clift/ Elizabeth Taylor film, with "A"
23 English county on the North Sea
24 Buckeyes' sch.
25 Place to wrestle
28 Kindergarten learning
32 Whinny
34 Missions, for short
37 Venus
40 Puppyish
42 Gullible
43 Suffix with cigar
44 Place to do business in the Old West
47 Use a Singer
48 Take ___ at (try)
49 Mlle., in Madrid
50 Luau souvenir
51 Goddess of the dawn
54 Lick of fire
59 1987 Prince song and album
64 Milliners' output
66 Scott who wrote "Presumed Innocent"
67 Dog that's a little of this, a little of that
68 Cotton swab
69 In unison
70 "That's clear"
71 Anatomical pouches
72 See 5-Across
73 "___ of the D'Urbervilles"

DOWN
1 Wide open, as the mouth
2 Lazes
3 Operatic solos
4 Cinnamon or cloves
5 Tenth: Prefix
6 Elvis's middle name
7 Part of M.I.T.: Abbr.
8 Many an art print, for short
9 Affirmatives
10 Bach's "___, Joy of Man's Desiring"
11 Hand protectors for bakers
12 It's between La. and N.M.
13 Using trickery
21 What a student crams for
22 Like lyrics
26 Playing marble
27 Passed
29 East Berlin's counterpart during the cold war
30 Rugged rock formation
31 Sounds in a barbershop
33 Opposite of WNW
34 In base eight
35 Total prize money
36 Earned run average, e.g.
38 Actor/ composer Novello
39 Hatchling's site
41 Author LeShan
45 "___ to differ"
46 President before Wilson
52 Not in bottles, as beer
53 Man of many marches
55 Maximum or minimum
56 Make laugh
57 Doles (out)
58 ___ Park, Colo.

by Andrew Ries

60 AOL and Road Runner: Abbr.
61 Too much: Fr.
62 Fine-tune
63 Still-life object
64 Mil. command bases
65 One ___ time

17

ACROSS
1 Do very well (at)
6 Alabama march city
11 U.K. news source
14 Pope before Paul V, whose papacy lasted less than four weeks
15 Loud, as a stadium crowd
16 Yahoo! competitor
17 Result of hitting the pause button on a movie
19 Dundee denial
20 Have concern
21 Authoritative order
23 Vegetarian's protein source
26 Volcanic emission
28 The "B" in L.B.J.
29 Hall-of-Fame QB Johnny
31 Enzyme suffix
33 Low-lying area
34 Uncovers
35 Chief Pontiac's tribe
37 Coast Guard rank: Abbr.
38 Extra
40 Nightwear, briefly
43 Buses and trains
45 "Honest to goodness!"
47 Sit for a picture
49 ___ compos mentis
50 Try hard
51 Book size
53 NNE's opposite
55 Part of a list
56 Chatty birds
58 "The Censor" of ancient Rome
60 Tire pressure meas.
61 Old-time songwriters' locale
66 "Horrors!"
67 Online birthday greeting, e.g.
68 Go out
69 Go blonde, say
70 Seized vehicles, for short
71 Channel with cameras in the Capitol

DOWN
1 North Pole toymaker
2 Generation ___ (thirty-something)
3 Cedar Rapids college
4 Carry out, as an assignment
5 Multitalented Minnelli
6 Bank fixtures
7 Goof up
8 Rich soil
9 "Goldilocks" character
10 Football bowl site
11 Dairy Queen offering
12 Overnight accommo-dations by the shore
13 John who starred in "A Fish Called Wanda"
18 Times on a timeline
22 Temperamental performer
23 TV, slangily, with "the"
24 ___ empty stomach
25 Attack before being attacked
27 Millinery accessories
30 "The Thin Man" canine
32 "Immediately," in the O.R.
35 ___ buco
36 Departed
39 Having been warned
41 Hepcat's talk
42 Appear to be
44 Derrière
46 Baltimore nine
47 Like some balloons, questions and corn
48 Playwright Sean
50 Ugly duckling, eventually
52 Person in a polling booth
54 A whole slew

by Allan E. Parrish

57 Jacket
fastener
59 After-bath
powder
62 Con's
opposite

63 Nascar
unit
64 Longoria of
"Desperate
Housewives"
63 Desire

18

ACROSS
1 Old __ tale
6 Fiction's opposite
10 Two-wheeler
14 Novelist Zola
15 "Are you __ out?"
16 Luau instruments, informally
17 Wee
18 Cost of an old phone call
19 Check for a landlord
20 Game equipment for an old sitcom star?
23 Son of Seth
24 Organic salt
25 Greek T
28 __ Kippur
29 Chem. or biol.
30 Captains of industry
32 Sudden outpouring
34 Mark in "piñata"
35 Game location for an actress?
38 Major mix-up

40 Deflect, as comments
41 IBM/Apple product starting in the early '90s
44 Pull tab site
45 Pinup's leg
48 Product pitches
49 Carved, as an image
51 Florence's river
52 Game site for a popular singer?
54 Plastic building block
57 Mélange
58 When repeated, classic song with the lyric "Me gotta go"
59 Rainbow goddess
60 Pasta sauce first sold in 1937
61 Ponders
62 Like some Steve Martin humor

63 "__ It Romantic?"
64 "Give it __!" ("Quit harping!")

DOWN
1 Actor Snipes of "Blade"
2 Prefix with suppressive
3 Owner of MTV and BET
4 New York Harbor's __ Island
5 Order in a bear market
6 Faithfulness
7 Licoricelike flavor
8 Hand-to-hand fighting
9 8-Down ender
10 Singer Ives
11 "I Like __" (old campaign slogan)
12 Barbie's doll partner
13 Inexact fig.
21 Train that makes all stops

22 Speaker's spot
25 Spilled the beans
26 &
27 "It's no __!" (cry of despair)
29 Go all out
31 Like a mechanic's hands
32 Ump's call with outstretched arms
33 Paranormal ability
35 Tools with teeth
36 Wasn't turned inward
37 Tehran native
38 Place for a mud bath
39 Doze (off)
42 A __ (kind of reasoning)
43 Maria of the Met
45 Bellyache
46 "__ Song" (John Denver #1 hit)
47 Not given to self-promotion

by Elizabeth A. Long

19

ACROSS

1 Toast to one's health
6 Whooping ___
11 Belle of the ball
14 Humiliate
15 Ship from the Mideast
16 Commercial cousin of crazy eights
17 Traps off the coast of Maine
19 Get-up-and-go
20 Horn sound
21 Urns
22 Nozzle site
23 Southerner in the Civil War
25 "___ you asked . . ."
26 Part of a TV catchphrase from Howie Mandel
28 Ball catcher behind a catcher
31 Thesis defenses
32 Identical to

33 Twisted, as humor
34 Source of disruption to satellites
36 "My man!"
39 Disobeys
40 Letter-shaped skyscraper support
42 Sleeveless shirts
45 Strained relations?
46 Bakery fixtures
47 Goad
48 Moist, as morning grass
49 Los Angeles's San ___ Bay
52 Mayberry lad
55 Santa ___ winds
56 Gotham tabloid
58 Yank
59 Kennel club classification
60 Guy
61 Wide shoe spec
62 Put a hex on
63 Fish basket

DOWN

1 Pepper's partner
2 "Peek-___"
3 Jerry Lewis telethon time
4 Andrew Carnegie corp.
5 Investigator: Abbr.
6 Reef material
7 Steals, with "off"
8 Skin cream ingredient
9 New Jersey hoopsters
10 Places to see M.D.'s in a hurry
11 Company behind nylon and Teflon
12 Georges who composed "Romanian Rhapsodies"
13 "Little" shepherdess of children's verse
18 Daredevil Knievel
22 Serpentine sound

24 Droopy-eared hounds
25 Rink activity
26 This instant
27 Bobby ___, the only N.H.L.'er to win the Hart, Norris, Ross and Smythe trophies in the same year
28 Points on a diamond?
29 Roadies' loads
30 Corporate V.I.P.
32 Salon sound
35 Roswell sighting
36 Tall, skinny guy
37 Like vegetables in salads
38 Mantra syllables
39 Designer letters
41 Knee-slapping goof
42 Thus far
43 Street
44 Music genre for Enya

by Randall J. Hartman

45 Aviation pioneer Sikorsky
47 Wash away, as soil
49 Andean land
50 Pitcher
51 Turns red, perhaps
53 "Survivor" setting, sometimes
54 And others, briefly
56 Peacock network
57 Col. Sanders's chain

20

ACROSS

1 Cutlass or 88, in the auto world
5 Result of a serious head injury
9 Refrigerates
14 Hilarious happening
15 Not new
16 Big foil maker
17 *It rolls across the Plains
19 Poverty-stricken
20 Church music maker
21 Bean from which sauce is made
23 18, e.g., as a minimum for voting
24 When repeated, a Hawaiian fish
27 Kevin of "Field of Dreams"
29 Psychiatrists' appointments
33 Western Indians
34 First responder, say: Abbr.
35 ESE's reverse
36 Spoke roughly
39 Former coin in the Trevi Fountain
41 Barely chewable
43 "It is so"
44 California city on a bay, slangily
46 Shooters' org.
47 Coach Parseghian
48 Edith who sang "La Vie en Rose"
49 Responsible for, as something bad
52 Wife of Marc Antony
55 Vivacity
56 "The Tell-Tale Heart" teller
57 1967 Montreal attraction
59 Saint ___, Caribbean nation
63 Range maker
65 *Beehive contents
68 Put back to 0000, say
69 Preppy shirt label
70 Jai ___
71 Birch and larch
72 Politicos with a donkey symbol
73 Barber's call

DOWN

1 Roughly
2 False witness
3 Rapper Snoop ___
4 Really ticks off
5 Snarling dog
6 The Buckeyes, for short
7 Result of a ransacking
8 Like some committees
9 Card game with melding
10 Bullfight cry
11 *Juice drink brand
12 Where Moose meet
13 Follower of nay or sooth
18 ___ B'rith
22 See 25-Down
25 With 22-Down, what the ends of the answers to the four starred clues are examples of
26 ___ way, shape or form
28 Try out
29 ___-help
30 Mideast leader
31 *Alluring dance
32 Moved like a pendulum
37 Coin across the Atlantic
38 Unhearing
40 Land east of the Urals
42 Eats
45 Cautions
50 Easter bloom
51 Big-billed bird
52 Bedazzling museum works
53 Person who shows promise

by Elizabeth A. Long

54 Green garden bug
58 Seep
60 ___ slaw
61 Large-screen cinema format
62 Not much
64 Maiden name preceder
66 ___ de plume
67 Mag. staffers

21

ACROSS

1 Warm-blooded animal
7 Polite concurrence
14 Neighbor of Sudan
16 Behind on payments, after "in"
17 Five-pointed ocean denizen
18 Short sleeps
19 Charged particles
20 1950s Wimbledon champ Lew
21 Singer Morissette
24 Justice div. that conducts raids
25 And so on: Abbr.
28 Pepsi and RC
29 Viewer-supported TV network
30 Sag
32 E. ___ (health menace)
33 Help
34 Sportscaster Howard
35 Opposite WSW
36 Creature suggested by this puzzle's circled letters
38 ___ v. Wade
39 Criticize in a petty way
41 Cleaning tool in a bucket
42 Turner who sang "Proud Mary"
43 ___ firma
44 ___ Bartlet, president on "The West Wing"
45 Trigonometric ratios
46 Michigan's ___ Canals
47 Sn, in chemistry
48 Unpaired
49 Threadbare
51 "What were ___ thinking?"
52 Driver's levy
55 Drinkers may run them up
59 Kansas expanse
60 Back: Fr.
61 Coarse-haired burrowers
62 2001 Sean Penn film

DOWN

1 Enero or febrero
2 "You ___ here"
3 "Mamma ___!"
4 Where Moses got the Ten Commandments
5 Stella ___ (Belgian beer)
6 Tilts
7 Regatta boats
8 ___ Good Feelings
9 Spanish Mlle.
10 Darners
11 Tiny battery type
12 Dadaist Jean
13 Editor's work: Abbr.
15 ___ poetica
21 One of two in "résumé"
22 Cuckoos
23 Fast, in music
24 Body's midsection
26 Jewelry for a sandal wearer
27 Rank below brigadier general
29 Cherry seed
30 Uno y uno
31 "The magic word"
33 1 or 11, in blackjack
34 Saucer's go-with
36 Suffix with pay
37 Pea's home
40 Fade
42 "Tip-Toe Thru' the Tulips" singer
44 They cause bad luck
45 ___ Mist (7 Up competitor)
47 Characteristic
48 Puppeteer Lewis
50 Other, south of the border
51 Abbr. in TV listings
52 Tach measure, for short
53 ". . . man ___ mouse?"
54 River to the Rhine
56 D.D.E. defeated him
57 Playtex item
58 Half a year of coll.

by Peter A. Collins

22

ACROSS

1 Gem units
7 Revolutionary Guevara
10 Sea creature that moves sideways
14 Common recipe amount
15 Actor Holbrook
16 Turner of Hollywood
17 Masonry work that may be smoothed with a trowel
19 Grace finisher
20 Deadly snake
21 Shoving away, football-style
23 Director Bob who won a Tony, Oscar and Emmy all in the same year
24 Evicts
25 Quester for the Golden Fleece
28 Hen's place
30 "It's a sin to tell ___"
31 Goes 80, say
34 Fellow
37 More rain and less light, e.g., to a pilot
40 Sault ___ Marie
41 Ill-___ gains
42 Hitchhiker's need
43 Tabbies
44 Person whose name appears on a museum plaque, e.g.
45 Zorro's weapon
48 Colorado resort
51 Some memorization in arithmetic class
54 Airport overseer: Abbr.
57 Director Kazan
58 Earlier . . . or a hint to the words circled in 17-, 21-, 37- and 51-Across
60 Book after John
61 Coach Parseghian
62 White fur
63 Two tablets every six hours, e.g.
64 Thieve
65 Target and J. C. Penney

DOWN

1 ___ Nostra
2 Six-legged intruders
3 Sign on, as for another tour of duty
4 N.C. State's group
5 University of Arizona's home
6 Leopard markings
7 Rub raw
8 .5
9 Singer Fitzgerald
10 Zip one's lip
11 Harold who directed "Groundhog Day"
12 Concerning
13 Hair over the forehead
18 State known for its cheese: Abbr.
22 Hen's place
23 Enemies
25 1975 thriller that took a big bite at the box office
26 Very much
27 Father
28 Give
29 Chief Norse god
31 Many a person whose name starts Mac
32 Flower holders
33 Suffix with differ
34 Enter
35 Ruin
36 Belgian river to the North Sea
38 "Zounds!"
39 Laundry implement that might make a 43-Down
43 See 39-Down
44 Gobi or Mojave
45 Lieu
46 Radio word after "Roger"
47 Skips
48 Popular BBC import, for short

by Peter A. Collins

23

ACROSS
1 "Get out of here!"
5 Scott who draws "Dilbert"
10 Heart problem
14 Tortoise's race opponent
15 Argue against
16 Attempt at a basket
17 Fe, chemically
18 Actress Verdugo
19 Loving strokes
20 Course option
23 Hold the wheel
24 "___ So Fine," #1 Chiffons hit
25 Double curve
28 Old photo shade
32 Space cut by a scythe
34 ___ Khan
37 Response option
40 Ballet skirt
42 Dweller along the Volga
43 Signal hello or goodbye
44 Electric light option
47 Hedge plant
48 Person under 21
49 Group singing "Hallelujah!"
51 Sault ___ Marie
52 Stout drink
55 Parts to play
59 Quiz option
64 Advertising award
66 "Praise be to ___"
67 Lhasa ___
68 Easter servings
69 String bean's opposite
70 Person under 20
71 Optometrists' concerns
72 Department of ___
73 Ocean eagle

DOWN
1 Freighters, e.g.
2 Diamond weight
3 Came up
4 Tightens, with "up"
5 Space
6 Place to get an egg salad sandwich
7 Eve's second son
8 Chew (on)
9 Old hat
10 Nile nippers
11 Shoo off
12 Mouth-burning
13 Travelers from another galaxy, for short
21 Glenn of the Eagles
22 Professional grp.
26 Comedian Martin
27 "The Taming of the ___"
29 Consumers of Purina and Iams food
30 Vidi in "Veni, vidi, vici"
31 Playful trick
33 Opposite ENE
34 They're smashed in a smasher
35 "Go fast!," to a driver
36 Back then
38 Courtroom affirmation
39 Western U.S. gas giant
41 Carrier of 13-Down
45 Berlin Mrs.
46 Take on, as employees
50 Spin
53 Pages (through)
54 Key of Mozart's Symphony No. 39
56 Outcast
57 Ruhr Valley city
58 Gem
60 One of TV's "Friends"
61 ___Vista (search engine)
62 Final
63 Mule or clog
64 Revolutionary Guevara
65 Make, as a wager

by Kurt Mengel and Jan-Michele Gianette

ACROSS

1 #1 number two who became the #2 number one
6 Actors who mug
10 Talking equine of '60s TV
14 Roll over, as a subscription
15 Neighbor of Yemen
16 Toy on a string
17 Food from heaven
18 Lot in life
19 ___-again (like some Christians)
20 She offered Excalibur to the future King Arthur
23 Garment accompanying a girdle
24 Last letter, in London
25 Gordon of "Oklahoma!"
29 Went out, as a fire
31 Club discussed in clubhouses: Abbr.

34 Guiding philosophy
35 Couch
36 Standard
37 Popular canned tuna
40 Word of invitation
41 Broadway award
42 Alleviates
43 Nile stinger
44 Hockey legend Gordie
45 Handles the food for the party
46 Big bird of the outback
47 Quilt locale
48 Columbia, in an old patriotic song
55 Witty Ephron
56 Lamb : ewe :: ___ : mare
57 Ram, astrologically
59 Voting no
60 Warren of the Supreme Court
61 Do, as a puzzle
62 Something to slip on?

63 Whirling current
64 County ENE of London

DOWN

1 Elbow's place
2 "Are we agreed?"
3 Late celebrity ___ Nicole Smith
4 Repair
5 Sag on a nag
6 Labor leader Jimmy who mysteriously disappeared
7 Amo, amas, ___ . . .
8 Trig or geometry
9 Take lightly
10 "Oops! I made a mistake"
11 Castle, in chess
12 "Jane ___"
13 "___ we now our gay apparel"
21 Valuable rock
22 ___ Zeppelin
25 Holy city of Islam
26 One of the Three Musketeers

27 Cheeta, in "Tarzan" films
28 Serving with chop suey
29 "Lorna ___"
30 Questionable
31 Rapper's entourage
32 Garson of "Mrs. Miniver"
33 Accumulate
35 The white in a whiteout
36 Tidy
38 Crayfish dish
39 One who could use a shrink
44 Medical care grp.
45 Corporate V.I.P.
46 EarthLink transmission
47 Stomach
48 Disappeared
49 Old Harper's Bazaar artist
50 Wart causer, in legend
51 Rocklike
52 Greek love god

by Randall J. Hartman

53 Needs
medicine
54 Campbell of
"Scream"
55 40 winks
58 Topic for
Dr. Ruth

25

ACROSS

1 Footlong sandwiches
5 Lost traction
9 Post office purchase
14 Fairy tale meanie
15 Hatcher of "Lois & Clark"
16 Himalayan kingdom
17 Short on dough
19 Play a role none too subtly
20 Kind of paper for gift-wrapping
21 Short on dough
23 ___ to stern
25 Dedicatory verse
26 Sports org. for scholars
29 Finger food at a Spanish restaurant
32 Over-the-top review
36 The "A" in A/V
38 Howard Stern's medium
40 Tiny criticism to "pick"
41 Short on dough
44 Part of an iceberg that's visible
45 Sarge's superior
46 Aquafina competitor
47 Aardvark's fare
49 Attack en masse, as a castle
51 Architect Saarinen
52 ___ Beta Kappa
54 Individually
56 Short on dough
61 Bits of wisdom?
65 One washing down a driveway, e.g.
66 Short on dough
68 Eye-teasing paintings
69 Saskatchewan Indian
70 Teeny bit
71 See 22-Down
72 "Thundering" group
73 Agts. looking for tax cheats

DOWN

1 Downy
2 Wrinkly fruit
3 Garments that usually clasp in the back
4 Takes off on a cruise
5 Avenue
6 Fierce type, astrologically
7 Annoys
8 Jenny Craig regimen
9 Three-time P.G.A. champ
10 Word repeated after someone starts to show anger
11 Individually
12 Chess ending
13 Begged
18 ". . . and nothing ___"
22 With 71-Across, "White Men Can't Jump" co-star
24 Ballet's Fonteyn
26 Can./U.S./ Mex. treaty
27 Give hints to
28 Good (at)
30 Barbecue area
31 Stick (to)
33 "___ Get Your Gun"
34 Church official
35 Prefix with -centric
37 Something good to strike
39 Unclose, poetically
42 Polite refusal
43 "Enough already!"
48 Globe
50 In an atlas, e.g.
53 #1 to Avis's #2
55 So-so grade
56 Restaurant acronym
57 "Uh-uh"
58 Nicholas I or II
59 Do art on glass, say
60 Partner of truth
62 "A ___ of One's Own"
63 Instrument that's plucked
64 Baseball's ___ the Man
67 Individually

by Harriet Clifton

26

ACROSS
1 In debt
6 Post-op locale
9 Bets build them
13 Workplace for some clowns
14 Melon exterior
16 Sign to heed
17 States confidently
18 Rice-shaped pasta
19 Late-night name
20 Number one #2?
22 Hunchbacked assistant
23 "All My ___ Live in Texas" (1987 #1 country hit)
24 Manorial worker
26 2 and 12, e.g., in dice
31 "I am such a dope!"
32 Bart's teacher, ___ Krabappel
33 Hen's home
35 Oslo is on one
39 Have-___ (poor people)
40 Traffic problem
42 Northamptonshire river
43 Yucky
45 Olympics blade
46 Toy with a cross frame
47 Dental problem calling for braces
49 Puts together hastily
51 Empty, as a stare
55 Baton Rouge sch.
56 Prefix with culture
57 Little woman?
63 Heist haul
64 Proceed slowly
65 Persian tongue
66 Cuzco native
67 Holding a grudge
68 "I surrender!"
69 Batik artist
70 In a funk
71 Manages to elude

DOWN
1 Like most folklore
2 Used a loom
3 Brainchild
4 Social misfit
5 Matthew or Mark
6 Hard porcelain
7 Magazine fig.
8 Loosen, as a parka
9 What a comedian might do before going onstage?
10 Alphabet ender
11 Carpentry joint part
12 Angry bull's sound
15 Apportioned, with "out"
21 Members of management
25 "___ Wiedersehen"
26 China's ___ Xiaoping
27 Dumpster emanation
28 Sermon preposition
29 Fish-shaped musical instrument?
30 Ivory, Coast and others
34 Made impossible
36 Alsace assents
37 Queue after Q
38 Tough to fathom
41 Most trivial
44 ___ Tomé
48 High-heel shoes
50 Really sorry
51 Not yet expired
52 Intense pain
53 Jim who sang "Time in a Bottle"
54 Missile sites
58 Ibsen's ___ Helmer
59 Hand, to Hernando
60 Rainbow shapes
61 Cruise stopover
62 Stamping tools

by Julie Ann Bowling

27

ACROSS

1 Missing Jimmy
6 Hit the slopes
9 General feeling
14 Paula of "American Idol"
15 Chum
16 Take forcibly
17 Big spender's woe?
19 "Mule Train" singer, 1949
20 Bête ___
21 Gum arabic-yielding tree
22 Where to find the headings Books, Dolls & Bears, and Collectibles
25 Revolver toter?
27 The Ewings' soap
29 ___ Tin Tin
30 Letter-shaped support
31 Huge expanses
33 Clinic name

37 MasterCard-carrying ecclesiastic?
40 New York home of Rensselaer Polytechnic Institute
41 Give the boot to
42 Greene of "Bonanza"
43 Mark, as a ballot square
44 "Blah, blah, blah . . ."
45 Peter?
51 Deck wood
52 Country singer Milsap
53 Quick Pick game
55 Worse than bad
56 Where this puzzle's theme pairs would like to meet
60 Chain unit
61 Reproductive cells
62 Condor's nest
63 Tender spots
64 Prickly husk
65 Pasta sauce brand

DOWN

1 Witchy woman
2 Sapporo sash
3 Rx watchdog
4 1975 Barbra Streisand sequel
5 Chorus voice
6 Richard's first vice president
7 Superman's birth name
8 Under the weather
9 Spock, on his father's side
10 Asimov of sci-fi
11 LaCrosse carmaker
12 Bert's Muppet pal
13 Pickle portion
18 Some ballpoints
21 Imitative in a silly way
22 Papal bull, e.g.
23 Kiddie lit elephant

24 Olds discontinued in 2004
26 Developer's plot
28 "___ Blue"
31 Spa feature
32 Overhead trains
33 Reggie Jackson nickname
34 Think alike
35 Buttinsky
36 Vacuum maker
38 Library no-no
39 Supermodel Carol
43 "Trust No One" TV series, with "The"
44 Sermon ending?
45 Lacking couth
46 Self-help category
47 Due to get, as punishment
48 Toughen
49 Romantic message, in shorthand
50 Without face value

by Larry Shearer

54 Pipe section
56 Cry out loud
57 Seam
material
58 Rug, of
a sort
59 Zodiac beast

28

ACROSS
1 Prefix with sphere
5 Assigned stars to
10 Thriving time
14 Jewish ritual
15 Visibly stunned
16 Humorist Bombeck
17 Ornery sort
18 Cutoffs fabric
19 Yemeni port
20 Striptease business?
23 Drive-thru convenience, perhaps
24 Having lunch, say
25 "___ to say this, but . . ."
26 Some auto deals
28 Stereotypical sandwich board diner
31 Young 'un
32 Younger brother, say
33 Knight's attendant
35 Wrestling business?
39 Former "Dateline NBC" co-host Jane
40 Beanery sign
43 Cockpit abbr.
46 Carefully arranged
47 Portugal's place
49 The March King
51 ___-Caps (Nestlé candy)
52 Row C abbr., maybe
53 Comb business?
58 Volcano known to locals as Mongibello
59 Dweller along the Arabian Sea
60 "Darn!"
62 Goatee site
63 Mullally of "Will & Grace"
64 ZZ Top, e.g.
65 Look after
66 Dummy Mortimer
67 Thanksgiving side dish

DOWN
1 "Dancing With the Stars" airer
2 One on a board
3 Jumble
4 ___ buco
5 Figure that's squared in a common formula
6 Go-between
7 Zesty flavor
8 Cast-of-thousands film
9 Floor model
10 Place for an umbrella
11 Tough time
12 Mafia code of silence
13 Unlike drone aircraft
21 Reason to cry "Alas!"
22 Some Japanese-Americans
23 Jungfrau or Eiger
27 Metro map feature
28 A singing Jackson
29 Bacchanalian revelry
30 Polar drudge
33 TV handyman Bob
34 Kind of diagram
36 The Pineapple Island
37 Expected in
38 Sauce for some seafood
41 Cratchit boy
42 Bummed out
43 Appearance
44 Not be able to stomach
45 Submit, as homework
47 Under consideration
48 Dizzy Gillespie's genre

by Fred Piscop

50 Witness's place
51 School locator?
54 Pierre, François, etc.
55 Hood fighters
56 Parakeet keeper
57 Pseudo-cultured
61 Brillo alternative

29

ACROSS

1 Home in an old warehouse district
5 Virus named for a river
10 Trans-Siberian Railroad stop
14 Peculiar: Prefix
15 U.S./Canada early warning syst.
16 City bond, for short
17 Eisenhower was one
20 Move unsteadily
21 Delon of "Purple Noon"
22 Cedar Rapids college
23 2:30, aboard ship
27 Dele undoers
29 Something new
30 Ho Chi Minh's capital
31 Boris Godunov, for one
32 Rove, with "about"
35 Full range
37 It's off the tip of Italy
40 Bad-mouth
41 __ war syndrome
45 __ plume
46 Chiang Kai-shek's capital
48 Mountain cats
49 Rests for a bit
52 Singleton
53 "Waiting for Lefty" playwright
54 Like Dickens's Dodger
57 Shortly after quitting time, for many
62 Forearm bone
63 Shul V.I.P.
64 Pizzeria fixture
65 Hot times in France
66 Befuddled
67 Try for a role

DOWN

1 Brit's elevator
2 Garfield's foil
3 Nickel
4 Slugging it out
5 __'acte
6 Feathery wrap
7 Bobby of the Bruins
8 Dillydally
9 Fruity quencher
10 Brunch dish
11 Wall art
12 Symbol of slowness
13 Ceramists' baking chambers
18 Welcomes, as a guest at one's home
19 Catches red-handed
23 Jack Sprat's taboo
24 Hypotheticals
25 Rome's __ Veneto
26 Blunders
27 Outbuilding
28 Vehicle with a medallion
32 Request for a congratula-tory slap
33 Pierce player
34 Gray concealers
36 End-of-workweek cry
38 At a cruise stop
39 Be worth
42 AP competitor
43 "My Name Is Asher __"
44 "For shame!"
46 Colorful fishes
47 Helper: Abbr.
49 Brimless cap
50 At least 21
51 "The Family Circus" cartoonist Bil
54 Home to most Turks
55 Iris's place
56 Libraries do it
58 Big Band __

by John Underwood

59 Turn state's evidence

60 "Sesame Street" channel

61 Honest __

30

ACROSS

1 Peak
5 Chattered incessantly
10 TV horse introduced in 1955 . . . or a Plymouth model introduced in 1956
14 Partiality
15 Seeing red
16 Prime draft status
17 Drug-yielding plant
18 Opposite of serenity
19 Cartoonist Al
20 Scary sound from the ocean?
23 Park, e.g., in N.Y.C.
25 "Sting like a bee" athlete
26 Having seniority
28 Scary sound from a war zone?
33 Juillet's season
34 Kodiak native
35 Physics unit
36 Theory's start

37 Scary sound from a cornfield?
41 Splinter group
44 Motel-discount grp.
45 Sales slips: Abbr.
49 Galley implement
50 Scary sound from a steeple?
53 Tedious
55 Boot part
56 "Whew!"
57 Misspells, say, as a ghost might at 20-, 28-, 37- and 50-Across?
62 Abominate
63 African antelope
64 Hot rod's rod
67 ___ Lackawanna Railroad
68 Countryish
69 Boot part
70 Card game for three
71 Walk leisurely
72 Stealth bomber org.

DOWN

1 Charles Gibson's network
2 A.F.L.-___
3 Cane cutter
4 Biblical son who sold his birthright
5 Wavelet
6 Language whose alphabet starts alif, ba, ta, tha . . .
7 Child's caretaker
8 Suffix with hypn-
9 Part of a bottle or a guitar
10 Kind of point
11 Helpless?
12 Filled to the gills
13 Big fat mouth
21 Country just south of Sicily
22 Moo goo gai pan pan
23 Lawyers' org.
24 Kilmer of "The Doors"

27 ___ Irvin, classic artist for The New Yorker
29 Cowlick, e.g.
30 Fit for a king
31 Blunder
32 "Long ___ and far away . . ."
36 Creep (along)
38 Name that's an anagram of 27-Down
39 ___ de mer
40 Egyptian dry measure equal to about five-and-a-half bushels
41 Soak (up)
42 Tag for a particular purpose
43 Neighbor of Slovenia
46 Co. addresses, often
47 A duo
48 Crafty
50 Tournament pass

by Gary Steinmehl

51 Like some
   music
52 Musically
   improvise
54 Sport
   utilizing
   a clay disk

58 Hospital
   shipments
59 Styptic
   agent
60 Part
   of a
   fishhook

61 Island with
   Waimea Bay
62 Gentlemen
65 Meadow
66 Shoemaker's
   helper, in a
   fairy tale

31

ACROSS

1 Play place
6 Ballroom dance
11 Chart-topper
14 Sign of spring
15 Mountaineer's tool
16 ET's ride
17 Play follower, usually
19 Unruly do
20 Amateurish
21 "___ economy is always beauty": Henry James
23 Buggy rider
26 Loofah, e.g.
30 108-card game
31 Start the pot
32 Pest control brand
33 Spoil
35 Bibliophile's suffix
36 Tipplers
37 Circulatory system flow
41 Singer ___ P. Morgan
43 Early 11th-century year
44 Back at sea?
47 Actress Chase of "Now, Voyager"
48 For dieters
51 Smidgen
52 Shoot-'em-up figure
54 Harmony, briefly
55 Clobber, biblically
56 Computer that uses OS X
58 Director Lee
59 What the starts of 17-, 26-, 37- and 52-Across are
66 Crib cry
67 Burger topper, maybe
68 Site of Ali's Rumble in the Jungle
69 Salon job
70 Cuts and pastes
71 TV awards

DOWN

1 Amniotic ___
2 Play about Capote
3 Put on TV
4 Manage, barely
5 Jacob's twin
6 G.I.'s helmet, slangily
7 Duke's sports org.
8 "Read Across America" grp.
9 Guy's partner
10 Primrose family member
11 Saroyan novel, with "The"
12 "It slipped my mind!"
13 Letterman lists
18 ID on a dust jacket
22 Acknowledges nonverbally
23 PC glitch
24 "Wheel of Fortune" buy
25 Hoops coach with the most N.C.A.A. Division I wins
27 Playful mockery
28 Rural event on horseback
29 Work out in the ring
31 Commotion
34 Red Sox div.
38 Old Dodge
39 Singer of the 1962 hit "The Wanderer"
40 Guinness Book suffix
41 Tools for making twisty cuts
42 Barnard grads
45 Bled, like dyes
46 "Deal or No Deal" network
49 Fakes, as an injury
50 Weaponry
53 Leave alone
54 "Beat it!"
57 Wood-shaping tool
60 Suffered from
61 Here, in Paris
62 "I'm kidding!"

by Alan Arbesfeld

63 Deadeye's
asset
64 Dryly
amusing
65 Nintendo's
Super ___

32

ACROSS
1 Show anger
5 Round before the final
9 Washroom tub
14 Ph.D. awarder
15 Gave the boot
16 Blessing-inducing sound
17 Flank
18 Gimlet garnish
19 Crockpot concoctions
20 Relax during a drill
23 Temp's work unit
24 Polite affirmation
25 Brazilian dance
27 Big Apple awards
30 Like hair, usually, after combing
33 Post-O.R. stop
36 Craps natural
38 Impoverished
39 Sgt. Friday's org.

41 Calendar units hidden in 20- and 61-Across and 11- and 35-Down
43 Worker's pay
44 Like a brainiac
46 Fire remnants
48 The "R" in Roy G. Biv
49 Trojan War hero
51 Popular snack chip
53 Surveyor Jeremiah, for whom a famous line is partly named
55 Beatle, endearingly
59 Meadow sound
61 Sunshine State school
64 Minute Maid Park player
66 Baylor's city
67 Sp. girl
68 Rodeo animal
69 From the top
70 Ticks off

71 TV shout-out from the team bench
72 It's sold in skeins
73 "Great" kid-lit detective

DOWN
1 Hard to please
2 Bring together
3 Greedy monarch
4 "Neverthe-less . . ."
5 On the payroll
6 Lighted sign in a theater
7 Hand-waver's cry
8 They may be bright
9 One in the infield
10 Follow direction?
11 Show sadness
12 Political caucus state
13 Like a yenta
21 "That's mine!"
22 Deplete, as energy

26 Cold one
28 FEMA recommen-dation, briefly
29 Play by a different ___ rules
31 Upper hand
32 Like batik fabrics
33 Ingrid's role in "Casablanca"
34 Showed up
35 "Time to rise, sleepyhead!"
37 Within earshot
40 Zwei follower
42 Lose the spare tire
45 Schedule B or C, e.g.
47 Ancient Greek colonnade
50 La preceder
52 Chooses to participate
54 "Impossible!"
56 ___ firma
57 Largish combo
58 Terrible twos, e.g.
59 Bad-mouth

by Michael Kaplan

60 Sparkling
wine city
62 ___ deficit
(lost money)
63 Pastry
prettifier
65 Vintage auto

33

ACROSS

1 Speaks, informally
4 Speak
9 Smokey Robinson's music genre, for short
14 ___ de France
15 End of a hangman's rope
16 Love to bits
17 BORE
20 Have ___ in one's head
21 ___ and outs
22 The "I" in T.G.I.F.
23 BOAR
28 Nap
29 "Golden" song
32 Ad-lib, musically
35 Sign before Virgo
36 Person performing an exorcism
37 Gives a stage cue
40 Honeybunch or cutie pie
41 Glowing remnants of a fire
42 Abbr. after many a general's name
43 Meyerbeer's "___ Huguenots"
44 Painting surface
45 Publisher of Cosmopolitan and Good Housekeeping
48 BOER
53 Before, in poetry
55 Baseballer Mel
56 "Maria ___," Jimmy Dorsey #1 hit
57 BOHR
62 Actress Garbo
63 "Er . . . um . . ."
64 Old tennis racket string material
65 Stand for a portrait
66 Taboos
67 Cry before "Get your hands off!"

DOWN

1 Have a chair by, as a table
2 ___ Yale, for whom Yale University is named
3 Six in 1,000,000
4 Out of sight
5 Also
6 ___ Sawyer
7 Reverse of WNW
8 Fix the electrical connections of
9 Didn't have enough supplies
10 Problem in focusing, for short
11 "Don't worry about it"
12 "Phooey!"
13 Panhandles
18 Club with a lodge
19 Bankbook abbr.
24 Knuckleheads
25 Tribulations
26 ___ dye
27 Lena or Ken of film
30 "This ___ . . . Then" (Jennifer Lopez album)
31 French summers
32 Computer image file format
33 French weapon
34 Sights at after-Christmas sales
36 Lab's ___ dish
38 Mini-plateau
39 "Will you marry me?," e.g.
40 Brandy fruit
42 Hoops official
45 Sticker through a lady's headgear
46 Coils of yarn
47 Soft powder
49 Biblical suffix
50 Stable sound

by Timothy Powell

51 Come
afterward
52 Wretched
53 Scoring
advantage
54 ___
avis

58 Suffix
with Israel
59 Dr. provider
60 Japanese
moolah
61 ___ Paulo,
Brazil

34

ACROSS

1 "Do you like green eggs and ham?" speaker
7 In the style of
10 Lao-tzu's way
13 Meeting handout
14 Broke from the band, maybe
17 Cosmopolitan staple
19 Date
20 Uncertainties
21 It can be silly
22 Spot en el mar
24 W.W. I German admiral
26 N.F.L. star
32 Slip
33 Conquistador's quest
34 Actress Turner
36 Opposite of WSW
37 Period of human benightedness
41 Stroke
42 Overall feel
44 Coquettish
45 Relative of a mole
47 Colorful bed cover
51 Corrida cheers
52 Pageant adornment
53 Highest peak of Crete
56 Egg: Prefix
57 Wide shoe spec
60 "Behave!" . . . and a hint to this puzzle's theme
65 Representative
66 Tie, as a score
67 Cry between "ready" and "go!"
68 "Kid-tested" breakfast cereal
69 Keep

DOWN

1 Fools
2 Author James
3 Slight
4 Special connections
5 Bustle
6 Port seized by Adm. Dewey, 1898
7 Poking tools
8 Luau offering
9 Queen of the hill?
10 Ballyhoo
11 Dismounted
12 Like mud
15 Easygoing
16 Sound at a greased pig contest
18 In the distance
22 Figs. clustered around 100
23 Like a malfeasant, often
24 Fluids in bags
25 Bull Moose party: Abbr.
26 Appeal
27 Incurred, as charges
28 "La Traviata," e.g.
29 Site of the first Asian Olympics
30 Kind of pants
31 Prepare to propose
35 1, for hydrogen: Abbr.
38 What a massage may ease
39 Theater seating
40 Titles for attys.
43 In disagreement
46 "Say what?"
48 Pottery materials
49 Reply, briefly
50 Onetime German leader
53 Mlles. after marriage
54 Red-bordered magazine
55 The "W" in Geo. W. Bush, e.g.
56 Straight-horned African animal
57 Author Ferber
58 Prefix with distant
59 "SportsCenter" channel
61 Yellow ribbon holder, in song
62 Geller with a psychic act
63 St. crosser
64 Bring home

by Oliver Hill

35

ACROSS

1 ___ Bartlet, president on "The West Wing"
4 John of "Full House"
10 Voodoo charm
14 Org. that publishes health studies
15 Butt in
16 One who may be caught off base?
17 Food transportation . . . that Harry Belafonte sang about
19 Place for a footballer's pad
20 Indiana and Ohio State are in it
21 Play ice hockey
23 Charles Lamb, pseudony-mously
24 . . . that's an ambulance, in slang
28 It ends in the fall: Abbr.
29 Shade of green
31 Helpful
32 Symbol of love
36 "Sometimes you feel like ___"
37 . . . that a rube might fall off
39 Al Jazeera viewer, typically
41 He danced in "Silk Stockings"
42 Put on the payroll
44 Stimpy's cartoon pal
45 Org. for drivers?
48 . . . that may be upset
52 Place to load and unload
53 R & B singer Mary J. ___
54 Sen. Feinstein
56 Pork chop?
59 . . . that's a source of easy money
61 Declare
62 Cliff hangers?
63 Some like it hot
64 Word with telephoto or zoom
65 San Fernando Valley district
66 Doofus

DOWN

1 Poked
2 Communi-cates with online
3 "Phooey!"
4 Trig function
5 Tax cheat chaser, informally
6 Alert for a fleeing prisoner, in brief
7 Bullwinkle, e.g.
8 Japanese city whose name means "large hill"
9 Go after
10 Stick out one's tongue, maybe
11 Hold title to
12 Coffee, slangily
13 Corrida cheer
18 One ___ time
22 Afternoon hour
24 Home run hero of '61
25 Icky stuff
26 Home of the Cowboys: Abbr.
27 New Jersey cager
29 Part of r.p.m.
30 Novelist Ferber
32 Mingle (with)
33 Make a choice
34 Crank up
35 Keystone State port
37 Rain delay roll-out
38 Caterer's coffee holder
39 "So it's you!"
40 Boot Hill letters
43 Actor Benicio ___ Toro
45 Party animal?
46 Wish offerers
47 Soccer venues
49 Prop for Groucho Marx

by Randall J. Hartman

50 See eye
to eye
51 Plays
parent
to
52 72, at
Augusta

54 Turned blue,
maybe
55 "___ deal!"
56 Kilmer
who once
played
Batman

57 She
raised
Cain
58 Bridge
capacity
unit
60 Compete

36

ACROSS

1 Inane
5 __ scan (biometric authentication method)
9 Districted
14 Cynic's comment
15 Payload delivery org.
16 Beam
17 Helpful person's line
20 Spiral in space
21 Most comfy
22 Jazz dance
23 Vice squad arrestees, perhaps
25 Perturbation
27 Autumn bloomer
32 With 42-Across, helpful person's line
37 Mesa tribe
38 Philosophy of bare existence?
39 Log-in info
41 Writer Waugh
42 See 32-Across
46 Like good pianos and engines
48 Levitated
49 Versatile fabric
51 Lives on
56 Spode ensembles
60 Coterie
61 Helpful person's line
64 Popular place for 18-Down
65 Tied up
66 Reel in
67 With cunning
68 St. Andrew's Day observer
69 Virtual mart

DOWN

1 Small jobs for a body shop
2 Kriegsmarine vessel
3 __ Park (noted lab site)
4 Substitute players
5 Annual racing classic
6 Squealer
7 Prefix with tonic
8 "Hello, Dolly!" jazzman
9 One of the Gabors
10 Bygone Dodge
11 Giant in footwear
12 Graceful shaders
13 It's repellent
18 Sojourners abroad, for short
19 Darlin'
23 Elbow
24 Prospecting find
26 1989's __ Prieta earthquake
28 Flushing stadium
29 Having a hard time deciding
30 Like "Paradise Lost"
31 Ferris wheel or bumper cars
32 Swarm member
33 "To Sir, With Love" singer, 1967
34 Mideast harbor city
35 Cubes at Harrah's
36 Bother
40 __ Artois beer
43 Agrees
44 Sellout letters
45 Lithium-__ battery
47 Stylish
50 Dough producer, briefly
52 Airplane seating request
53 Fowl entree
54 __ deaf ear to
55 Not yet gentrified
56 Much of a waitress's income
57 And others, for short
58 Cockeyed
59 Clipper's sheet
60 ¢
62 Piping compound, briefly
63 Fierce type, astrologically

by Chuck Deodene

ACROSS

1 The whole ball of wax
5 Court cry
9 Last budget category, usually: Abbr.
13 Loafer, for one
14 Fabricate
15 Mediterranean island country
16 Golf club used in a bunker
18 Bird-related
19 USAir rival
20 Like Methuselah
21 Invent
22 Butcher's device
25 Examine
29 Pizazz
30 At full speed
31 Xerox machine output
36 Architect Ludwig Mies van der ___
37 Krispy ___ Doughnuts
38 Nabisco cookie
39 Tourist shop purchases
41 Avoid, as work
42 N.Y.C. cultural institution
43 Taste bud locale
44 U.S.S. Nautilus, for one
49 Show to be false
50 Computer file name extension
51 Haw's partner
54 Sierra ___
55 Spider-Man or the Green Lantern
58 Religion of the Koran
59 Like the Sahara
60 Singer Fitzgerald
61 Cop's path
62 "Toodles," in Milan
63 Marvel Comics mutants

DOWN

1 Secretary: Abbr.
2 Microwave option
3 Mrs. Chaplin
4 1-Across's end, in England
5 Frittata, e.g.
6 When said three times, et cetera
7 Heart chart, for short
8 New York's Tappan ___ Bridge
9 Expert
10 Troy story?
11 Union member
12 Chair person?
15 Name after Dan or San
17 "Pretty ___" (Richard Gere/Julia Roberts movie)
21 Shipping container
23 Iran's capital
24 ___ on to (grabs)
25 Swedish version of Lawrence
26 Melville novel
27 Waikiki Beach locale
28 Ukraine's capital
31 ___ ballerina
32 Big band saxophonist Al
33 Not a reproduction: Abbr.
34 The Pan-American Highway runs through it
35 Oxen holder
37 Séance sound
40 Rapper Marshall Mathers, familiarly
41 On the wagon
43 Some supper club attire
44 Improvise
45 Reagan cabinet member
46 Deadly virus
47 Charge
48 Brownish photo tint
51 Captain's position
52 Writer ___ Stanley Gardner

by Christina Houlihan Kelly

53 Séance
sound
55 Pouch
56 "Psychic"
Geller
57 Voodoo
doctor's doing

38

ACROSS
1 Trots
5 Seaweed product
9 Visual movement popularized in the 1960s
14 Twist-apart treat
15 God, for George Burns or Morgan Freeman
16 U.P.S. supply
17 One . . .
20 Artist's mishap
21 79, for gold: Abbr.
22 Brenner Pass locale
23 Many a TV clip
25 "i" completer
27 Helpless?
30 Headed out
32 Averse
36 Noted polonaise composer
38 Kind of vaccine
40 Horse course
41 Two . . .
44 Prefix with con
45 W.W. I German admiral
46 Rafael's wrap
47 On edge
49 Big atlas section
51 Fateful March date
52 Mother's hermana
54 Cable for money?
56 Iolani Palace locale
59 Simmer (down)
61 "I wanna!"
65 Three . . .
68 End of a fight
69 Langston Hughes poem
70 Largest volcano in Europe
71 Athenian lawgiver who introduced trial by jury
72 Big do
73 "Durn it!"

DOWN
1 Writes quickly
2 City near Provo
3 Subject of modern "mapping"
4 Fizzy drinks at a five-and-ten
5 J.F.K. posting: Abbr.
6 Start limping
7 One, two and three . . . or this puzzle's title
8 Guide strap
9 Baby docs, briefly
10 It has eyes that can't see
11 1½ rotation leap
12 Bring in the sheaves
13 Tut's kin?
18 Goof
19 O.K. sign
24 Confess (to)
26 Half an old comedy duo
27 Bloodhound's trail
28 "Golly"
29 Access the Web
31 "Don't give up!"
33 In first place
34 Brownish gray
35 Ballyhoos
37 Immigrant from Japan
39 Analyze, as ore
42 Grant-giving org.
43 High school course, for short
48 Wall plaster
50 "Yes, you are!" retort
53 Crackerjack
55 Mom's skill, briefly
56 Makes up one's mind (to)
57 Sleek, in auto talk
58 Burglar's booty
60 "You wish!"
62 Prefix with physical
63 Thomas who wrote "The Magic Mountain"

by Manny Nosowsky

64 Slate, e.g.,
for short
66 Rooster's
mate
67 It goes
for a
buck

39

ACROSS

1 Russian space station
4 "The Song of ___," old French epic
10 Spill the beans
14 Half of dos
15 Blackboard appurtenance
16 Like hands after eating potato chips
17 It's worth listening to
19 Info in a used car ad
20 Toll
21 Conduct a survey
23 Republic from which Montenegro gained its independence
25 ___-jongg
26 Sherlock Holmes portrayer
33 Nabokov heroine
35 "Don't ___ on me" (slogan of the American Revolution)
36 Where San Diego is: Abbr.
37 Art ___
39 Expensive coat
41 Cravings
42 Not silently
44 Laughing
46 Drivers' org.
47 Perfect shape
50 Building wing
51 Sale markdown indicator
54 Variety of rose
60 Decorative sofa fabric
61 River of Switzerland
62 Where the first words of 17-, 26- and 47-Across may be found
64 It may be in the doghouse
65 Its alphabet starts with alif
66 Bard's "before"
67 Hightail it
68 Tennessee team
69 "Help!"

DOWN

1 Scents used for perfume
2 Senseless
3 English philosopher called "Doctor Mirabilis"
4 One who sees it like it is
5 Fort ___, former Army post on Monterey Bay
6 Source of basalt
7 Purchase stipulation
8 Place for a crick
9 Imagined
10 Cry of glee
11 Stead
12 Chester Arthur's middle name
13 Polar explorer Richard
18 Isle of exile
22 Sis-boom-bahs
24 Snobs put them on
27 Memorize, as lines
28 Raging mad
29 He lost to Dwight
30 They're controlled by the moon
31 "Peter Pan" dog
32 Actress Lanchester, who married Charles Laughton
33 "Madam, I'm ___"
34 Place to get a Reuben
38 Catcher of sound waves
40 ___'acte
43 Mid seventh-century date

by Linda Schechet Tucker

45 Haber-
dashery
items: Var.
48 Dated
49 Smell
52 Old Olds-
mobile

53 They
may be
dominant
54 Knife handle
55 Where Bill
and Hillary
met

56 La ___
Tar
Pits
57 Hatcher
or Garr
58 Part of
Q.E.D.

59 "I Do, I Do,
I Do, I Do,
I Do" group
63 Winning
cry in
a card
game

ACROSS

1 Private stash
6 Eighty-six
10 Very smart
14 Earthy pigment
15 Double-reed woodwind
16 Ruffian
17 Police ploys
20 Old Russian ruler
21 Lid trouble
22 Omar of TV's "House"
23 ___ of Man
25 Farm milk producers
27 Type
30 End-of-day spousal salutation
35 Clear, as a winter windshield
37 Crossed out
38 Sign of things to come
39 When said three times, a W.W. II movie
40 Give the giggles

42 Gallery showing works by Turner, Reynolds and Constable
43 Calendario units
44 Debussy's "La ___"
45 Lead down the aisle
46 "Call when you get the chance"
50 Flutter
51 Pocket particles
52 Sandbox item
54 Univ. lecturer
56 Way to go
58 Duchess of ___, Goya subject
62 Bogart/ Hepburn film
65 Work in the garden
66 Use of a company car or private washroom, say
67 Took a shot at

68 Birds whose heads can rotate 135° left or right
69 "Got it"
70 Full of lip

DOWN

1 How much to pay
2 Play parts
3 Quickly growing "pet"
4 Painter Matisse
5 Wee bit of work
6 Best-seller list
7 Toe the line
8 What a welcome sight relieves
9 Neptune's realm
10 Lofted approaches to the green
11 Earring shape
12 Charged particles
13 They may be burned and boxed
18 1993 Israeli/ Palestinian accords site

19 Swarm
24 "___ Drives Me Crazy," #1 hit by the Fine Young Cannibals
26 Like some smiles and loads
27 Holder of a dog's name and owner info
28 Téa of "Spanglish"
29 Russian ballet company
31 Outlying community
32 D-Day beach
33 Apportioned
34 First month in Madrid
36 Social workers' work
40 "You got that right!"
41 Pastries in "Sweeney Todd"
45 Action film firearm
47 Tick off
48 Mental grasp

by Tom Heilman

41

ACROSS

1 David or Victoria Beckham, e.g.
5 Bit of surveillance evidence
9 Muffin ingredient
13 When doubled, an old sitcom goodbye
14 Film format for domed theaters
15 Vibes
17 Derive (from)
18 Doofus
20 ___ flour
22 Sun. morning lecture
23 Novel on which "Clueless" is based
24 English philosopher who wrote "Wherever Law ends, Tyranny begins"
27 Doofus
29 Cheri
30 Parrot

31 Tablet
32 Part of U.S.P.S.
33 CD players
36 Stanley's love in "A Streetcar Named Desire"
38 Shown the door
40 Suffix with priest
41 Craggy mountain ridges
45 Computer command
46 Runaway bride or groom
47 Eyeliner problem
48 Doofus
51 Overweight plus
52 In awe
53 Airport stat.
54 Priestly vestment
55 Doofus
58 Catch sight of
62 RCA competitors
63 Wry Bombeck

64 AT&T's stylized globe, e.g.
65 Crave
66 Former Russian royalty
67 Pig and poi feast

DOWN

1 ___ and outs
2 Calico, e.g.
3 Sole
4 Doofus
5 Itsy-bitsy
6 Pierre's pal
7 Pretty violets
8 Sound bite, e.g.
9 "Pow!"
10 Media executive Murdoch
11 Scent
12 Mama Judd
16 Stretch of time
19 Difficult experiences
21 Opposite of 'neath
24 Expire
25 Cuts out

26 Nat and Natalie
27 Sis's sib
28 It's bound with twine
32 Many an ex-con
33 Recipient
34 Traitor
35 Kmart or Target
37 ___ land
39 Doofus
42 Nickname
43 Chicken ___
44 Work unit
46 Eastertime product
47 Pine-___
48 QB Marino and others
49 "Shall ___?" ("Want me to continue?")
50 Nary a soul
54 Hebrew month
56 Psychedelic drug
57 Doc's org.
59 Pittance
60 Organizer of one of four Grand Slam events: Abbr.
61 A person who is not a doofus

by C. W. Stewart

42

ACROSS
1 Liquor holder in a coat pocket
6 Wonderment
9 Taxi sounds
14 Milk: Prefix
15 First word of every Robert Ludlum title but one
16 Extreme
17 Ward off
18 Texas tea
19 Sectors
20 "Just like that!"
22 Electronic toll-collecting system in the Northeast
23 Walk in water
24 In the past
25 "Not on your life!"
30 Torment
31 ___ in Show (Westminster prize)
32 Temporary drop
34 Subj. in drawing class
35 Cargo area
36 Rick's "Casablanca" love

37 Holiday ___
38 Planning detail
40 Gold standards
42 "Yeah, wanna start somethin'?"
45 War ender
46 Create, as a phrase
47 No-goodnik
50 "The Sopranos" clip? . . . or where you might hear 20-, 25- and 42-Across
54 Continent separator
55 Embargo
56 One of the Carpenters
57 Make joyous
58 Israeli-invented gun
59 Goaded, with "on"
60 Like notepaper or subjects of a king
61 Fed. monitor of stock fraud
62 Midterms and finals

DOWN
1 "Spare tire"
2 Content of some cones
3 Nailed
4 Farmer's headwear
5 Toiletries holders
6 Made amends (for)
7 Henry Clay, politically
8 Conger or moray
9 Army barber's specialty
10 Ran off to the marrying judge
11 Italian source of 2-Down
12 White House occupant: Abbr.
13 Snippiness
21 Midmonth time
22 Grandson of Adam
24 Love, honor and ___

25 Rear end
26 Heavens: Prefix
27 Taken ___ (surprised)
28 Religion with the Five Pillars
29 Small bite
30 "Bali ___"
33 Good time, slangily
35 Frequent target of engine wear
36 Circus animal enclosure
38 Tarnished
39 Walk to and fro
40 Old TV feature
41 Start of an Ella Fitzgerald standard
43 Timely news bulletin
44 Like some sacred art
47 Afrikaner
48 Legal rights org.
49 Successful conclusion of a negotiation
50 Labyrinth

F¹	L²	A³	S⁴	K⁵		6	7	8		9	10	11	12	13
14						15				16				
17						18				19				
20				21					22					
			23					24						
	25	26				27					28	29		
30						31					32		33	
34					35					36				
37				38	39				40	41				
	42		43				44							
		45					46							
47	48	49				50					51	52	53	
54					55				56					
57					58				59					
60					61				62					

by Daniel Kantor

51 Pieces of
work?

52 Nair
competitor

53 Conclusions

55 Vehicle with
a route

43

ACROSS

1 Chews the fat
5 Cleveland cagers, briefly
9 1986 Indy winner Bobby
14 ___ breve
15 Writer Waugh
16 Maine college town
17 Paper quantity
18 Zig or zag
19 Pooh's creator
20 *Line formatting option
23 Go off course
24 Blockbuster aisle
25 Prerequisite for sainthood
27 Nixon's 1968 running mate
30 Big top noise
31 Coke competitor
34 Not of the cloth
36 Pawn
39 In the style of
40 *Hipster
43 Cyndi Lauper's "___ Bop"
44 Accompanying
46 Explorer Zebulon
47 Book before Joel
49 Lacking slack
51 Get going
53 Kind of pool or medal
56 Common TV dinner
60 Part of Ascap: Abbr.
61 *Education overseers
64 Ring-tailed mammal
66 Jason's craft
67 Wharton degs.
68 Sought answers
69 Old female country teacher
70 Der ___ (Konrad Adenauer)
71 Model/ volleyballer Gabrielle
72 Commoner
73 Coward of the stage

DOWN

1 Singer Brooks
2 Last Oldsmobile to be made
3 Britain's P.M. until 2007
4 Tennis star Pete
5 Grotto
6 Pub servings
7 27-Across, e.g., informally
8 "Get out!"
9 Cesar who played the Joker
10 "Exodus" hero
11 *College in Worcester, Mass.
12 One-year record
13 Lerner's musical partner
21 Sound reasoning
22 About, in dates
26 Satisfied sigh
28 "The Time Machine" race
29 Word following the last parts of the answers to the five starred clues
31 Pussy foot?
32 QB Manning
33 *Kids' game
35 "Ricochet" co-star
37 Rebel Guevara
38 Mauna ___
41 Fiber-___ cable
42 Pulsate
45 Prosciutto
48 Living room piece
50 Positive aspect
52 Self-assurance
53 Musician/wit Levant
54 Not tied down
55 Titleholder
57 Artist Picasso
58 Really steamed
59 Collectible Ford product
62 Voiced
63 Fairy-tale fiend
65 Private eye, slangily

by Allan E. Parrish

44

ACROSS

1 Language in which plurals are formed by adding -oj
10 Wrist timer
15 Christian Dior, e.g.
16 Drop a line from a pier, say
17 Angry rabbits in August?
19 Windsor's prov.
20 Prefix with identification
21 Hard-to-miss hoops shots
22 Handheld computer, briefly
24 Give a card hand
25 Hens at the greatest altitude?
32 Battery part
33 Houston skaters
34 Horse at the track
36 Villain's reception
37 Green card holder
38 Whence Goya's duchess
39 Memphis-to-Chicago dir.
40 Tourneys for all
41 Have ___ (revel)
42 Cat lady's mission?
45 Channel
46 Finder's ___
47 Shortly, after "in"
50 Have a bug
52 Tussaud's title: Abbr.
55 What a Chicago ballpark bench holds?
59 Apply, as coat of paint
60 Beach cookouts
61 Mensa-eligible
62 Private chat

DOWN

1 Greek nymph who pined away for Narcissus
2 "Any day now"
3 Any miniature golf shot
4 And more: Abbr.
5 Play about robots
6 Scents
7 Not yet final, in law
8 Trueheart of "Dick Tracy"
9 Poet's planet
10 Classifieds
11 Tree rings
12 Happy hour cry
13 Staff symbol
14 Dame Myra
18 Given experimentally
22 Many profs.
23 Actor Billy ___ Williams
24 Most calamitous
25 1944 Chemistry Nobelist Otto
26 Permanently written
27 "Take a look!"
28 Scouts seek it
29 Life form
30 China's Zhou ___
31 Luxurious fur
35 Guys' pals
37 Zeniths
38 French cleric
40 Luxuriant
41 Face on a fiver
43 Masthead title
44 On fire
47 Pointy tools
48 Impact sound
49 Informal "Welcome!"
50 Auto shaft
51 "___ first . . ."
52 Karaoke need
53 Track event
54 In ___ (existing)
56 Columbus Day mo.
57 Hoops org.
58 Rebellious Turner

by Bruce Adams

45

ACROSS

1 Rocker Ocasek
4 "American Pie" beauty
9 Window area
13 Sufficient, old-style
15 Walt Whitman's "___ the Body Electric"
16 Far from harbor
17 *1942 film with the line "What makes saloonkeepers so snobbish?"
19 Look inside?
20 Prefix with mural
21 Long-distance letters
23 Commercials
24 *Bench sharer
28 One with fingers crossed
30 Lead-in to while
31 "Illmatic" rapper
32 Like a clock that has hands
34 Ensembles of eight
37 You might crack one while playing
38 Word before pool or park
41 *Japanese grill
43 "Get it?"
44 "Me, Myself & ___," 2000 Jim Carrey film
46 Peter of "Goodbye, Mr. Chips"
48 When Alexander Hamilton and Aaron Burr dueled
50 Goof
51 Letters
55 Actor Milo
56 *Underwater creature whose males give birth
58 "Finger-lickin' good" restaurant
59 Fort ___, N.J.
61 Had dinner at home
62 Not at home
64 How the answer to each of the nine starred clues repeats
68 Barely cooked
69 Bor-r-ring voice
70 Alternative to truth in a party game
71 Uno + uno + uno
72 The "S" in WASP
73 "Help!"

DOWN

1 Say, as a pledge
2 More ludicrous
3 Sportscaster Bob
4 Nothing
5 Blind ___ bat
6 Clamor
7 Old llama herder
8 Christie who created Hercule Poirot
9 Instrument that wails
10 *They live on acres of Acre's
11 *Rick Blaine in 17-Across, e.g.
12 Sets (down)
14 Start liking
18 "Kapow!"
22 Throat part
25 "Nay" sayer
26 Popular aerobic program
27 *Many-acred homes
29 Bobby's wife on "Dallas"
33 "Well, that beats all!"
35 Bawled (out)
36 It might need to be settled
38 Secretive org.
39 *Classic Chinese military treatise, with "The"
40 *Fearful 1917–20 period
42 Bar mitzvah dance
45 Slangy denial
47 Hammed it up
49 River nymphs, in Greek myth
52 Basketball venues

by Natan Last

53 San ___, Argentina
54 Camera eyes
57 Derisive laugh
58 Mario ___, Nintendo racing game
60 More, in commercialese
63 Verbal nod
65 Be a pugilist
66 Plastic ___ Band
67 Evening hour

46

ACROSS
1 Completely wreck
6 Pipe shape
9 Twin Falls's home
14 High home
15 Finder's reward
16 Generous soul
17 Loan to a company before it goes public, say
20 Computer command after cut
21 Gill opening
22 D.C. insider
24 N.F.L. position: Abbr.
26 Lake that is a source of the Mississippi
30 Spilling out
34 Director Browning
35 Russian country house
36 Slangy turndown
37 History chapters
38 Periods of unrest
42 Life stories
43 Unedited
44 South Beach plan and others
46 Seating info
47 Remover of impurities
50 "___ Song" (John Denver tune)
52 ___ one-eighty
53 Mormons, initially
54 Crash-probing agcy.
56 Place to shop in Tokyo
59 The starts to 17-, 30-, 38- and 47-Across, collectively
65 Arboreal Aussie
66 Be short
67 Pour out from
68 On the tail of
69 Ernie of golf
70 Social level

DOWN
1 Treater's pickup
2 "___ the land of the free . . ."
3 Racing feat
4 Broadway musical with the song "The Gods Love Nubia"
5 Crab morsels
6 Lacking vigor
7 Handout at a tiki bar
8 Shutterbug's purchase
9 Set off
10 Formal rulings
11 Bird: Prefix
12 Old biddy
13 .com alternative
18 Impress clearly
19 Land (on)
22 Part of a commercial name after "i"
23 It may be standing
25 Extended, as a membership
27 Lights on posts, perhaps
28 Didn't work that hard
29 They may pop up nowadays
31 Greek R's
32 Greek T
33 Nascar ___
37 Expressionist Nolde
39 Harsh and metallic
40 Long. crosser
41 ___ Amin
42 It has a supporting role
45 Grads-to-be: Abbr.
47 Home mixologist's spot
48 ___ gallery
49 Go bankrupt
51 Fireplace
55 Fraternal org.
57 Tiny fraction of a min.
58 Coors brand
59 Calypso cousin
60 Punch-in-the-gut response
61 Rebellious Turner

by Pete Muller

62 Saddler's
tool
63 Baseball's
Master
Melvin
64 Carrie of
"Creepshow"

ACROSS
1 It's a no-no
6 Up for it
10 Hook attachment
14 Shia's deity
15 Letter-shaped beam
16 Long ago
17 Colorful food fish
18 Kid around
19 Mix up
20 Deeply hurt
23 Benevolent fellow
25 Poem of exaltation
26 Quitter's cry
27 Abs strengtheners
29 Big bash
32 Partner of poivre
33 Ark complement
34 Checks for errors
36 Ramadan observance
41 Be testy with
42 Pride member
44 Little terror
47 Genesis garden
48 Attached, in a way
50 Racial equality org.
52 Whale group
53 Suffix with butyl
54 Gulliver's creator
59 Mineralogists' samples
60 Met solo
61 Game played on a wall
64 Scot's attire
65 Took a turn
66 Like leprechauns
67 To be, to Brutus
68 Scots' turndowns
69 Conical dwelling

DOWN
1 "___ Te Ching"
2 Yodeler's setting
3 Semiformal
4 Pearl Harbor site
5 "Come on, that's enough!"
6 Doll for boys
7 Help in wrongdoing
8 Kind of note
9 Art Deco notable
10 Petty officer
11 Class clown's doings
12 Yule tree hanging
13 Pulitzer winner Studs
21 N.F.L. six-pointers
22 Drink heartily
23 "I know what you're thinking" ability
24 Fish story teller
28 www addresses
29 Wordless "Ouch!"
30 Summer month, in Paris
31 Rock's ___ Lobos
34 Sherlock Holmes prop
35 Red tag event
37 Klutzy
38 ___ about (rove)
39 Excursion diversion
40 Cel character
43 S.F.-to-Spokane direction
44 Bit of humor most people can't get
45 Native New Zealanders
46 Discussion groups
48 Wrecker's job
49 "Finally finished!"
51 Social stratum
52 Jr.-year exams
55 Goldie of "Laugh-In"
56 General vicinity
57 Punch-in time for many
58 MetroCard cost
62 "The Waste Land" monogram
63 ___-crab soup

by Norma Johnson

48

ACROSS

1 Director Kazan
5 Actress Lane of old TV
9 Challenge in a western
13 Artist Chagall
14 Developer's land
16 A pop
17 Computer introduced by Steve Jobs
18 __ dish (lab item)
19 Full of pep
20 First showing at an all-day film festival? (1988)
23 Genetic material
24 Prankster's bit
25 Second showing (1970)
34 First sign, astrologically
35 Crystal-lined rock
36 Rocky peak
37 Highland headgear
38 Paycheck booster
39 Packed away
40 Greek H
41 Von Richthofen's title
42 Disloyal
44 Third showing (1975)
47 Taking after
48 Motorists' org.
49 Final showing (2004)
57 Graph line
58 Wipe clean
59 The Hawkeyes of college sports
60 Beanery handout
61 Hearing-related
62 "Beg pardon . . ."
63 Mideast's Gulf of __
64 Avian sources of red meat
65 Ticked off

DOWN

1 Send out
2 Poor, as excuses go
3 It includes Mesopotamia
4 Damn
5 Having fun
6 La __ Tar Pits
7 Upside-down sleepers
8 Neutral shade
9 Create fashions
10 Speaks ill of
11 Plot unit
12 Tot's repeated query
15 Self-important sorts
21 Printers' supplies
22 Red in the middle
25 Assigned stars to
26 Muse with a lyre
27 Joltin' Joe
28 Ancient marketplace
29 A little before the hour
30 Climb onto
31 Novelist Calvino
32 "That's a lie!"
33 Eco-friendly
38 San Francisco and environs
41 Place for a hayfork
42 Herr's mate
43 Biblical liar
45 Nissan, once
46 Atelier sights
49 Pink-slipped
50 Speeder's risk
51 Loyal
52 Damage
53 Biblical twin
54 Gallery-filled part of the Big Apple
55 Basin accompanier
56 Unlikely to bite
57 Physicians' grp.

by Ray Fontenot

49

ACROSS
1 The gamut
5 Places to kick habits
11 Merino mother
14 Comic Chappelle
15 Like a paradise
16 Gen ___
17 Cool treats
18 Wildlife manager
20 Home of Smith College
22 Like some heirs
23 Flop or lop follower
26 100 square meters
29 Home of the U.S. Military Academy
33 Run out
35 Like a greenhorn
36 Start the kitty
37 Suffix with psych-
38 Leopold Bloom's creator
40 Maryland collegian
41 Unicorn in a 1998 movie
42 Words of commitment
43 Correo ___ (words on an envelope)
44 Home of Notre Dame
48 In position
49 "Blame It ___" (Michael Caine film)
50 Most-cooked parts of roasts
52 Home of Michigan State
59 Sites for stargazers
61 With 64-Across, 2005 Charlize Theron title role
62 Author Rand
63 Way past ripe
64 See 61-Across
65 "Absolutely!"
66 Ball
67 Puts into play

DOWN
1 Score after deuce
2 Food in a shell
3 [see other side]
4 Citrus peels
5 Wine and dine
6 Mingo player on "Daniel Boone"
7 Source of hashish
8 Work without ___
9 Steven ___, real-life subject of the 1987 film "Cry Freedom"
10 Act starter
11 Former lovers, e.g.
12 Minuscule
13 Mess up
19 Flow out
21 "The Battle Hymn of the Republic" writer
24 It may come with more than one side
25 Colorist's vessel
26 "The Tempest" king
27 Mete out
28 Devotees of fine dining
30 Test for fit
31 ___-Man
32 Have a tab
34 Nova ___
38 Triangular sail
39 Lyric poem
43 "The King ___"
45 Boorish sorts, in Canada
46 Naysayer
47 Ready for the rubber room
51 Major mess
53 Sporty auto roof
54 Plasterer's strip
55 Johnson of "Laugh-In"
56 Salon goos
57 Pouting look
58 "Need You Tonight" band
59 Compensation
60 Caustic alkali

by John Underwood

50

ACROSS

1 Former U.N. chief Javier ___ de Cuéllar
6 Colorist
10 Black Power symbol
14 Site of Crockett's demise
15 Gutter site
16 Creep (along)
17 Spoonerism, usually
20 Something that may be brought back from the beach
21 Abbr. in a help wanted ad
22 Instruments played with bows
23 Sight along the Thames
28 Most acute
30 Bran material
31 Draft org.
32 Get on one's nerves
33 Indiana ___
35 Actress Roseanne
36 Word that can follow the starts of 17-, 23-, 51- and 59-Across
38 Clickable image
42 Baby screecher
44 Observe Yom Kippur
45 Deadly viper
48 "The Star-Spangled Banner" contraction
49 Like some dental floss
51 Hoedown folks
54 Author Vonnegut and others
55 General on a Chinese menu
56 Lilliputian
59 San Francisco tourist attraction
64 Modern ice cream flavor
65 Little explorer on Nickelodeon
66 Raise
67 Pete Rose's team
68 Small bit
69 Actress Moorehead

DOWN

1 Previous
2 Singer Fitzgerald
3 Slickers and the like
4 Akihito's title: Abbr.
5 Madhouse
6 Abhor
7 Popular e-mail provider
8 Grandmother of Enoch
9 Abbr. after some generals' names
10 That's all
11 Metal bars
12 Crews' craft
13 Postdocs often publish them
18 Gangsters' foes
19 Elliptical
24 Emcee's delivery
25 Word between two last names
26 Etymological basis
27 Axes
28 Putin's former org.
29 Pitcher's stat
33 Small bit
34 Instrument often accompanied by a pair of small drums
36 Swiss painter Paul
37 "Happy Days" put-down
39 Crew's leader
40 Atomic number of hydrogen
41 Flanders of "The Simpsons"
43 "It's ___ than that!"
44 Great reverence
45 Request
46 Future knight
47 Puckered
49 Open, in a way
50 Cpls. and others

by Jonathan Gersch

51

ACROSS

1 Bird in the "Arabian Nights"
4 Traffic tie-up
9 Morning hour
14 Actor Gulager
15 Playful sprite
16 Throat dangler
17 Alphabetic trio
18 38-Across, in a sense
20 Decides one will
22 Afternoon social
23 Request to a switchboard oper.
24 Secular
25 Composer of the "Brandenburg Concertos," in brief
28 38-Across, in a sense
31 Throw out
35 Verdi aria
36 Squanders
38 1964 #1 hit by the Shangri-Las . . . or this puzzle's theme
42 Excite
43 Italian flowers
44 Mural site
45 38-Across, in a sense
49 Personify
52 Five-star
53 Letters before a pseudonym
56 U.R.L. ending
57 "Uncle" of old TV
59 38-Across, in a sense
63 Former Vladimir Putin org.
64 Zhou ___
65 Being of service
66 Funnyman Philips
67 Seat that may have a swivel top
68 All-night trucker's aid
69 Tibetan beast

DOWN

1 Soft drink since 1905
2 Friend since high school, say
3 Place for chalk
4 Petty quarrel
5 One-named singer for the 1960s Velvet Underground
6 Firefighter's tool
7 Resort city that shares its name with a Duran Duran hit
8 Did not disturb
9 Rapper Shakur
10 "Little" '60s singer
11 Hosiery shade
12 Third baseman Rodriguez
13 Schooner part
19 Pirate's domain
21 Plan
25 Mil. plane's boosted launch
26 Discarded: Var.
27 Setting for TV's "House"
29 War god on Olympus
30 Muddy area
32 Actress Hagen
33 Jiffy
34 "Naughty!"
36 Often-misused pronoun
37 Prefix with space
38 Murphy's is well known
39 Period to remember
40 Gmail alternative
41 Microscopic
45 Area connected to a kennel
46 Computer user's shortcut
47 Conundrum
48 Adidas competitor
50 It merged with Exxon
51 "What's shakin', ___?"
53 Skunk River city

by Barry C. Silk

54 Categorical imperative philosopher

55 Guthrie who sang about Alice

57 Opposite of bueno

58 "Mocking-bird" singer Foxx, 1963

60 Southeast Asian language

61 Oklahoma native

62 Prefix with afternoon

52

ACROSS

1 King who united England
7 Game period: Abbr.
10 Hinged closer
14 Friend
15 Laramie's state: Abbr.
16 They lean to the right: Abbr.
17 Teleologist's concern
20 Word on a Mexican stop sign
21 Bugged
22 French flower
23 ¹⁄₁₀₀ of a euro
24 Vainglory
25 On the side of
26 Part of the verb "to be," to Popeye
28 Overlook
32 "September 1, 1939" poet
35 Old Asian ruler
37 Jaffa's land: Abbr.
38 Figuring something out
42 A hallucinogen
43 Hanging ___ a thread
44 August 15, 1945
45 Nosedive
47 Indent setter
48 Carrier with the in-flight magazine Scanorama
49 Actress Gardner
51 Cries during a paso doble
53 "It's not TV. It's ___"
56 Make worse
60 Clunker of a car
61 Part of a city code
63 Bring to naught
64 Give the coup de grâce
65 Lamebrain, in slang
66 ___ extra cost
67 Some ESPN highlights, for short
68 Oliver Twist and others

DOWN

1 Like two dimes and four nickels
2 Without much intelligence
3 Actress Naomi of "Mulholland Dr."
4 Sony co-founder Morita
5 Post-retirement activity?
6 Bureau part
7 Places to find the letters circled in the grid
8 Use 7-Down
9 Worker who makes rounds
10 Zoo heavyweights, informally
11 On
12 MS. enclosure
13 Argued (for)
18 10th anniversary gift
19 Scandal sheet
23 Neighbor of Gabon
25 Quagmire
27 Sounds leading up to a sneeze
29 Pirate captain of legend
30 La Española, e.g.
31 Hunted animals
32 "___ Lang Syne"
33 U.S. ally in W.W. II
34 One-named singer with the 2001 hit "Thank You"
36 Exploding stars
39 Meeting expectations
40 Cagers' grp.
41 Breakfast drinks, for short
46 "Scent of a Woman" Oscar winner
48 Going out with
50 Title for one on the way to sainthood: Abbr.
52 British "Inc."
53 Artist Matisse
54 Strips for breakfast

by John Farmer

53

ACROSS

1 Harsh criticism
5 Presidential middle name
10 Active vocabulary?
15 Priest in an Ogden Nash verse
16 Point a finger at
17 It may include a cc or bcc list
18 "Little Shop of Horrors" dentist
19 Consumer Reports offering
21 Film showing for V.I.P.'s, in the army?
23 Ludd, the original Luddite
24 Doctor's request
25 ___ de Jouy (fabric)
27 Carte blanche offer
32 Worked the garden
35 "Chances ___"
38 Use the H.O.V. lane, say
40 Driver's warning
41 Big studio release, in the army?
44 Fit to serve
45 Gary's home
46 Med. unit
47 Add to the kitty
49 Like many oaths
51 Shapes up
53 Oktoberfest music
57 Islands fare
59 Common ticket category, in the army?
64 Means of visual communication
66 Foam
67 Queen ___ lace
68 Bit of monkey business
69 Give a come-hither look
70 Quaint denial
71 Lets up
72 Get tiresome

DOWN

1 Lays an egg
2 Maggot, e.g.
3 Cordial quality
4 Bob Dole, by birth
5 E.g., e.g.
6 Smurf-colored
7 Comic Martha
8 Final word
9 Scholarship criterion
10 Meatless, informally
11 Outback runner
12 Postponed, in a way
13 Patiently wait
14 Inuit's ride
20 Demarcation affected by warming
22 ___ Canyon (Pueblo cultural area)
26 Not right
28 Shows with lower-priced seats, usually
29 Yeats's land, poetically
30 Popular MP3 players
31 "Pagliacci" clown
33 Slips up
34 Tough to fathom
35 In a frenzied way
36 Sari-clad royal
37 Bouncers' tasks
39 Nevada gemstone
42 Cousin of a hammerhead
43 Roughs it
48 Consume
50 Standby's salvation
52 Take potshots
54 Feudal lord
55 "Bear" that's not a bear
56 Florida congressman Crenshaw
57 Jr.'s exam
58 ___ Hotels (luxury chain)
60 Indian tourist city
61 Double-helix molecules
62 Lippizaner's locks
63 Kinds
65 Classic Mattel doll

by Kelsey Blakley

54

ACROSS
1 NPR host ___ Conan
5 Prevents, in legalspeak
11 Dental device
14 Chamber music piece
15 Blubber
16 When to get to the airport to pick someone up: Abbr.
17 A la a free-for-all
19 It's definite
20 Western lily
21 Granny, for one
22 ___ Rio, Tex.
23 Become bored by
25 Really easy decision
28 Bum
30 Mimieux of "Where the Boys Are"
31 "Newhart" setting
32 World Series prize
35 Double curves

36 Slogan popularized in the 1980s . . . and a hint to 17-, 25-, 28-, 48-, 51- and 60-Across
39 Fabled "snowmen"
42 Call at home
43 Unruly do
46 Hunky sort
48 Restricted airspace
51 Pitcher's coup
53 Good horseshoe toss
54 Eastern "path"
55 BB's and shells
58 "Whoso diggeth ___ shall fall therein": Proverbs
59 Museum hanging
60 Mediocre
63 Mag. info
64 Suffragist Bloomer
65 Hatcher of film

66 Whatever amount
67 Hal David output
68 ___ race

DOWN
1 To the ___ power
2 Wind and rain cause it
3 Wing part
4 Stuck
5 Fall back
6 Overcharge
7 Of two minds
8 "The Dick Van Dyke Show" catchphrase
9 "The bill and coo of sex" per Elbert Hubbard
10 Lawn base
11 Warming, of sorts
12 Wheaties box adorner
13 Singer Ella ___ Morse
18 Shortly
22 Muralist Rivera
23 ___ Friday's
24 Holiday trees

26 "___ calling!"
27 Hi-___ monitor
29 Little foxes
33 Code-cracking org.
34 Large fishing hook
36 Self-professed ultrapatriot
37 Old Voice of America org.
38 "Gimme a C . . . !," e.g.
39 Derisive word
40 Bibliophile's concern
41 100%
43 Handle
44 Like Carter's presidency
45 ___ diem
47 Excessively flattering
49 Repeated word in "She Loves You"
50 1952 Brando role
52 Mideast V.I.P.
56 Saharan land
57 Ear-related
59 Things in tubes

by Jim Page

60 Hoedown
    partner
61 Airline to
    Oslo
62 Family
    nickname

55

ACROSS

1 Scores, as a victory, with "up"
7 Blunted blade
11 Hipster
14 Door sign
15 Fancy club trophies
16 Pale ___
17 Mongol horde, e.g.
18 Romantic goings-on
20 "Rose is a rose is a rose is a rose" writer
21 Clinton cabinet member
22 Poetic land
23 Tupperware sale event
25 Takes a turn
26 City limits sign abbr.
27 Dept. of Labor agcy.
29 N.L. Central team
32 Society column word
34 Erie Canal city
38 What 18-, 23-, 55- and 63-Across each comprises
43 Early time to rise
44 Mahmoud Abbas's grp.
45 Pro-gun org.
46 Catches Z's
49 Star pitchers
52 Chorus after a bad call
55 Catching cold?
60 Annika Sorenstam's org.
61 Fraternity letters
62 Good-looker
63 Cockpit datum
65 Whodunit plot element
66 Vane dir.
67 "You lookin' ___?"
68 Spring bloomers
69 ___ Moines
70 North Sea feeder
71 When many stores open

DOWN

1 Don't go together
2 Must
3 It means "Go with God"
4 Act as a go-between
5 Boarding site
6 Sound of a leak
7 Calculus pioneer
8 Chop-chop
9 Embassy figures
10 Suffix with Brooklyn
11 Where "Aida" premiered
12 Jude Law title role
13 Many Justin Timberlake fans
19 Smooth, musically
21 Was incoherent
24 "All the King's Men" star, 2006
28 Important airport
29 They cross aves.
30 ___-night double-header
31 Deli delicacy
33 Eerie ability
35 Novelist Fleming
36 N.B.A. position: Abbr.
37 "___ friend, I . . ."
39 Toto's home
40 "___ Believer"
41 Five Norse kings
42 Points that may have rays
47 Lab tubes
48 Intrigue
50 Debutante's date
51 Confined
52 Short on flavor
53 Say one's piece
54 Shrek's ilk
56 Pillow filler
57 Answer to "Who's there?"
58 David of Pink Panther movies

by Richard Chisholm

59 Foie gras sources

64 Pony up

65 "Mamma ___!"

56

ACROSS
1 Big stingers
6 Johnny Fever's workplace, in 1970s–'80s TV
10 Amt. at a car dealership
14 Ancient marketplace
15 Mixed bag
16 Siouan tribe
17 Some horizontal lines
18 Carries
19 Birthstone of someone born on Halloween
20 Professional secrets
23 Muslim holy man
26 Amanda of "The Whole Nine Yards"
27 Off-site meetings, maybe
28 Promoted, as a pawn
30 Took to court
32 Went bad
33 Formal discourse
34 "Choosy moms choose ___"
37 Ham it up
38 ___ pop
39 Ride the ___ (sit out a baseball game)
40 Heros
41 Red in the middle
42 Large, at Starbucks
43 Elec. Day, e.g.
44 Hockey feat
45 Some urban legends
46 Aussie's neighbor
47 Like some old stores
48 Early seventh-century year
50 Wander
52 Whirlpool
53 U.N. ambassador under Reagan
56 Shows
57 Entr'___
58 Certain flower girl
62 Focal point
63 Honolulu's home
64 Reese of "Touched by an Angel"
65 Plea
66 Swill
67 Balance sheet listing

DOWN
1 Candle material
2 Turkish title
3 Red ___
4 Stain looseners on washday
5 Lip
6 Gobbled up, with "down"
7 Movie for which Jane Fonda won an Oscar
8 Starboard
9 You might strike one
10 Docked
11 Mid-March honoree
12 Map lines
13 New York Cosmos star
21 Like some columns
22 Fig or fir
23 Hurdle for Mensa membership
24 Hawaiian dress
25 Organism needing oxygen
29 Born
31 Can. neighbor
33 Something said while holding a bag
34 Having bad luck, say
35 Mean
36 Spunky
38 Like The Onion
39 War enders
41 Uncooked
42 Designer Diane ___ Furstenberg
44 Honey site
45 Rope material
46 "Sexual Behavior in the Human Male" author
47 Begin, as a hobby
48 Two-sport Sanders
49 Entertainment from a magician
51 Brand name in lawn care

by Ken Stern

57

ACROSS

1 7 Up flavor
5 Easter serving
9 Funny ones
14 "Just ___!"
15 Succulent plant
16 Clinker
17 Locker room supply
18 *Solid ground*
20 *You should have the body*
22 Online currency
23 Catches in the act
24 Pro at balancing
27 Big pet food brand
30 Pageant wear
32 Erica who wrote "Any Woman's Blues"
35 Bottom of a lily
38 Bank rights
39 Schoenberg's "Moses und ___"
40 *From the beginning*

42 Gray-brown goose
43 "The Taming of the Shrew" setting
45 Sport whose name means "gentle way"
46 Formerly, once
47 Kind of number
49 7'1" N.B.A. star, informally
51 Pince-___
52 Shout to a team, maybe
55 Fall colors
59 *The die is cast*
62 *Always the same*
65 "Warm"
66 They're rather pointless
67 "Camelot" actor Franco
68 Other, in the barrio
69 Charges
70 Innovative 1982 Disney film
71 Like a busybody

DOWN

1 Wood-turning tool
2 Stern that bows
3 Nellie of opera
4 *Behold the proof*
5 Back muscles, for short
6 "The Black Stallion" boy
7 Idiot
8 He said "Slump? I ain't in no slump. I just ain't hitting"
9 Turndown
10 Van Gogh floral subject
11 Bobby of Boston
12 Male cat
13 Title in S. Amer.
19 Getaway alerts, for short
21 Cry before "It's you!"
24 All alternative
25 ___ Grove, N.J.
26 Money in the bank, e.g.

28 Part of a C.E.O.'s résumé
29 Topic: Abbr.
31 *Without which not*
32 Black lacquer
33 Filibuster, in a way
34 Alertness aid
36 Bud's comedy sidekick
37 Briefs, briefly
41 "Isn't that beautiful?!"
44 Lacking purpose
48 Round dance official
50 Gallery display
53 Canonized figure
54 One who's not "it"
56 Look after
57 Some Peters
58 Homeless animal
59 Mimicked
60 Pertaining to flying
61 "Follow me!"
62 Leave in stitches?
63 Air quality org.
64 Debussy's "La ___"

by Patrick Blindauer

58

ACROSS

1 The Velvet Fog
6 Casino pair
10 Cabaret, e.g.
14 Smuggler's stock
15 Giant-screen film format
16 Summer wine selection
17 All the rockets in existence?
20 Ask for
21 Some emergency cases, for short
22 Place for shots
23 Noughts-and-crosses win
25 Brand of shaving products
26 "Dry-clean only," e.g.?
33 Empty (of)
34 Small, as a Beanie Baby
35 First course option
36 Does as told
38 ___ Andreas fault
39 Like déjà vu
40 Turner who sang "The Best"
41 Marzipan ingredient
43 Piggy
44 Cooking utensil from central Spain?
47 Like a starless sky
48 Alt. spelling
49 Iran-___
52 Debtor's letters
54 ___ buco
58 HAL 9000, in "2001: A Space Odyssey"?
61 First-year J.D. candidate
62 Restaurant chain acronym
63 Thus far
64 A sergeant might ask a soldier to pick it up
65 I.R.S. ID's
66 Recipe parts

DOWN

1 Tabbies' mates
2 Mayberry boy
3 Angry reaction
4 Animal with a shaggy coat
5 U.K. record label
6 Fizzled out
7 Radio's former "___ in the Morning"
8 Poky
9 Mutual fund redemption charge
10 Deep fissure
11 Oral history
12 "Evil empire" of the '80s
13 "It's ___ real!"
18 Sarge's superior
19 Brewery units
24 Baseball's Ed and Mel
25 Relative key of C major
26 Second-longest human bone
27 Utopias
28 Stahl of "60 Minutes"
29 As a friend, to the French
30 Outlet of the left ventricle
31 Astronaut ___ Bluford, the first African-American in space
32 Sport with lunges
33 Mil. option
37 First N.F.L. QB with consecutive 30-touchdown passing seasons
39 Novelist Ferber
41 Acid neutralizers
42 "___ Organum" (1620 Francis Bacon work)
45 Crucifix inscription
46 Subject of the 1999 film "Le Temps Retrouvé"

by Paula Gamache

59

ACROSS

1 C-shaped gadget
6 Breastplate, e.g.
11 "Kinda" suffix
14 Spokes, essentially
15 Break from service
16 E-file preparer, briefly
17 Good-looking, briefly
19 Part of a confession
20 Oscar winner Tomei
21 Like a woodland
23 Inventor Rubik
24 Bounty letters
26 Thumbscrew ridges
27 Final Four org.
29 Dom or earl
30 Low man
33 Taylor Hicks, e.g.
35 Sharp as a tack
38 Cable network owned by NBC Universal
39 Oh-so-cute carnival prizes, briefly
42 Pirouette pivot
43 Adoption agcy.
45 Projector unit
46 "Jerusalem Delivered" poet
48 Of yore
50 Fall setting
52 Dry rot, e.g.
54 Bustle
55 "Don't forget . . ."
59 Prayer wheel inscriptions
61 "Oops!" list
63 Phoenix-to-Albuquerque dir.
64 Risky person to do business with, briefly
66 Holy ones: Abbr.
67 Made public
68 Possessive pronoun in an old hymn
69 It may be cocked
70 Some are proper
71 Church assembly

DOWN

1 ___ fraîche
2 Agent Swifty
3 Deck out
4 Flunkies
5 Places to refuel
6 Toby filler
7 Marine hazards
8 Deli supply
9 It's too much
10 Take umbrage at
11 Winter hazards, briefly
12 Hawker's line
13 Deck crew
18 "That's a laugh!"
22 Be a sourpuss
25 Fair one?
28 "Le ___ d'Or"
29 Rang out
30 H.O.V. lane user
31 Shakespeare's "poor venomous fool"
32 Student writing competition, briefly
34 Buck's mate
36 Aurora, to the Greeks
37 Opposite of paleo-
40 Fortress of old
41 Sault ___ Marie Canals
44 Kelp, for one
47 Possible result of a natural disaster
49 Victim of Macbeth
51 Active sort
52 Crayola color changed to "peach"
53 ___ Mountains, home of King's Peak
54 Ghostly pale

by Robert Zimmerman

56 Like most South Americans
57 Note taker
58 Propelled a shell
60 Hose shade
62 Mafiosi who "flip"
65 Online revenue sources

60

ACROSS

1 A diehard enemy might want yours
6 Gather
11 QB's goals
14 Amor vincit ___
15 Milk: Prefix
16 In
17 Call in roulette
19 Suffix with fish
20 For smaller government, presumably
21 One who supplies the means
23 Knocks off
25 Gun dealer's stock
26 Norway's patron saint
30 Call in blackjack
34 Robot maid on "The Jetsons"
36 Buttresses
37 Call in many a betting game
44 Impart
45 Broadcast portion
46 Call in draw poker
52 John P. Marquand detective
53 Signify
54 Prefix with carpal
56 Sounds of walking in moccasins
60 Deicing tool
65 Detroit-to-Philadelphia dir.
66 Call in craps
68 Family room
69 Challenge to ___
70 Family girl
71 Inexact fig.
72 Request to meet in person
73 Photographer Adams

DOWN

1 It has arms, legs and a back
2 "Let's go!"
3 "Sometimes you feel like ___ . . ."
4 Italian river valley in W.W. II fighting
5 Page of music
6 Cosmonaut Leonov, the first human to walk in space
7 "Holy moly!"
8 Fair-sized plot
9 Old British gun
10 Fountain offering
11 1991 Geena Davis title role
12 "The Sound of Music" hit
13 "Sophie's Choice" author
18 Per
22 Catch
24 Celebrity
26 Fort ___ on Monterey Bay
27 W.C.
28 Tempe sch.
29 Tiny tale
31 Part of r.p.m.: Abbr.
32 Pre-1868 Tokyo
33 Dog in 1930s films
35 Fitzgerald who sang "A-Tisket, A-Tasket"
38 Comics cry
39 Start of long-distance dialing
40 Make music on a comb
41 Answer before exchanging rings
42 Have a ___ to pick
43 Sentimental drivel
46 Hinder
47 Some auto deals
48 Present but not active
49 Contents of some shells
50 Be cozy
51 Write permanently
55 Rock concert setting
57 Pitchers' stats
58 Depended (on)
59 Pivot
61 Score after deuce
62 Bakery display
63 "___ homo"
64 Line holder
67 NASA vehicle

by Robert Dillman

61

The answers to the 13 starred clues have something in common.

ACROSS

1 *Stone in Hollywood
7 *Home for Will Rogers and Garth Brooks
15 1950s All-Star outfielder Minnie
16 *What some unscrupulous e-businesses do?
17 Arthurian paradise
18 Bejeweled pendant
19 *Torn
20 Regatta crew leaders
21 Govt. code-breaking group
22 Wish to take back
23 Song syllable
25 U.S. mil. medal
27 Whence the line "A soft answer turneth away wrath"
31 *Extremely narrow winning margin
35 *Kind of club
37 Mother of Queen Elizabeth I
38 Lingerie shade
41 *A Perón
42 Mercury model
43 TV Dr. of note
44 *Student of Dr. Pangloss
46 *Lover of Radames
47 Like some nursery care
50 Cape Town's country: Abbr.
53 Oz. and kg.
54 Washington ballplayer, briefly
56 Study
59 Class ___
62 *Renown
63 Nullify
65 Air ___
67 *Site of much horsing around?
68 Architectural decoration
69 *Perform ostentatiously
70 *Destiny

DOWN

1 Astrologer Sydney
2 Meet, as expectations, with "to"
3 Goofier
4 Battery unit
5 That, in Tijuana
6 Friend of Harry and Hermione
7 Capital near the 60th parallel
8 2001 film set in a mental institution
9 Washed
10 Collect
11 Anthropo-morphic cinema computer
12 Lena of "Chocolat"
13 Place to which Bart Simpson makes prank calls
14 Gillette brand
20 Dodge on the road
23 New Deal program, for short
24 Renaissance instrument
26 Home in the Alps
28 Eyepiece
29 Curer of feta cheese
30 Lay
32 Even one
33 Wayfarer's stop
34 King's title
36 Sully
38 Clean Air Act org.
39 The Bears, on scoreboards
40 Completely free
45 Some "Law & Order" figs.
48 Ancient garland
49 Kind of class
51 Cancel
52 ___ Viejo (California city near Laguna Beach)
55 Creed element
56 Medics
57 Cole Porter's "Well, Did You ___?"
58 "Quo Vadis" role

by Lee Glickstein and Craig Kasper

60 Old music halls

61 Result of a whipping

62 End-of-wk. times

64 Big fight

65 1991 film directed by 1-Across

66 "Either he goes ___ go!"

62

ACROSS

1 "That stinks!," quaintly
4 Ladder danger
8 It makes Frisky frisky
14 Evangelical sch. with a 4,000+ enrollment
15 On the deep
16 Top gun
17 Alternative to Gleem
18 "Pretty Woman" and "Waiting to Exhale"
20 Shul's shepherd
22 On its way
23 Stew (over)
24 Shepherds' locales
26 Like harp seals
28 Actor who got his start on TV's "Gimme a Break!"
32 Roadie's load
33 "Master"
34 "I Love Lucy" co-star
38 Wing, e.g.
40 Archie Bunker, famously
42 Belgrade resident
43 Dummy Mortimer
45 Hit Sega title character
47 Gene material
48 Shooter of westerns
51 What virgin drinks lack
54 1847 novel subtitled "A Narrative of Adventures in the South Seas"
55 Gladly
56 Oscar-winning role for Helen Mirren, in brief
59 Part of a metropolitan area
62 They're exercised when cycling
65 ___ Canals
66 Rival of Old El Paso
67 Opera's ___ Te Kanawa
68 Useful insect secretion
69 Not just hypothesize
70 It's hard to believe
71 Singer Sumac

DOWN

1 Animal hunted in one of Hercules' 12 labors
2 ___ da capo
3 It's embarrassing to eat
4 Spa offerings
5 Tree of life, in Norse myth
6 Kauai keepsakes
7 Some needlework
8 Beach cover-up
9 Be indisposed
10 Those who don't behave seriously
11 Mother-of-pearl
12 Clinton adviser Harold
13 Termites and such
19 Patella
21 Old Turkish title
25 Fashion designer Elie
27 Pioneer in 33⅓ r.p.m. records
28 Photocopier woes
29 Land on the end of a peninsula
30 Sounds from a teakettle
31 Ordeal's quality
35 With shaking hands, perhaps
36 "Rule, Britannia" composer
37 Letter-shaped beam
39 Automatic-drip machine maker
41 Busy viewer's convenience
44 "What an idiot I am!"
46 Arrives
49 Plumlike Chinese fruit
50 Fish eaten cold
51 Foil-making giant
52 Specialists in storytelling?

by Stella Daily and Bruce Venzke

53 Druids, e.g.
57 Totally gross
58 Pelvic bones
60 Go far and wide
61 Part of Florida's Gold Coast, informally
63 Restaurant V.I.P.: Abbr.
64 Misreckon

63

ACROSS

1 Mountain goat's spot
5 Letter-shaped fastener
10 Shake up
14 Hold sway
15 "Socrate" composer
16 Co. bigwig
17 "You said it!"
18 Dress design
19 "Jaywalking" personality
20 Smash
23 Pipe type
24 Once-common skyline sights
28 Head of state?
29 Athlete seated at a table, maybe
33 "Shrek" princess
34 "It's Impossible" crooner
35 Advice to a Harley passenger
39 Cracked a bit
41 County near Tyrone
42 Fits perfectly
46 Jiffy
49 Soccer forward
50 Put on
52 Sprint to the tape . . . and a hint to this puzzle's theme
56 Pacific retreat
59 Like any of seven Nolan Ryan games
60 Similar
61 Tom Joad, for one
62 With 57-Down, 1950s campaign slogan
63 Hawaii's state bird
64 Does a dog trick
65 Break off
66 Windsor, for one

DOWN

1 Tarzan portrayer
2 They spread fast
3 Joan's "Dynasty" role
4 Salami variety
5 B-1 letters
6 Hope/Crosby "Road" destination
7 Ear-related
8 Going from A to B, say
9 [Giggle]
10 Suffered from an allergy, maybe
11 Send packing
12 Meditative sect
13 "Foucault's Pendulum" author
21 Hardly robust
22 Employer of many auditors: Abbr.
25 Plenty
26 Apollo vehicle, for short
27 Good sign for an angel
30 Retinal cell
31 Phone trigram
32 Fish in a John Cleese film
33 Enriches with vitamins
35 "Aquarius" musical
36 Asian holiday
37 High dudgeon
38 Destined for the record books
39 Onager
40 Stick out
43 Do moguls, say
44 Court action
45 A.L. East player
46 Not tacit
47 Cause of weird weather
48 Young swan
51 Short-sheeting, e.g.
53 Weapon in a rumble
54 Scout outing

by Alan Arbesfeld

55 Poll closing?
56 Watch
    attachment
57 See
    62-Across
58 Energetic
    dance

64

ACROSS

1 It may be held together by twine
5 Bit of broccoli
10 Tussle
15 ___ Turing, the Father of Computer Science
16 Usher's domain
17 Incinerator deposit
18 Do a post office job
19 Prenatal
20 It leaves the left ventricle
21 Start of an idle question
24 Long look
25 Canasta plays
26 Kon-Tiki Museum site
30 Mid sixth-century year
31 ___-cow
34 Robbie Knievel's father
38 Blow a mean horn
40 Ruby's victim
42 Middle of the question
45 Book before Jeremiah
46 Drink with tempura
47 Antelope's playmate
48 Inc., in St. Ives
49 Insolence
51 Rover's pal
53 Low-fat breakfast dish
55 Cambria, today
60 End of the question
66 Tenth of a decathlon
67 Manhattan Project result
68 Contact at a hospital, say
69 Pad paper?
70 Bottom line
71 Tropical spot
72 Went white
73 In need of middle management?
74 "Bang Bang" singer, 1966

DOWN

1 Groundwork
2 In the air
3 Pre-chrysalis stage
4 Record
5 Call at first
6 Painter Mondrian
7 Is, to Isabella
8 Chili rating unit?
9 Depended
10 Miles from Plymouth
11 Boxing punch
12 Few and far between
13 Hammett pooch
14 Excellent, slangily
22 Prefix with thermal
23 Licit
27 Language from which "safari" comes
28 Part of a science course
29 Museum display
31 Final check
32 Ye follower
33 Gas leak giveaway
34 Satanic
35 Endow with authority
36 "Zounds!"
37 Luau favor
39 Fall faller
41 Chewing gum mouthful
43 Masterful
44 Runner with a turned-up nose
50 Victim of ring rot
52 Have title to
53 Parson's place
54 Big shot
56 Molded jelly
57 Collar attachment
58 Top scout
59 Have the tiller
60 Fab Four film
61 Part of the eye
62 Square thing
63 Learning method
64 "___ corny . . ."
65 Up to snuff

by Richard Silvestri

65

ACROSS
1 Steering wheel option
5 Superior to
10 Pacific island nation
14 Gas leak evidence
15 20 Mule Team compound
16 Canadian dollar bird
17 Nativity trio
18 Ain't grammatical?
19 Wilson of "Zoolander"
20 Expresses scorn
22 Means' partner
23 Swiss artist Paul
24 Early TV comic Louis
26 Blowhard's speech
29 1966 Rolling Stones hit
34 Give a keynote
35 Eco-friendly
36 Author Fleming
37 Hose woes
38 Nymph of Greek myth
39 ___ breve
40 Upper-left key
41 Prison-related
42 Prefix with task
43 Scan
45 Start a new hand
46 Part of H.R.H.
47 Tubular pasta
48 Place to dock
51 Human hand characteristic
57 In good shape
58 Rhone feeder
59 Back muscles, for short
60 Loafing
61 Word before tube or self
62 Neutral shade
63 Face, slangily
64 They may be the pits
65 Percolate

DOWN
1 Barnum midget
2 Actress Lupino and others
3 Business card graphic
4 Tchotchkes
5 Brought down
6 Held up
7 Creme-filled snack
8 U-Haul rentals
9 Like some warranties
10 Lapel insert
11 Corn Belt state
12 "Friends" spinoff
13 Roadside stops
21 Gen. Robert ___
25 Nikkei average currency
26 It may stick out
27 Pie part
28 Dressing choice
29 Dickens's ___ Heep
30 Boortz of talk radio
31 ___ Lacs, Minn.
32 Big Three meeting place
33 Kind of sketch
35 What a prisoner's tattoo may signify
38 Anxiety may be a symptom of it
39 Quarter-backs' play changes
41 Rue Morgue's creator
42 Prefix with physics
44 Rappers' skill
45 Stair parts
47 Stopped listening, with "out"
48 Swab name
49 Pakistani tongue
50 Has a fever, say
52 Plexiglas unit
53 Corn bread

by Jayne and Alex Boisvert

54 Queen
Anne's ___
55 To be, in
France
56 Encouraging
sign

66

ACROSS
1 Lovers' scrap
5 Nanki-Poo's father
11 Cabinet dept.
14 Samovars
15 Artillery unit member
16 Some eggs
17 McGarrett's TV catchphrase
19 Unit of RAM
20 Father figure?
21 By way of
22 600-homer club member
23 Alights
24 Question for a hitchhiker
26 Giant in Cooperstown
27 Eggs, in labs
29 Biblical landing spot
30 Putting a toe in the water, say
32 Hockey position
35 Paris Métro station next to a music center

36 Shout from the phone
39 Resident of Medina
42 ___' Pea
43 Type size
47 Cause of odd weather
49 Wrap up
51 ___ de plume
52 Chevy truck slogan, once
55 John of London
57 Ward (off)
58 Sellout sign
59 World Cup chant
60 Italian diminutive suffix
61 Singles bar repertoire (and a hint to 17-, 24-, 36- and 52-Across)
63 Make darts, say
64 Cry after "Psst!"
65 For fear that
66 Farm brooder
67 Casually add
68 Pseudo-cultured

DOWN
1 Side story
2 Apportion, as costs
3 Rubs oil on
4 Clicked one's tongue
5 Ones minding the store: Abbr.
6 Birth control option, briefly
7 Scalawag
8 ___ Hall, Diane Keaton role
9 "Gracias" response
10 Cortés's prize
11 Tall wardrobe
12 Succeeds in a big way
13 Yachting event
18 "Happy Motoring" brand
22 Top-notch, to a Brit
24 Innocents
25 Suffix with buck
28 Bugs on a highway

31 Straightened (up)
33 "___ what?"
34 Rosetta stone language
37 Yothers of "Family Ties"
38 Kobe cash
39 Me-first
40 Property recipient, in law
41 Hardly a celebrity
44 Chanter
45 Least ruffled
46 General pardon
48 "Twelfth Night" lover
50 Secluded valley
53 Violists' places: Abbr.
54 Burger go-withs
56 Hyams of 1920s–'30s films
59 Shop window sign
61 Word with boss or bull
62 New England state sch.

by Patrick Blindauer

67

ACROSS

1 Did one leg of an Ironman competition
5 Mike holder on a film set
9 Luxuriant fur
14 Wheeling's river
15 Castaway's spot
16 Ballerinas' skirts
17 Queen of Carthage who loved Aeneas
18 Part of a blind
19 Paradises
20 Start of a newspaper headline about a workplace mishap
23 HBO competitor
24 U.N. workers' grp.
25 Mil. decoration
28 Special __
30 Not subtle at all
34 Headline, part 2

37 Mideast ruler: Var.
38 Ingenuous
39 Flight info, for short
40 Subject for a chiropractor
41 Feudal serf
42 Headline, part 3
44 Stung
46 I, in old Rome
47 C.I.A. predecessor
48 __ Lanka
49 Something that may be drawn in a fight
51 End of the headline
59 Soothing plants
60 Shook, maybe
61 Panache
63 Map detail
64 Beige
65 Muse of history
66 Blacksmiths' tools
67 Bubble source
68 Soviet news agency

DOWN

1 Greenskeeper's supply
2 Caprice
3 "Celeste __" (aria)
4 Gazes dreamily
5 Knights' neighbors
6 1952 Winter Olympics site
7 Minnesota's St. __ College
8 Hand (out)
9 Designer McCartney, daughter of Paul and Linda
10 Sound recording
11 Bingo call
12 Broadway's __-Fontanne Theater
13 Brand name that's coincidentally Italian for "it"
21 Alternative to 1% or 2%
22 Easter decoration
25 Beach sights
26 Twitch

27 Great Wall site
29 Lieu
30 Astronomer Tycho __
31 Protein acid, for short
32 Boys, in Bogotá
33 Close-fitting tartan pants
35 Ignore the alarm?
36 List ender
40 [How boring!]
42 Rabin's predecessor
43 "Go ahead, tell me"
45 No-tell motel happenings
50 Construct
51 Evenhanded
52 It's hinged with the humerus
53 Red ink entry
54 Meadow mamas
55 Fashion's Chanel
56 Gumbo ingredient
57 "__ Enchanted" (Gail Carson Levine book)

by Ray Fontenot

58 Place for a seat of honor

62 Dissenting chorus

68

ACROSS

1 Toyota Camry model
7 Dietary needs
11 Balaam's beast
14 1980 John Carpenter chiller
15 Sarcastic reply
16 Rap's Dr. ___
17 Channel swimmer Gertrude
18 Novelist Jaffe
19 Crude, e.g.
20 Back-to-the-slammer order?
23 Readies, briefly
24 "___ a traveler from an antique land": "Ozymandias"
25 Son of Judah
27 Opposite of ecto-
28 Hard-rock connector
29 Cheerful
30 Reason the kids were left alone?
34 Eiger, e.g.
37 A/C meas.
38 ___ Na Na
39 Get stuck with, as the cost
40 Reward for a Ringling invention?
44 In progress
45 La-la lead-in
46 Devil Ray or Blue Jay, for short
50 Prefix with cab or cure
51 Baba ___, Gilda Radner "S.N.L." character
53 Coward's lack
54 Scuff marks on the prairie?
57 Bespectacled dwarf
58 "Young Frankenstein" hunchback
59 TV's Howser
60 "Norma ___"
61 Poetic times
62 Museum guide
63 Since Jan. 1
64 Be in a stew
65 Alley pickups

DOWN

1 Grassy expanse
2 "Shoot!"
3 Looked like a wolf
4 Music from across the Atlantic
5 Diner basketful
6 Posthumous Pulitzer winner
7 Dalmatian's master, sometimes
8 Superior to
9 Group doctrine
10 Marquee topper
11 "Oklahoma!" gal
12 Ceylon, now
13 Condiment for pommes frites
21 Revolt
22 Go bad
26 Duma denial
28 Graphic ___
29 1970s tennis great Smith
31 Border on
32 Woman's shoe style
33 1969 and 2000 World Series venue
34 Put ___ on (limit)
35 1944 Hitchcock classic
36 Cranked out
41 Do
42 Least favorably
43 Starchy dessert
47 Hang around
48 Object of a tuneup
49 Turns to 0, say
51 It might be placed at a window
52 Without equal
53 Hawk's descent
55 Feudal estate
56 Throws in
57 Prohibitionist

by Donna S. Levin

69

ACROSS

1 Playground retort
6 Pre-bedtime ritual
10 Flower people?: Abbr.
13 Passes over
14 Made an overthrow, say
16 Milne baby
17 Rectory
19 Coastal bird
20 Super server
21 Multivolume refs.
22 Neckline?
24 Minor-league club, in baseball
26 Jumper alternative
28 Locked up
32 Make secure
33 Christopher of "Back to the Future"
34 Kinski title role
36 Look after
39 Delicacy that may be pickled

40 Worthless pile
43 Fish spawn
44 Speaker in the Hall of Fame
46 "___ were . . ."
47 Easy pace
49 Keep one's distance from
51 Glare blocker
53 Erudite sort
56 Foot specialist?
57 ___ water
58 Part of A.M.A.: Abbr.
60 Autocrat of old
64 ___ fault
65 Feast of Trumpets
68 Balance provider, for short
69 ___-Detoo
70 Sounds to shop by
71 Hi-___ monitor
72 Harsh cry
73 Tickle

DOWN

1 L-___ (treatment for parkinsonism)
2 Apple variety
3 Desperate
4 Wok preparation
5 Bygone covert org.
6 Whales, elephants, etc.
7 Dominican-American major-league slugger, to fans
8 Tie up tightly
9 Cock and bull
10 Sprigs from the garden
11 Sculpted form
12 "___ disturb!" (and a hint for 17-, 40- and 65-Across, and 10- and 30-Down)
15 American rival
18 ___ de combat

23 Tel. message taker, maybe
25 1953 Loren title role
27 Mrs. Einstein
28 "Why should ___ you?"
29 D-back, for one
30 Deli selections
31 Classic sodas
35 Go into business
37 Court plea, for short
38 They're game
41 Mideast capital
42 Cobble, for example
45 "Amscray!"
48 "The Night of the Hunter" star, 1955
50 To-the-max prefix
52 Hendryx of the group Labelle
53 "Norwegian Wood" instrument
54 Franklin's on it

by Jim Page

55 Dreadlocked one
59 Keep an appointment
61 Bird in "The Lion King"
62 Literary olios
63 Croupier's tool
66 Suffix with direct
67 Little, to a lass

70

ACROSS
1 "Vissi d'arte" opera
6 Rx, for short
11 Fed. holiday, often
14 Not just question
15 Evidence of pain
16 So-so grade
17 Part 1 of a snarky quote by 54-Across
19 D.C. clock setting
20 Admiral Bobby who directed the N.S.A. under Jimmy Carter
21 Unwordy
23 Prime status
24 Photo ___
27 Sibling of 54-Across
28 With 53-Across, noted comedy group, in brief
29 Geisel's pen name
32 ___-chef (kitchen #2)

33 "It's nobody ___ business"
35 Picks off, as a pass
37 Proposal fig.
38 Middle of the quote
41 Take steps
44 Showed fright
45 ___ Ark
49 "Cheers" character
51 Baseball exec Bud
53 See 28-Across
54 Speaker of the quote
56 General on Chinese menus
57 Celeb fired in 2007
58 Pale yellow Danish cheese
61 Ribbed, like corduroy
63 Japanese waist material?
64 End of the quote
68 Narrow inlet
69 Some are Dutch
70 Web mag

71 N.L. insignia
72 Iran-Contra name
73 Prepare to fire again

DOWN
1 ___ Friday's
2 1st or 2nd, e.g.
3 Parties to a contract
4 Punch lines, e.g.
5 Menlo Park middle name
6 Farm enclosure
7 Golden parachute receiver, maybe: Abbr.
8 Actor Julia
9 Rombauer of cookery
10 Coll. course
11 Tennis star-turned-analyst
12 Antigone's father
13 What you pay
18 Slaughter in baseball

22 Western treaty grp.
23 Cockney's abode
25 Apothecary tool
26 Snowbirds' destination
30 Some OPEC officials
31 ___ Snorkel of the funnies
34 National Chicken Mo.
36 Thing to confess
39 Some batteries
40 Put into action
41 Firmly ties (to)
42 Share digs
43 Worth bubkes
46 Yerevan's land
47 Master escapologist
48 Radiator sound
50 Longtime Elton John label
52 Cap's partner
55 Bean on-screen

by Ed Early

59 Record for later viewing
60 Anatomical canal
62 Golden ___ (senior)
65 "We know drama" channel
66 Sort of: Suffix
67 Pro ___ (for now)

71

ACROSS

1 Example of 41-Across
7 Example of 41-Across
15 Like "Survivor" groups
16 "That's fine"
17 __ Quimby of children's books
18 Most finicky
19 Not fighting
21 Squeezed (out)
22 Ballerina's digit
23 Suffix with racket or rocket
25 Weakens, as support
29 Line up
32 Push (for)
36 Needle part
37 Mauna __
39 Example of 41-Across
41 Theme of this puzzle
45 Example of 41-Across
46 90° pipe joint
47 Result of getting worked up

48 Call the whole thing off
50 On the wagon
54 Eton students, e.g.
56 Symbol of sturdiness
58 City map abbr.
59 Tacks on
63 Works of Swift and Wilde
66 They're over the hill
70 Dancing locale
71 "Be delighted"
72 Low tie
73 Example of 41-Across
74 Example of 41-Across

DOWN

1 Rock bands?
2 Keynote speaker, e.g.
3 Less firm
4 Instrument with a conical bore
5 Sha follower
6 French ice cream

7 Bush league?: Abbr.
8 Merle Haggard, self-descriptively
9 Sail a zigzag course
10 Little one
11 Put up with
12 Bread for a Reuben
13 Speakers' no-nos
14 Amount left after all is said and done
20 Unagi, at a sushi restaurant
24 Actress Dawson of "Rent"
26 Polar denizen
27 Polar explorer
28 Salty septet
30 Therapeutic plant
31 "__ got mail"
33 Humanities degs.

34 Memory unit
35 Cries from the woods
38 "I love him like __"
40 Defendant's plea, informally
41 Not work out
42 Kirlian photography image
43 Four-footed TV character
44 Jar part
49 Thank-yous along the Thames
51 Black Russians may go on it
52 __ Brothers
53 Fix, as a shoe
55 Buffalo hockey player
57 Barbecue offering
60 Bug juice?
61 Like Radio City Music Hall, informally
62 Hitch
64 Pint-size

by Tibor Derencsenyi

65 "Mm-hmm"
66 Chart
   topper
67 "Do ___ do"
68 It may be
   tidy
69 ___-Cat

ACROSS

1 SeaWorld attractions
6 50 Cent piece
9 Constantly change lanes
14 "Peachy!"
15 Voters liked him twice
16 Stan's partner in old films
17 Poke, in a way
18 Mature before being picked
20 Sport played on the first word of its name
22 Ax user, e.g.
23 Page turner
28 Eerie
29 Tot's wheels
32 Say "uncle"
33 Popular clog-buster
34 California's state bird
35 Sport played in the first word of its name
39 Gucci competitor
40 Scrabble draw
41 Prefix with -gon
42 The lion in "The Lion, the Witch and the Wardrobe"
43 Go out, as embers
46 Organized crime
48 "You can come out now"
51 Sport played on the first word of its name
54 It may get stuck in a movie theater
58 Home of Brigham Young University
59 Fictional Scarlett
60 Lead-in to many a chef's name
61 Fan's opposite
62 "Shucks!"
63 Horse color
64 Alley pickup

DOWN

1 Boxing combo
2 Installed anew, as flooring
3 Took a taxi, with "it"
4 Ringlike island
5 Scattered over the earth
6 They run rapids
7 Related
8 William for whom a colony was named
9 Not as good
10 Inventor Whitney
11 European peak
12 Compete
13 Poetic darkness
19 Limerick's home
21 Neon ___ (fish)
24 Contents of una fontana
25 Use a rotary phone
26 Dr. ___ of "Austin Powers" films
27 Divinity sch. subject
30 How sardines are often packed
31 Pitcher who says "Oh, yeaahh!"
33 Crime lab evidence
34 Some hikers' targets, for short
35 St. Louis attraction
36 Appraise
37 Noted cheese town
38 Tither's amount
39 Poker payoff
42 Irish Rose's beau
43 Some Plains Indians
44 "Should that come to pass"
45 Pooh's mopey pal
47 Words after court or rule
49 Frosh, next year
50 Consign to the junkyard
52 "Yikes!"
53 Corker

by Patrick Merrell

54 Conk
55 Dull responses
56 Cry from Scrooge
57 Strapped wear

73

When this puzzle has been completed, shade in the letters of 35-Across everywhere they appear in the grid, revealing three letters and three lines.

ACROSS

1 Karate blow
5 Winkler role, with "the"
9 Cartoon pics
13 Wertmuller who directed "Seven Beauties"
14 "___ Gold"
16 Sky lights?
17 Brewery fixture
18 Knocking sound
20 Solid alcohol
22 All you need, in a Beatles song
23 Have a TV dinner, say
24 Fire sign?
26 Late singer Rawls
29 Classic Mercedes-Benz roadsters
30 Homes that may have circular drives
32 Long, long time
33 Soviet labor camp
34 Automaker Ferrari
35 July 4th message to America
40 Theological schools: Abbr.
41 Buys for brew lovers
42 Grand ___ Opry
43 How many teens go to movies
46 Not many
49 160, once
50 Mentholated cigarettes
51 Gawk (at)
53 Brief moments
54 Regains one's senses, with "up"
55 Memorable title film role of 1971
60 Some nest eggs, for short
61 Risk-taking Knievel
62 Prod
63 ___-Rooter
64 Old comics boy
65 Those, to Carlos
66 Official with a list

DOWN

1 Shutters
2 Having a gap
3 Initiations
4 "Gloria ___" (hymn start)
5 Roll up
6 Suffix with pay
7 Web
8 Fanatic
9 Adorable
10 Pond denizen
11 Mauna ___
12 Sound barrier breaker: Abbr.
15 Tend the hearth
19 Greetings of long ago
21 Early Ping-Pong score
24 Puncture
25 Enchanting
26 Horne who sang "Stormy Weather"
27 Like mud
28 3 – 2, en español
31 Cunning
33 Some docs
34 Masthead names, for short
35 "War is ___"
36 Green card?
37 "Phooey!"
38 Lao-___
39 "___ Fine" (1963 Chiffons hit)
40 Assn.
43 ___-doke
44 Opposite of día
45 Medicinal amount
46 Denmark's ___ Islands
47 Mistakes
48 Big name in oil
52 Snazzy Ford debut of 1955
53 Capital of Manche
54 Dict. offerings
55 Opium ___
56 Correct ending?
57 Part of a sleep cycle
58 Some football linemen: Abbr.
59 Down Under hopper

by Patrick Blindauer

74

ACROSS

1 Great Trek participant of the 1830s
5 Courtroom fig.
11 Bake sale grp.
14 Bowed, in music
15 "Yippee!"
16 Alley ___
17 Newts and such
19 "The Addams Family" cousin
20 Nocturnal beetle
21 Sugar suffix
22 ___ equal footing
23 Senior Saarinen
24 Take apart
26 Setting for a chaise longue
28 In groups
29 Deflating sound
30 When repeated, part of a Beatles refrain
33 Services' partner
34 Go-between, and a clue to 17-, 24-, 49- and 57-Across
37 Prized violin, briefly
40 Canned fare since 1937
41 Univ. staffers
44 School papers
46 Downsize, maybe
49 Salon job
52 ___ Potti
53 Totally confused
54 In the style of
55 Hit close to home?
56 Kick ___ storm
57 Locale of Uhuru Peak
59 Israeli airport city
60 Lover of Cesario, in "Twelfth Night"
61 Neighbor of Wash.

62 City grid: Abbr.
63 Take stock of
64 Features of greenhouses

DOWN

1 Stout-legged hounds
2 Sources of wisdom
3 Bakery treats
4 Lion, for one
5 Ill-fated captain
6 Trinity member
7 "Me too"
8 Long lock
9 Risktaker's challenge
10 "I see" sounds
11 Indicate, in a way
12 Came to
13 Suitability
18 Actress Powers of "Cyrano de Bergerac"
22 Something to cry over?
24 Knight's list

25 Bit of plankton
27 Dancer Charisse
31 Eiger, for one
32 Soul mate?
34 "___ mia!"
35 It pops into the head
36 Tussaud's title: Abbr.
37 Wren's cathedral
38 X marks it
39 Double-checks
41 Rarer than rare
42 Took in, perhaps
43 Old salts
45 Garden pests
47 Worked like Rumpelstiltskin
48 Swindler's work
50 ___ Island (museum site)
51 Dewy-eyed
55 Lambs' laments
57 R.V. hookup provider
58 Wrong start?

by Barbara Olson

75

ACROSS

1 With 1-Down, 1982 Richard Pryor/Jackie Gleason film
4 Half court game?
7 Part of an auto accident
13 Crude structure?
15 Tourist's aid
16 "Understood!"
17 Like a band of Amazons
18 Iran-Contra grp.
19 Draftsman's tool (and a hint to this puzzle's theme)
20 Satchel in the Hall of Fame
23 Little squirt
24 Poli ___
25 Aunt of Prince Harry
26 Dogma
28 Conclusion, in Germany
31 Levy on a 33-Across
33 Place to build

35 63-Across, in Málaga
36 Like vinegar
37 Cookout sites
39 Foundation exec.
40 Frank McCourt memoir
42 A few
43 Suffix with exist
45 Means of fortunetelling
47 ___ account (never)
48 "___ got it!"
50 King in a celebrated 1970s U.S. tour
51 Clampett player
52 Attend to the final detail
54 Crimson foe
55 Commits to, as an interest rate
56 Ferris in film
60 Intent, as a listener
61 Field of unknowns?
62 Hand-color, in a way
63 Rotation period
64 Muesli morsel

DOWN

1 See 1-Across
2 Shake a leg
3 Old N.Y.C. lines
4 Title guy in a 1980 Carly Simon hit
5 A Waugh
6 Any part of Polynésie
7 Where Mosul is
8 Waiter's armload
9 Guard's workplace
10 Iroquois and others
11 Grammar concern
12 Plays a campus prank on, informally
14 Gridiron formation
15 Dutch beer brand
19 Big load
20 1974 Medicine Nobelist George ___
21 Bayer alternative

22 Influential group
23 Singing Ritter
26 Implied
27 Go ___ (deteriorate)
29 Quints' name
30 Hardly strict with
32 Relative of a chickadee
34 Fashion a doily
38 Big name in cellular service
41 "___ Cheerleaders" (1977 film)
42 "I'm kidding!"
44 Brought forth
46 Endless 9-to-5 job, e.g.
49 Op-Ed, typically
51 Poem of lament
52 E. ___
53 What to call a king
54 Faulkner's ___ Varner
55 Iron pumper's muscle

by Bonnie L. Gentry and Victor Fleming

56 No longer edible
57 Wall St. action
58 Diamond stat
59 Disloyal sort

76

ACROSS
1 Classic muscle cars
5 Stellar bear
9 Not be able to take
14 Juillet's follower
15 Gad about
16 Valuable find
17 Scrap the original strategy
19 Party spreads
20 Bikini, for one
21 Part of a suit
23 Rap's Dr. ___
24 Big spread
26 Mrs., in Madrid
27 ___ Mae (Whoopi's "Ghost" role)
28 Broke ground
30 Loop looper
33 Restrained
35 Chapel fixture
36 Three-time 60-homer man
37 Personal quirk
39 Anthem starter
43 Bandleader Eubanks, familiarly

46 Metropolis figure
49 Muscle shirt, e.g.
53 Rock's ___ Lonely Boys
54 Pewter component
55 Glass of "This American Life"
56 Lock
58 Common Market inits.
59 Cyclist Armstrong
61 "Cool!"
64 Unaided
66 What the ends of 17-, 30- and 49-Across spell
68 Comic Amsterdam
69 Pandora's boxful
70 Cry after the sound of a bell
71 Dag Hammar-skjöld, for one
72 Cry after the sound of a bell
73 PC suite components

DOWN
1 Totally smitten
2 Attention-getting sound
3 On empty
4 Took off with
5 Location to bookmark: Abbr.
6 Driver's license prerequisite
7 All there
8 Plot feature in many a western
9 Calm
10 Support, of a sort
11 Ballpark buy
12 Take too far
13 Use again, as a Ziploc bag
18 Catcher's place
22 Blood's rival
25 ___ Na Na
28 When added to 29-Down, tres
29 See 28-Down
31 Big copper exporter
32 Wanted G.I.

34 One of 10,000 in Minnesota
38 "Who's on first?" asker
40 Spicy bowlful
41 2008, por ejemplo
42 What a nod may mean
44 Curse, of sorts
45 Designer Wang
47 Neighbor of Leb.
48 Gregg pro
49 Cooks, in a way
50 Stay out of sight
51 Call for more
52 "The Blues Brothers" director John
57 Mattress giant
60 Knick rival
62 Fill-in
63 Bauxite and others
65 Prof. Brainard of "The Absent-Minded Professor"
67 AOL, e.g.

by Curtis Yee

77

ACROSS
1 Slightly
5 Got rid of a chaw
9 Perfume from petals
14 Formal fabric
15 Corrida creature
16 Pleasant Island, today
17 Kelly Clarkson or Taylor Hicks
18 Broadway's ___ Jay Lerner
19 Like unfortunate bullfighters
20 Stealing some computer memory?
23 Roll-call vote
24 Go off course
25 "Too bad!"
27 Squeegees' kin
30 Homework assignments
33 Stash away
34 Jackknife, for one

35 Tale of the gods
37 Stateside Ltd.
38 Narrow pieces
41 Kung fu star
42 Most of I-76 across Pennsylvania
44 Word of agreement
45 Lincoln Center offering
47 Beermat, e.g.
49 Drank slowly
50 Sig Chi, e.g.
51 Where Fermi went to university
52 Queasy
54 Always use the term "coloring agent"?
60 Sent out beams
62 Graph line
63 Tiger club
64 Where the action is
65 Bean town?
66 Maritime: Abbr.

67 Twangy
68 School in Berkshire, England
69 Sandwich from a sidewalk stand

DOWN
1 Found a perch
2 Vocal fanfare
3 Running ___
4 Come through
5 Puts on
6 Arctic
7 Djellaba wearer
8 "West Side Story" role
9 San ___, Tex.
10 Chinese cosmic order
11 Ways to make lefts and rights?
12 Realtor's calculation
13 Basketball's Tomjanovich
21 "Revenge of the ___"
22 Get to the point?
26 Outfielder's asset

27 Senate figure
28 Ancient Greek dialect
29 Assorted hydroxides?
30 Don or Lena
31 Square
32 Cordwood measure
34 Makeshift screwdriver
36 John, at sea
39 Coffeehouse order
40 "El Capitan" composer
43 Audio receiver
46 Saying grace
48 Huarache
49 Toyota rival
51 First-rate
52 Where Farsi is spoken
53 1965 Julie Christie role
55 Lowland
56 Take off
57 Sledge
58 Part of B.Y.O.B.
59 Inner, in combinations
61 Faline's mother, in "Bambi"

by Richard Silvestri

78

ACROSS
1 "I'm glad that's over!"
5 "Green" sci.
9 Schindler of "Schindler's List"
14 Sound from a 57-Down
15 Writer Ephron
16 Like some Groucho Marx humor
17 Himalayan legend
18 Sketched
19 Speak histrionically
20 Revolve
23 "Honest!"
26 Put chips in a pot
27 "Don't miss the next episode . . ."
32 "Bye Bye Bye" boy band
33 Kind of sleep
34 Sleeping, say
36 Gave the thumbs-up
37 Start of many a pickup line

41 Tall tale
42 Cry
44 Luau serving
45 Set straight
47 Become a recluse, perhaps
51 Campaign fund-raising grp.
52 Rest stop features
53 Speaker of the catchphrase that starts 20-, 27- and 47-Across
58 Shade of green
59 Word with pepper or saw
60 Congregation's location
64 Signal to clear the road
65 Nat or Natalie
66 Hertz competitor
67 Courage
68 Give __ to (approve)
69 Stun

DOWN
1 Like some humor
2 Weed whacker
3 Chow down
4 On paper
5 Evasive maneuver
6 Relative of a trumpet
7 Creme-filled snack
8 Croquet site
9 Act before the headliner
10 Indonesian island crossed by the Equator
11 The "K" in James K. Polk
12 Naysayer
13 Deli loaves
21 Robert of "Spenser: For Hire"
22 Weapon in 1940s headlines
23 Edward R. Murrow's "See __"
24 Like a walrus
25 Talk show host Tom

28 Go around and around
29 __ culpa
30 Do a favor
31 Pound, for example
35 Jobs for body shops
38 Geologic period
39 "__ and whose army?"
40 Arafat of the P.L.O.
43 Light muffin
46 Frog's perch
48 Inventor's goal
49 Verdi opera featuring "Ave Maria"
50 Gave birth in a stable
53 "Poppycock!"
54 Tennis's Nastase
55 Actress Sorvino
56 Org. that organizes camps
57 Big prowler
61 Longoria of "Desperate Housewives"

by Mike Nothnagel

62 Diana Ross
musical,
with "The"
63 Dir. from
Seattle
to Las Vegas

79

ACROSS
1 Moisten, in a way
6 Q-tip, e.g.
10 In the sack
14 Really enjoyed
15 Sign of a saint
16 MS. accompanier
17 Junction points
18 Yemeni port
19 Part of a bird's gullet
20 Org. with a noted journal
21 Start of a quip from a hunter
24 Composer Rimsky-Korsakov
26 "___ hath an enemy called Ignorance": Ben Jonson
27 Quip, part 2
33 One putting out feelers?
34 Visa alternative, informally
35 "Little piggy"
36 Partner of trembling
39 Person with a code name, maybe
40 Fraction of a euro
41 Clumsy ox
42 Pump, e.g.
44 Federal property agcy.
46 Quip, part 3
52 Gal of song
53 Be fond of
54 End of the quip
59 Pa. nuclear plant site
60 Word repeated in a Doris Day song
61 Spring shape
62 Little laugh
64 Not of the cloth
65 Russian city on the Oka
66 Not pimply
67 Tram loads
68 Forms a union
69 Solving helpers

DOWN
1 Yogurt flavor
2 Like some energy
3 Neil who wrote "Stupid Cupid"
4 Calendar column: Abbr.
5 Delta follower
6 See 25-Down
7 Dry riverbed
8 Protected, in a way
9 Slave's state
10 Fancy neckwear
11 Stinging comment
12 Biblical "hairy one"
13 Like morning grass
22 Lacking slack
23 Fearsome dino
25 With 6-Down, Doctor Zhivago's portrayer
28 Boutonniere's place
29 "Little Women" sister
30 Western tribe
31 Cl⁻ or Na⁺
32 Lunar New Year
36 Watch spot
37 Évian, par exemple
38 Toward the stern
39 Mere pittance
40 Place to have a brioche
42 Do a cashier's job
43 "Geez Louise!"
44 Make a snarling sound
45 Pre-workout ritual
47 "Almost Paradise" author Susan
48 Some batteries
49 Kind of statement, to a programmer
50 Vegetarian's stipulation

by Bruce Venzke and Stella Daily

80

ACROSS

1 Birthplace of Galileo
5 Up
10 Not much
14 Bad time for Caesar
15 Word with press or Marine
16 Broccoli ___ (leafy vegetable)
17 Thrill
19 Critical hosp. areas
20 Close communication?
21 Emmy winner for "Chicago Hope"
22 Couple
23 Part of a chemistry group
25 Conservatory graduate
28 Heartless one?
31 Companion of 28-Across
32 It merged with Mobil
36 Plane prefix

37 Seaport of New Guinea
38 Part of a coach's chalk-talk diagram
39 Start of a countdown
40 Baseball's Ed and Mel
42 ". . . like a ___ chocolates"
44 Tennis great Lacoste
45 Bernstein's "Trouble in ___"
47 Eye passionately
49 Jong who wrote "Fanny"
51 Boohoo
52 Roman septet
54 Flo Ziegfeld's specialty
59 Athens's setting
60 "Piece of cake!" (and a hint to the starts of 17-Across and 11- and 27-Down)
61 Musical Mitchell

62 One of Homer's in-laws
63 Maglie and Mineo
64 Diner sign
65 On pins and needles
66 Give out

DOWN

1 Willis's "Twelve Monkeys" co-star
2 Romeo's last words
3 Group of prayers
4 Didn't leave waiting at the door
5 Film overlay
6 Imbibed
7 One who watches the telly
8 Breathing problem
9 "Ba-a-a-ad!"
10 Huffington who wrote "Fanatics & Fools"
11 Part of a dash
12 Go up against

13 Half a classic sitcom couple
18 Places
21 Year before Trajan was born
24 Fuji, e.g.: Abbr.
25 Apportion
26 Rope with a slipknot
27 Do what is expected
29 Sporting site
30 Three trios
33 Kiss and hugs, in a love letter
34 Adults-only
35 Big name in kitchen gadgets
41 Certain cut
42 Certain razor
43 June 14
44 Medical setback
46 "___ a pity"
48 Mas with baas
50 Blanched
51 Soothers
52 Breakfast spot, briefly
53 Breakfast spot, briefly
55 Feature of the earth

by Patrick Blindauer

56 Quahog,
e.g.
57 Anklebones
58 Part of
DOS: Abbr.
60 Gen. Lee's
cause

81

ACROSS
1 Churn
5 Tale with a point
10 Pre-Communist leader
14 It's a killer
15 Tubular instruments
16 Doing
17 Winston Churchill's description of a fanatic, part 1
19 Gymnastics apparatus, for short
20 Layout
21 Opposite of Mar. on a calendar
23 American Depression, e.g.
24 Part of A/C
25 Secured, as a fish on a line
27 Description, part 2
31 Suffer
32 Not the brainiest sort
33 December celebrations
36 Chooses
39 Dreadful
41 Rock's ___ Van Halen
42 Lug
43 "Lead ___ King Eternal" (hymn)
44 Description, part 3
49 How often federal elections are held
51 Science fiction author Stanislaw
52 "Well, ___ be!"
53 Free (of)
54 Formally speaks
58 Résumé addenda
60 Description's end
63 Rangy
64 Like a despot, typically
65 Western Indian
66 Pushing the envelope
67 Collars worn outside the lapels
68 Payment in Monopoly

DOWN
1 Part of the mouth
2 "Yes ___?"
3 Froster
4 Tin star wearer
5 Barber chair feature
6 "Dancing With the Stars" airer
7 It has some feathers around the neck
8 Contacts, e.g.
9 Revere
10 Margarine container
11 Leadfoot
12 Pong creator
13 Not italic
18 Alexander who said "I'm in control here"
22 "Elder" of ancient history
25 Tear (up)
26 Orbiting chimp of 1961
27 Legal assignment
28 Double-timed
29 From dawn till dusk
30 Owns
34 "Metropolis" director Fritz
35 Gin fruit
37 Bild article
38 Moth deterrent
39 Bldg. unit
40 Obscures
42 Indiscriminate amount
45 Squirm
46 Common-place
47 Spearmint, e.g.
48 Key with three sharps
49 Oath taker's aid
50 Classic epic
55 Head, in an école
56 College course, briefly
57 Mark indicating "O.K. as is"
59 Heavens
61 Abbr. on W.W. II maps
62 Bayh or Biden: Abbr.

by Patrick Merrell

82

ACROSS
1 Rock's Green Day, for one
5 Worker during a walkout
9 First-stringers
14 Hebrides island
15 Manger visitors
16 Pulitzer Prize category
17 Closet pest
18 Concerning
19 Long-billed wader
20 Coin thrown for good luck?
23 Work started by London's Philological Soc.
24 Geeky guy
25 Grand Canyon beast
29 All lit up
31 Letterman letters
34 Kurds and Nepalis
36 My ___, Vietnam
37 Stones from the sky

38 Result of sitting on a court bench too long?
41 "The Morning Watch" author
42 River to the Rhine
43 Feed for livestock
44 Neurotic TV dog
45 Lusted after, visually
47 Palette choice
48 Scott Turow work set at Harvard
49 Sound of amazement
51 Bugged Bugs?
57 Edible shells
58 Neighbor of an Arkie
59 Projecting edge
61 Waters seen on Broadway
62 Creatures of habit?
63 Pinnacle
64 Shade of gray

65 Learned
66 Battery component

DOWN
1 The youngest Cratchit
2 It may be raised
3 Having as a hobby
4 Waikiki locale
5 Deal a mighty blow
6 Dudley Do-Right's home
7 Cultural beginning?
8 Like House elections
9 Stick
10 What a line on a chart may show
11 Be worthy of
12 Taiwan Strait city
13 Answer to the riddle of the Sphinx
21 Before Oedipus, who could answer the riddle of the Sphinx

22 Risks
25 Storybook elephant
26 Subject of Fowler's handbook
27 Up
28 Make copiously, with "in"
30 "Accident ahead" indicator
31 Alimentary ___
32 "You got it!"
33 Less straight-forward
35 One putting on a show
37 Holy ring
39 Puffs out
40 Woman's shoulder wrap
45 Standing by
46 Plying with pills
48 Cousin of a mink
50 Much too big for one's britches?
51 "Haughty Juno's unrelenting ___": Dryden

by Richard Silvestri

83

ACROSS

1 Parts of churches appropriate to this puzzle
9 TV news crew
15 Decks
16 Put up
17 Really bizarre
18 Loads
19 Angular opening?
20 Follower of Max or Paul?
21 Ones with cool jobs?
22 Veronica of "Hill Street Blues"
24 Frenzied
26 "Do ___ others . . ."
28 Petri dish gel
29 Touch up, as text
30 Italian leaders
31 Quick change artist?
33 Pal
35 Sounds of ambivalence
36 Consequence
39 Roast V.I.P.'s
42 Old Testament book: Abbr.
43 Winter Olympics event
47 "Midnight Cowboy" role
49 Thumb locale: Abbr.
51 Rice-A-___
52 Computer once with an egg-shaped design
53 City south of Delray Beach, for short
54 Carpenter's pin
55 It ends with something found four times in this puzzle
57 Sales rep's assignment: Abbr.
59 Month before juin
60 Writer Rushdie
61 Graphic in a business report
63 Rare play
64 Bach's Branden-burgs, e.g.
65 Factor in a hotel rating
66 Egyptian royal

DOWN

1 "You sure said it!"
2 "Be brave!"
3 Best
4 Alphabet trio
5 It meant nothing to Nero
6 Fall place
7 Like favorite books, often
8 Reno-to-L.A. dir.
9 Wood block for holding an object steady
10 Primo
11 Roomy dress
12 Perfume
13 Type in, as lost data
14 Adds to or subtracts from
21 Smidgens
23 First name in mysteries
25 Imitative
27 C.I.A. forerunner
29 Mahler's "Das Lied von der ___"
30 Hollow
32 Prefix with spore
34 Sitting spot
37 Buzz
38 Hawaiian root
39 Dr.'s order
40 Trattoria order
41 Twinkly, in a way
44 D, for one
45 Where "Thy will" will be done, in part
46 Citizen soldiers
48 Trattoria order
50 Tony winner for "Sweeney Todd," 1979
53 Edvard ___, Czech president and patriot
54 Label of Bing Crosby's "White Christmas"

by Elizabeth C. Gorski

56 Setting for many episodes of TV's "Gilmore Girls"

58 Roomy dress

60 Filament holder

61 Polling abbr.

62 Mother ___

84

ACROSS
1 Crosses and such
7 Rid of persistent dinginess, say
13 Crunchy salad ingredient
14 Sluggishness
16 *See diagram*
18 Word with ceiling or football
19 Son of David
20 N.Y.C. commuter option
21 Prefix with skeleton
23 Author of "Winning Bridge Made Easy"
24 Wisconsin senator Feingold
25 Trick
27 "Gnarly!"
28 "The Da Vinci Code" albino
29 Some camp sights
31 Beast that bugles

32 T. ___
33 Marks (out)
34 ___ Press, classic Venetian printer that introduced italics
39 Half of a 1991 film title duo
44 Children's doctor?
45 ___ Lawrence Orchestra (British big band since the 1960s)
47 Domains
48 Slew
49 Los Angeles's ___ Verdes Peninsula
51 A long time
52 Hill creator
53 Thumb's end
55 Feeling in a cathedral, maybe
56 *See diagram*
59 What x makes
60 Superlatively Halloween-like

61 High point
62 Small harpsichord

DOWN
1 Medium tempo
2 Tense
3 Poking tool
4 Sch. papers
5 Clear up
6 Crew member
7 Barely missed, as a hole
8 Corporation in 2001 headlines
9 Withdraw (from)
10 "All nature is but ___": Pope
11 Bright lights, at times
12 Suggests
13 Like blue-chip stocks
15 Sampras rival
17 44-Across character, with "the"
22 A
24 Light (into)
26 Gull relatives

28 Skater Cohen
30 Spot
31 Soggy
34 B flat, enharmonically
35 "Fidelio" protagonist
36 It's shaken outside a house, not in
37 Suffix with sex
38 Tree tissue
40 Pitching stat
41 Heir
42 Who said "I believe in censorship. After all I made a fortune out of it"
43 Yes
45 Private response?
46 Nonprofit groups, often
49 ___-nez
50 Throat ailment
53 Cozy
54 Adriatic port
57 Hustle and bustle
58 Architect Maya

by Oliver Hill

85

ACROSS

1 Eventful times
5 Gin flavor
9 Prince Valiant's wife
14 Unlucky board game square
16 Intoxicate
17 Palindromic thought about preparing to pay down massive debt
19 It might set off a light
20 Extra winning opportunities
21 Prefix with natal
23 Sea flier
24 With 47-Across, palindromic Senate worker looks with amazement upon job payment inconsistency
29 "Is that someone I should know?"
32 Cheese in a ball
33 Lemon ___
34 Annoy
36 1960s singer Terrell
38 It has M.S.G. in it
40 Group-mailing aid
41 "Um . . . sure"
43 Hot tub reaction
45 Line starter in "Hot Cross Buns"
46 Asian holiday
47 See 24-Across
50 Seal
51 Ukraine was one: Abbr.
52 Completely
56 Michigan is part of it
61 Palindromic plan for freshening part of a lab
63 Boxes
64 Meeting
65 Role played in films by Chief Thundercloud
66 Overseas denial
67 Somewhat, musically

DOWN

1 Landmark Newport mansion, with "the"
2 Womanizer
3 A.A.A. member?: Abbr.
4 Preceders of spikes in volleyball
5 Ogle
6 Cutesy letter closer
7 Some bank deposits
8 Is green?
9 Like some ballots
10 Not bother
11 Latin 101 verb
12 Talk up
13 20 places?
15 "___ to Remember," biopic on Frédéric Chopin
18 Play to ___
22 Wilson of "Wedding Crashers"
24 Minor, at law
25 Bit of old wisdom
26 Range
27 One-named supermodel
28 Vessel in icy waters
29 Squeeze out
30 Whence the line "They have sown the wind, and they shall reap the whirlwind"
31 Ready
35 Soother
37 "Really?"
39 Harsh cries
42 Cook in a skillet, maybe
44 Star no more
48 Drop by
49 Breakfast serving
50 Feel the pain
52 How a painkiller should act
53 Defaulter's concern

by Joe Krozel

86

ACROSS
1 Quarrel (with)
5 Contents of a scoop
9 Glass substitute
13 Child's plea
14 "Jabberwocky," for one
15 Real ___
16 Former southern constellation in the shape of a ship
17 Billet-doux writer
18 "Skunk egg"
19 Internal-combustion device
22 Executor's concern
23 When someone 27-Across
27 See 23-Across
30 "Très sexy!"
31 "American Psycho" author
35 One of the first to raise a hand, usually
36 Barn adjunct
37 Scented gift
38 Loser in a staring contest
45 Temper, as metal
46 Vaccine target
47 Acts as a middleman
49 Began
53 Unfeeling nature . . . or a literal hint to 19-, 31- and 38-Across
56 Lustrous black
59 "What ___?"
60 Type choice: Abbr.
61 Apply
62 Not worth ___
63 Equipment in chuck-a-luck
64 Best of the early Beatles
65 Chop ___
66 Tolkien's talking trees

DOWN
1 Suffix with land or sea
2 Setting for "La Traviata"
3 Inner tension
4 It's read to the unruly
5 Beach adjacent to Copacabana
6 The ___ Nugget, Alaska's oldest newspaper
7 Sinn ___
8 The end
9 Historian William H. ___, author of "The Rise of the West"
10 Here, abroad
11 Be lovey-dovey
12 Philosopher Rand
15 Secretary of state during the War of 1812
20 Siouan speaker
21 Monopoly token
24 "Rag Doll" singer, 1964
25 Visitor from afar
26 Kind of surgery for the eyes
28 Home of "Monday Night Football"
29 Soak
31 Without question
32 Marie Antoinette, par exemple
33 Gets
34 Hang ___
39 "You pay attention!"
40 Factor in pageant judging
41 Stewpot
42 One who's late to adopt the latest
43 Leaning
44 Beach maximizer
48 Mex. misses
50 Away
51 Pass
52 Strikes out
54 Vegan's protein source

by Paula Gamache

55 Cartoon
canine
56 Agent,
for short
57 Sturdy feller?
58 A.S.P.C.A.
worker

87

The clues in this puzzle appear in a single list, combining Across and Down. Where two answers share a number, they also share a clue.

CLUES
1 Maintain
2 In ___ (form of research)
3 Concert halls
4 They're unlikely to work
5 Fiddle with
6 Goofed (around)
7 Quod ___ faciendum
8 Negative connector
9 Spy supply
10 Rubberneck
11 Composition of the Spanish Main
12 Hit the road
13 Florida ___
14 Part of Caesar's boast
15 ___ Soleil (Louis XIV)
16 "The Night of the Hunter" screenwriter
17 First name in daredeviltry
18 Some Romanovs

19 Runtish
20 Motor Trend job
21 Prohibition agents
22 Legends
23 Author Jaffe
24 2002 Literature Nobelist ___ Kertész
25 Pair
26 Dodge
27 Sun protection
28 All bark ___ bite
29 Start of a phrase meaning "always"
30 "Sounds like ___!"
31 Gusto
32 Put to rest
33 Changers of 34
34 See 33
35 Cartoon character with feminine wiles
36 Annual parade site
37 Death jokes and such
38 Stamp letters

39 ___ mer
40 Lover of Tess in "Tess of the D'Urbervilles"
41 Part of the Constitution after the Preamble: Abbr.
42 N.F.L. coach who was undefeated in 1972
43 Relative of a cod
44 Like tennis balls and dinners
45 Wicked witch's home in "The Wizard of Oz"
46 Ranch closing?
47 Bowl
48 Comic, e.g.
49 N.F.L. placekicker David
50 Fast-food franchise that started in S. Salt Lake, Ut.
51 Squoosh

52 Impersonator's work
53 It's all downhill from here
54 Gene group
55 "I goofed"
56 Delight
57 Tore
58 Don Juan
59 Old Testament book
60 Cry made with a handshake
61 Nippy
62 Benny Goodman's "___ Foolish Things"
63 Savage
64 Challenge for Theseus, in myth
65 Be a gloomy Gus
66 Radio part
67 Pod holder
68 Something ___ (a wow)
69 Door
70 Unexaggerated

by Larry Shearer

88

ACROSS

1 "Thou art not lovelier than ___, — no" (Millay sonnet start)
7 Make even
10 Neighbor of Afghanistan: Abbr.
13 Cadillac model
14 ___ jam
15 Word with pick or pack
16 With 55-Across, description of 23-, 36- and 44-Across
17 Wither
19 Atlanta's ___ Center
20 College square
22 Playwright Edward and others
23 Beginning of some folk wisdom
26 Clod buster
27 Pacific islands in W.W. II fighting, with "the"
30 Hugh ___, successor to Louis V as king of France
33 Kind of cup
34 Les poissons swim in it
35 Charter
36 Folk wisdom, part 2
37 Doggone
38 Nabokov novel
39 Biblical prophet thrown overboard by his shipmates
40 Formal dress shoes
41 Sane
43 Norwegian coin
44 End of the folk wisdom
49 Obliquely
51 Bishoprics
52 Old Eur. domain
53 Cutout to fill in
55 See 16-Across
57 Additionally
58 Green: Prefix
59 Corrida combatants
60 Have
61 Shade of blue
62 Makeshift hatrack

DOWN

1 ". . . ___ man put asunder" (wedding words)
2 "___ to be alone" (words attributed to Greta Garbo)
3 Wee, quickly
4 Exact proper divisor, in math
5 Part of a contract
6 French legislature
7 Spanish aunt
8 Incised printing method
9 Pendant place
10 Bit of wishful thinking
11 Yearn
12 Phi Beta Kappa mementos
13 Webster's, e.g.: Abbr.
18 Melancholy woodwind
21 Medicinal cardiac stimulant
24 Syngman ___, first president of South Korea
25 The last Pope Paul, e.g.
28 Infield cover
29 Heavenly orbs
30 Scorch
31 She dies with Radames
32 Talk, talk, talk
33 Robert of "The 39 Steps"
36 Teflon, e.g.
37 Any Sonny and Cher song
39 Bumps on a ride
40 Do some advance organizing
42 Ayatollah's home
43 Titania's husband

by Susan Harrington Smith

45 Dividing membranes
46 When doubled, comforting words
47 Cause for an erasure
48 Fighters for Jeff Davis
49 Regarding
50 Pack
54 Powell's co-star in "The Thin Man"
56 Speed: Abbr.

89

ACROSS

1 Lady abroad
5 With 50-Down, steak go-with
10 With 68-Across, fish filet go-with
14 Wedding parties?: Abbr.
15 Water, for one
16 Tel ___
17 Psyche components
18 Fix, as a hitch
19 Unnerve
20 "Yep" negator
21 Behind closed doors
23 Drug-free
25 Well-founded
29 He-man
33 With 44-Across, hot sandwich go-with
34 Like waves on a shoreline
37 It's on the St. Lawrence River: Abbr.
38 Hilarious . . . or a hint to this puzzle's theme
42 Brown, in ads
43 Passed
44 See 33-Across
47 Closed tight
51 White-knuckle
54 Make a ship stop by facing the wind
55 Newscast lead
59 Drift ___
60 Airline rarity, nowadays
63 "May ___ your order?"
64 Bob Dylan's first wife and the title of a song about her
65 Makeover
66 Stinky
67 Dirty magazines and such
68 See 10-Across
69 See 1-Down
70 Neither good nor bad

DOWN

1 With 69-Across, burger go-with
2 Treat splendidly
3 One saying "I do"
4 Letters before Liberty or Constitution
5 Sprung (from)
6 x, y and z
7 Toy sometimes seen on a beach
8 Order
9 Big name in balers
10 Unisex dress
11 Female gametes
12 1995 showbiz biography by C. David Heymann
13 December 31, e.g.
21 Harden
22 Musician Brian
24 Breezed through
26 One of a series of joint Soviet/U.S. space satellites
27 Dragged out
28 Suffix with absorb
30 Shake, in a way
31 Cable inits. since 1979
32 Albino in "The Da Vinci Code"
35 Police target
36 Jazzy James
38 Something to take in a car
39 Fred Astaire's "___ This a Lovely Day"
40 The Beeb is seen on it
41 "The very ___!"
42 The Rams of the Atlantic 10 Conf.
45 2003 #2 hit for Lil Jon and the East Side Boyz
46 ___-Cat
48 Go-getter
49 Womb
50 See 5-Across
52 Spruce (up)

by Lucy Gardner Anderson

53 Perfume ingredient

56 1955 Oscar nominee for "Mr. Hulot's Holiday"

57 Tex's neighbor to the north

58 Some wines

60 Partner, informally, with "the"

61 Underwater cave dweller

62 Oral health org.

64 Draft org.

90

ACROSS

1 Any one of a trio of Hollywood sisters
6 Reason to get some cosmetic dental work
10 ___-Americans (about 3.5 million people)
14 Say "amen," say
15 Gadzooks, e.g.
16 "You've Got Mail" actress
17 People's 2006 Sexiest Man Alive
19 Just
20 City southeast of 64-Across
21 Starting
22 Beverage brand
24 Mouth's locale
26 Cage for hawks
27 Subway stop: Abbr.
28 New York's ___ Mansion
30 Hen, e.g.
32 Julius Caesar portrayer, 1963
34 What a drinker may enter
38 Chevrolet model
39 Big exporter of coconut cream and coconut oil
41 Prefix with kinetic
42 O.K.'s
44 Frat Pack actor
46 Tasty
48 Smirk
49 Fertilized things
52 Wander
53 Like some checks
54 Quarter
56 City with una torre pendente
57 Particularly: Abbr.
60 R & B singer with a hit 1990s sitcom
61 Wishful things? . . . or a literal description of 16-, 17-, 32-, 44- and 60-Across
64 City along the Chisholm Trail
65 Fidel Castro's brother
66 Part of a printing press
67 Refuse
68 Starchy side dish
69 Points on a crescent moon

DOWN

1 Crazy
2 Like relics
3 Timber hewers
4 Poetic contraction
5 Robes, tiaras, etc.
6 Shade of brown
7 Game division
8 "Were ___ do it over . . ."
9 Insincere
10 Partner in an old radio comedy duo
11 Lets
12 Shoelace tip
13 Presidential candidate who said "No one can earn a million dollars honestly"
18 Some organic compounds
23 Water holder
25 Repeats
26 Construction worker
28 South side?
29 French dream
30 Like many cared-for lawns
31 Measure again, as a movie's length
33 Fervent
35 Computer technicians' positions
36 Everyone, in Essen
37 Blast constituent?
40 Historic Umbrian town
43 Palm type
45 Enormous
47 Sauté
49 Like an eyeball
50 "From the Earth to the Moon" author
51 "Encore!"
53 Volleyball stat
55 Annual May event, informally

by E. J. Platt

56 Windfall
58 When repeated, a dance instructor's call
59 Most are 3, 4 or 5
62 Top bond rating
63 Bearded beast

91

ACROSS

1 Twinge
5 W.W. II blast makers
11 Realm of Proteus, in Greek myth
14 ___ patriae
15 Pack again, as hay
16 ___ Rose
17 Leading Russian in the 32-Down
19 One to one, e.g.
20 Regard
21 Attitudes
23 Pilgrim in Chaucer's "The Canterbury Tales"
24 Florida island resort
25 Once, once
27 Prayer word
30 Paul McCartney played it for the Beatles
33 NASA launch vehicle
36 Record producer Davis

37 Connection for an electric guitar
38 Newsmaker of October 4, 1957
40 Result of a road emergency
41 Be hot under the collar
43 New Mexico county or its seat
44 Basted
45 Orders
46 Korea's Syngman
48 "20 Hrs., 40 Min." author, 1928
52 Catch on the range
56 Detroit suburb named for the plants the area was once overgrown with
58 Blocked, as a harbor, with "up"
59 Victorian ___
60 Leading American in the 32-Down

62 Twitch
63 Personally handle
64 Egg on
65 Bridge topper?
66 Finishes
67 Earl, for one

DOWN

1 One with checks and balances?
2 Beguile
3 Durango direction
4 Distresses
5 Composer Khachaturian
6 Have a hand out, say
7 Future senator who delivered the 2004 Democratic convention keynote address
8 California county
9 Shrovetide dish
10 Remit
11 38-Across, e.g.

12 "No ___"
13 Stein fillers
18 "The Waltons" actor
22 Dump, e.g.
24 Show pride, in a way
26 Bonehead
28 Profess
29 Chopped
30 Odist, e.g.
31 Parisian possessive
32 Event started by 38-Across
34 ___ Pi (dessert lover's fraternity?)
35 Stallion's sound
38 Enterprise log entry
39 Suffix with sheep or goat
42 1972 Wimbledon winner Smith
44 Arctic newborn
47 First name at the 1986 Nobel Prize ceremony

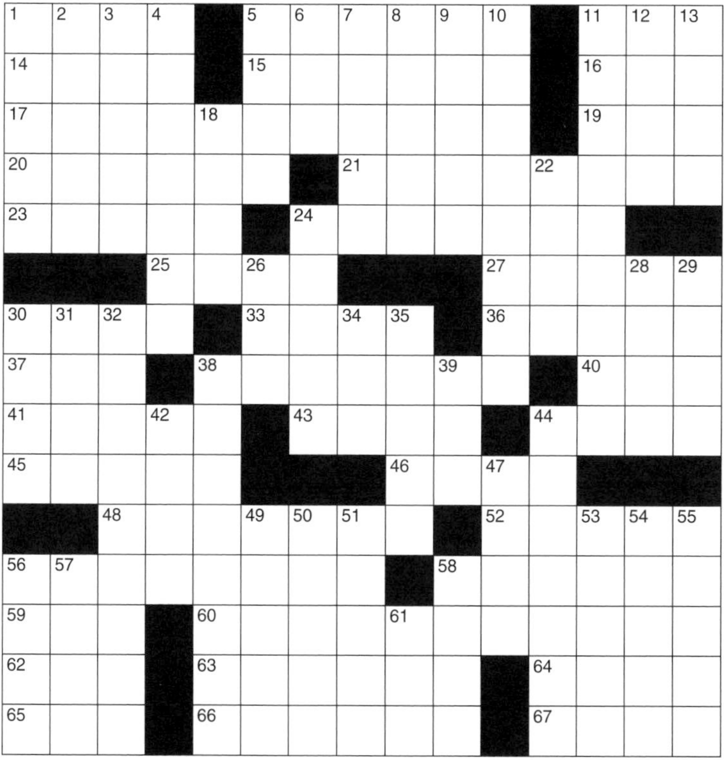

by Sheldon Benardo

49 Van ___

50 "___ flowing with milk and honey" (Canaan, in the Bible)

51 Tears

53 Intimidate, in a way, with "down"

54 Suit material

55 Comparatively uncon-ventional

56 Kind of cheese

57 Newsman Sevareid

58 Butcher's, baker's or candlestick maker's

61 Disco guy on "The Simpsons"

92

ACROSS

1 End of many college addresses
7 Fictional pirate
11 Suffix with official
14 "I do," e.g.
15 King's position, in a game
16 "Another Green World" musician
17 90
19 The Silver State: Abbr.
20 Like white elephants
21 Damp basement cause
23 One way to stand
26 Prime Cuts maker
28 This and that
29 Shia leaders
32 3
35 Jai alai ball
37 Lake ___
38 1

43 Present-day Persian
44 Don't stop
45 7
49 Criticize sneakily
50 Skittles variety
51 Weary worker's cry
53 Roll call call
54 Auto accident sound
57 Cruise ship Empress of the ___
60 Turner in the Rock and Roll Hall of Fame
61 What is being held in 17-, 32-, 38- and 45-Across
66 Receive
67 Captain of literature
68 "The Power and the Glory" novelist, 1940
69 Walletful, informally

70 Like many games
71 Hunter-gatherer types

DOWN

1 Drop bait lightly on the water
2 Eggs in labs
3 A.L. team, on scoreboards
4 Still-life object
5 Carvey of "Wayne's World"
6 Extreme sort
7 Alan Jay Lerner's "___ Wasn't You"
8 ___ Valley Conference in college sports
9 Gen. Robt. ___
10 Alternatively
11 20,320-foot Alaskan peak
12 Capacity of many a flash drive, informally

13 Not dawdle
18 Information desk offering
22 Some carriers
23 Old King Cole accessory
24 Kind of card
25 Soapstone, e.g.
27 Plant nursery activity
30 Pseudonym of Jean Baptiste Poquelin
31 ___ Report of the 1990s
33 Breakfast place
34 Beach sights
36 Second in a Latin series
39 Damned one
40 Samoan capital
41 Like some muscles
42 Common injury site
45 Franciscan locale

by Peter Wentz

46 Unpopular, in a way
47 Makes applesauce, e.g.
48 One helping
52 Pretend
55 Locale of many Italian vineyards
56 Bawl (out)
58 It's rarely seen under a hat
59 Originate
62 Sauce ingredient
63 Mauna ___
64 Culmination
65 "You bet!"

93

ACROSS

1 "Wait ___!"
5 Terrif
10 Andrew of "Melrose Place"
14 Longtime Vicki Lawrence character
15 Burn slowly
16 One of the Munsters
17 Popular depilatory
18 Static
19 Baryshnikov's birthplace
20 "Jolly good!"
22 Pioneer in I.Q. testing
23 Honoraria
24 Takeout choice
26 Home of São Miguel Island
29 Lab container
30 British general in the American Revolution
31 Light-colored stogie
32 Dallas-to-Austin dir.

35 Author of a 1952 novel published in full in Life magazine
39 "No ___!"
40 Occupy
41 Nutritionist Paul who founded a pet food company
42 Pear-shaped instrument
43 Rodeo sights
45 "I"-opening experience?
48 Throw out water
49 Ticks off
50 Accessory for many a game
54 Winnebago owner
55 Amber, e.g.
57 Height
58 Like llamas
59 Truck stop sign
60 Unpleasant feeling
61 Some personal data: Abbr.
62 A Stooge
63 Many a D.C. org.

DOWN

1 Peloponnesian War participant
2 Part of a Three Stooges shtick
3 Dr. Skoda of "Law & Order"
4 Happy-go-lucky
5 Elvis's "Hound Dog" and "Anyway You Want Me"
6 Some chain hotels
7 Gave up one's hand
8 Suffix with two
9 Morsel
10 3-Down's profession
11 German poet who wrote "Don't send a poet to London"
12 Presses
13 Flow out
21 Formerly known as
22 Animal on the backs of three state quarters

24 Surgical aid
25 Mata ___
26 Faux cough
27 Author ___ Neale Hurston
28 Fesses (up to)
29 Part of un jardin
31 Badly made
32 End of a fly? . . . or the start of one?
33 All the ___
34 "The Swiss Family Robinson" author Johann
36 Rouses oneself
37 South American monkey
38 Politician who wrote the book "Leadership"
42 Rears
43 Oscar winner for "Yankee Doodle Dandy"
44 Baseball datum
45 Odd jobs
46 Buckles

by Alex Boisvert

47 Ingredient in some potato chips
48 Old nightclub employee
50 Old Testament book
51 Thom ___ shoes
52 Layers of eggs weighing more than a pound
53 Move to first class, e.g.
55 Boombox button
56 Évian or Perrier

94

ACROSS

1 Times to call, in some classifieds
4 Johnny Carson persona
9 Sauce
14 Serious crimes
17 Perry Mason line
18 Crest bearer in heraldry
19 Showed enthusiasm for, with "up"
20 Highest bond rating
21 Passes more than once
24 Annually
26 "__ Robin Gray" (classic Scottish ballad)
28 Dr. __ Schneider, historian who was a love interest of Indiana Jones
32 Order sought by an accused before trial
39 Hearing, e.g.
40 Lawyers' requests at trials
41 You are, in Aragón
42 De bene __ (of conditional validity)
43 Kind of hand
47 Title locale in a Cheech Marin film
52 Neighbor of Libya: Abbr.
55 Energy
56 Hombres en la familia
57 Equals at a trial
63 Specialist's offering
64 Snappish
65 Relative of -ish
66 __ Tamid (synagogue lamp)

DOWN

1 Part of a company
2 Family name in Olympic skiing
3 Period of time
4 Montréal's Rue __-Catherine
5 Erstwhile military aux.
6 Drink in "The Taming of the Shrew"
7 "Hey, __!" (Jamaican greeting)
8 Suppose
9 First multiracial coeducational college in the South
10 Night stand leader?
11 Mythical mount
12 Certain sorority woman
13 What she is in Italy
15 Bean sprout?
16 Grand affair
22 Meal, in Milan
23 Lazy __
24 Like many pets
25 Steel support for concrete
27 Kissers
29 Legal scholar Guinier
30 Twisted
31 On the less windy side
32 Crown
33 Entrance
34 Remote option
35 Lucky sorts?
36 Modernists
37 French cup
38 "Coffee __?"
44 Key component
45 Falling-out
46 Overplay
48 The brain has one
49 Fastenable, as labels
50 Emmy-winning Michaels
51 From Nineveh: Abbr.
52 "Leaving on __ Plane"
53 Elegance
54 Assns. and orgs.
58 Still

by Joe Krozel and Victor Fleming

59 Old video game inits.

60 Abbr. on a firm's letterhead

61 Good name for a flight attendant?

62 Bake sale offering

95

ACROSS

1 Burns's tongue
6 Popular desktops since 1998
11 Camel's end?
14 Cul-de-sac
15 Wearer of the Yankees' retired #9
16 3.2 million-member org. with a pi in its logo
17 Wardrobe malfunction?
19 Atlantic City hotel, informally, with "the"
20 "Blah blah blah blah blah"
21 Start of a musical scale
22 Arias, usually
23 "___ Time" (1952 million-selling Eddie Fisher hit)
24 Unit of punishment
26 Result of punishment
28 Mood after a military victory?
32 Polling results, e.g.
35 Tries
36 Beastly
39 Ranges
40 Akin
42 Estuaries
43 Where porcine pilots arrive?
46 Narc's discovery, maybe
47 Believed
48 Grand Canyon area
51 Early English actress Nell ___
53 Not just threaten
55 Threats to World War shipping
57 Certain southeast Asian
58 Hint to 17-, 28- and 43-Across
60 Hospital dept.
61 YouTube feature
62 Hardly futuristic
63 A.L. city, on scoreboards
64 A lot
65 Beaker

DOWN

1 Kind of tank
2 First name in late-night
3 Over near
4 Old New York paper, for short
5 Artist Frank ___, pioneer in Minimalism
6 Org. that lends to countries
7 Arrive with authority
8 Nickname among major-league sluggers
9 It has many pictures
10 Boomer, once
11 Director Michelangelo
12 Warranty feature
13 Muslim honorific
18 "___ me"
22 Emmy-winning Phil
25 Trial position, for short
27 Like ___ out of hell
28 Late editorial cartoonist Bill
29 Carol starter
30 Abbr. on an envelope to Mexico
31 Flat sound
32 Radio feature
33 Eleanor Roosevelt's first name
34 Certain notes
37 Work hard
38 Doubter
41 Like wedding attendees, often
44 "___ U"
45 Tennis great Stefan
48 Dreadlocks wearer
49 Anatomical passages
50 Old PC standard
51 Smooth

by Daniel C. Bryant

96

ACROSS
1 Seinfeld's "sworn enemy"
7 En route
15 Dig up
16 Vicious sorts
17 1961 Connie Francis hit
19 Up to no good
20 Sterile, in a way
21 Debussy's "Air de ___"
22 Word before Oscar or Orloff
24 Madras title
25 Intl. agreement since 1993
27 Class-conscious grps.?
29 Prefix with skeleton
32 Hold 'em challenge
34 Fourth book of the Book of Mormon
36 Gore follower
37 Eponymous rink jump
39 Bring up

41 View from Long Is.
42 Tennyson woman called "the Fair"
44 ___ Beach, Fla.
45 ___ Jordan, who wrote "The Crying Game"
47 A writer may work on it
49 Bolero, e.g.
50 Long on screen
52 First name in architecture
54 One-third of a Morse "O"
55 Children's author/photographer Alda
58 "Here, I can help you"
61 End of a line about "friends"
63 Not be honest about oneself
64 Ingredients in many stews
65 Derides
66 Become, as mush

DOWN
1 Google heading
2 Thrill
3 1952 Doris Day hit that was an even bigger hit for the Lettermen in 1961
4 ___ acid (old name for hydrochloric acid)
5 Bob ___, young man in Dreiser's "Sister Carrie"
6 Web-based service
7 Be in charge of
8 Pointed extremity
9 Suffix with beta
10 First sitting president to visit the West Coast
11 Protect
12 "Huh?!"

13 It rises in the Bernese Alps
14 Battle of the ___, 1914
18 Mr. Wickfield's clerk, in literature
23 Narrow way
25 Passover month
26 Gentleman of the court
28 "Deal!"
30 Troop group
31 Kind of daisy
33 Eternities
35 Starting point
38 Efface, with "off"
40 One of the men waiting in "Waiting for Godot"
43 Like some eyes
46 Mortgagor, e.g.
48 Canadian native
51 At hand, in poems

by Victor Fleming and Bruce Venzke

97

The clues in this puzzle appear in a single list, combining Across and Down. Where two answers share a number, the unclued Down answer is a homophone of the corresponding Across answer.

CLUES

1 Obstruction at the entrance to a cave, maybe

2 Rarely used golf club

3 Picture on a $50 bill

4 Drip, say

5 Seventh-century year

6 Want ad abbr.

7 Some needle holders, for short

8 Like jail cells

9 Makes like

10 Connecticut or Colorado: Abbr.

11 Touch up, as a painting

12 Country named for its location on the globe

13 Bring down

14 Having hit a double

15 Neuter

16 For one

17 Party of the first part and party of the second part, e.g.

18 Gets going

19 Weapon in old hand-to-hand fighting

20 Does some yard work

21 One famously begins "O Wild West Wind, thou breath of Autumn's being"

22 Carcinogenic substance

23 Victorian ___

24 Head-quartered

25 Lowers the cuffs on, maybe

26 Legis. period

27 Point to

28 Wood of the Rolling Stones

29 ___ Nikolaevich, last czarevitch of Russia

30 Queen of France in Shakespeare's "Henry V"

31 Rich Spanish decorations

32 Big blasts, informally

33 Duck down

34 Tailors

35 Social register listees

36 Residents: Suffix

37 Seat at a hootenanny

38 Place for a guard

39 Recondite

40 Shoulder muscle

41 Tolerates

42 Logged

43 Singer who founded Reprise Records

44 Letter before Peter in old radio lingo

45 Bygone council

46 Donations at some clinics

47 Essential

48 "___ for nest"

49 Accent

50 NASA subj.

51 French town

52 Contents of some shells

53 Audio equipment pioneer

54 Wiped out

55 Verb of which "sum" is a form

56 Campsite visitor

57 Job specifications

58 ___ B. Wells, early civil rights advocate

59 Individually

60 Race unit

61 Blood type letters

62 Calculator button

63 Wears down

64 Work force

65 Grade again

66 Pretended to be

by Joe Krozel

98

ACROSS

1 Union demand
6 2001 Oscar nominee for the song "May It Be"
10 With 37-Across, theme of this puzzle
14 Monkey's ___
15 Sugar source
16 Some artwork
17 Super bargain
18 Reason to renovate an opera house?
20 One cauterizing a skin blemish?
22 Prom wear
23 Prefix with warrior
24 Night school subj.
27 What flowers do, in poetry
28 Abbr. on a toothpaste box
31 Caballero
33 Wrinkly-skinned fruit
36 Poem about Paris, in part
37 See 10-Across
40 Kingdom
41 "When I am dead and gone, remember to ___ me . . .": "Henry VI, Part I"
42 Throws out
44 Hieroglyphic symbol for the ancient Egyptian "M"
45 Bud's bud
48 Salon supply
49 Blesses
51 Pantomime
54 Narc operation on Amtrak?
57 Dropped "The Simpsons" from the TV schedule?
60 Florence's ___ Vecchio
61 Toni Morrison novel
62 Iris's place
63 Tee off
64 Wax remover
65 Rectify
66 Can't do without

DOWN

1 Hurry in the direction of
2 Make a stud payment
3 Climber's chopper
4 Ballot listing
5 Caught congers
6 Battle of the ___, in the Spanish Civil War
7 Nine, in Nantes
8 "___ Have No Bananas"
9 War cry
10 Helvetica, for one
11 A dunker may grab it
12 Soccer cheer
13 Boulder hrs.
19 A household chore
21 Comical tribute
24 Sponsorship: Var.
25 Ruler toppled in 1979
26 Bygone Ford
29 Bank contents
30 From the beginning
32 "Would ___?"
33 Racer Yarborough
34 Big bag of groceries, e.g.
35 Some
37 Hot
38 Marathon terminus
39 Dental work
40 Brave opponent
43 Slopes devotee
45 Waiting area
46 Given the boot
47 Comes out with
50 Work like a dog
52 Hearings airer

by Alan Arbesfeld

99

ACROSS

1 Moon and Starr, for short
4 Where Home Depot was founded
11 The J aguars, on scoreboards
14 Sharjah's locale: Abbr.
15 Tinseltown doings
16 TV title character voiced by Paul Fusco
17 Mess up
18 Where to see a crown
19 The Engineers of coll. athletics
20 & 22 Actor with a black belt in aikido
24 Office expense
25 Cigarette detritus
28 "I'll Have to Say I Love You in a Song" singer, 1974
29 Card game with no cards below seven
30 Force along
32 Some in Spain
33 Item sought in the spring
36 President with a bridge in Montreal named after him
42 Consumer's enticement
43 More smarmy
44 Protein building block, for short
45 Snap
48 Don't do it
49 Univ. with an annual mystery hunt since 1980
50 Champion figure skater Cohen
52 Some dashes
53 He said "Great art picks up where nature ends"
58 Be disqualified, in the 8-Down
60 Comparable
63 Wall in
64 Bring up
65 "Who Let the Dogs Out" group
66 Like some friendships

DOWN

1 Knights' journeys
2 Hungarian composer who wrote "The Miraculous Mandarin"
3 Star near Venus?
4 ___ usual
5 Word with greater or rather
6 A captain might keep one
7 Blow away
8 Rockets' and Suns' org.
9 Spam holders
10 Tenochtitlán dweller
11 Computerese, e.g.
12 Wool source
13 1998 film thriller based on a TV series, with "The"
21 Longtime
23 Salad bar offering
25 Qtys.
26 Blew (through)
27 "Take this!"
30 "Gotcha"
31 Toy name preceding "land"
34 High, in Honduras
35 Jog, say
36 Stuff
37 Kind of engine
38 Too-too
39 Protection against smearing
40 Rock singer Russell
41 Psyche's love
45 Washington and Oregon are in it
46 Suffix with hell and bull

by Tyler Hinman

47 Beer, often
50 Italian apologies
51 Unlike klutzes
54 ___ breve (musical direction)
55 Space
56 "That's what I'm talking about!"
57 Like some wires
58 Winter mo.
59 ___ whim
61 Downed
62 Like second-place ribbons

100

ACROSS

1 Whiz
6 Prefix with structure
11 Kind of instinct
14 Minneapolis suburb
15 Dimwit
16 1992 U2 top 10 hit
17 "Shake a leg!"
19 Busy co. on Mother's Day
20 Generally
21 Target of some testing
23 Territory on the Arabian Peninsula
25 Alternative to Le Bourget
26 Sobriquet for Charles V, with "the"
29 Suddenly changes course
30 You might get in this at work
31 Start of many Arabic names
32 Car driven by Seinfeld on "Seinfeld"
33 Residue
36 Go by
38 Ayres who played filmdom's Dr. Kildare
40 Get on
41 Tired-looking
42 Unit of punishment at sea
44 Common car decal
45 Basketball champ's souvenir
46 Go bonkers
47 Warthog feature
48 River through the Steppes of Asia
50 Lose freshness
52 Ones standing around monuments?
54 Jeer
58 Mate
59 Sound out?
61 Summer in Québec
62 Farm letters?
63 Picture
64 Bit of light
65 More roguish
66 Visual put-down

DOWN

1 Prefix with phone
2 Sweet drinks
3 Lucio's life
4 Dining highlight
5 Prophet who predicted the destruction of Nineveh
6 Like old Rome
7 Certain jack, in cribbage
8 Ticks off
9 Trail
10 Put up
11 Try to win
12 Before
13 Nightwear
18 "Uncle Tom's Cabin" woman
22 Stir
24 Christmas song since the 1950s
26 Uncombed, say
27 Letter-shaped part of a grate
28 Songwriters' home
30 Reckless
32 Launched
34 Some fraternity men
35 Overcharge and how
37 Super
39 Expects
43 Vacuum
46 Anthropologist Dian
47 Kitchen coat
48 Bunk option
49 Lasso
50 Object of a knight's quest
51 Farm soils
53 Great, in slang
55 V
56 "___ Baby" ("Hair" song)
57 Stadium part
60 Equal, in a way

by Robert Dillman

101

While some Across clues in this puzzle appear to be missing, every answer is in fact clued.

ACROSS

4 Common Halloween costumes
10 Opposite of all
14 Went on and on
15 Loser
17 Hosts
18 Try, as something new
21 Engine meas.
22 Like some low-rise buildings
23 West Indies, e.g.
25 Suffix with super
29 Inaugural oath starter
30 Places where fans may gather to watch a game
35 End of a match
36 Noted 1829 West Point graduate
38 Summer clock setting: Abbr.
39 Buffoon
40 Deem appropriate
43 Imitate
44 Irish playwright who wrote "The Shadow of a Gunman"
46 Bill of Rights freedom: Abbr.
47 Countryman of Chancellor Konrad Adenauer
48 "Monsters, ___" (2001 Pixar film)
49 Long-billed wading bird
54 Shade of green
55 Target of chondrolaryngoplasty surgery
60 English king who was the youngest son of William the Conqueror
62 Barely
64 Canine coat?
65 Comforting words
67 Some dips
68 What some browsers browse

DOWN

1 Spanish card suit
2 Kind of mile: Abbr.
3 Inner: Prefix
4 London shades
5 Part of a western sandwich
6 One way to buy things
7 Hamlet, to Claudius
8 Abound (with)
9 Radical '60s org.
10 Card, e.g
11 Bone: Prefix
12 Bear
15 Like a thumb struck with a hammer
20 Spring (from)
22 ___ the morning
24 Not really sing
25 Certain Middle Easterner
26 Cloud up
27 One of the Honeymooners
28 Fix, as a road
31 Visit anew
32 Mint dept.
33 Blockage fix
38 Early American patriot Silas
39 Guests may be greeted with them
42 Symbol in Wal-Mart ads
43 Magazine locale
44 Scand. language
50 Parts of beach kits
51 Like some online forum postings: Abbr.
52 Move slowly (along)
53 H.S. exam
54 Former Royals manager Tony

by Joe Krozel

102

ACROSS
1 Restraint
5 Project Blue Book subject
9 Ex-
13 Not berthed
14 Big name in skin care
16 Talk radio's ___ & Anthony
17 Hospital count
18 Turns around, as a mast
19 Abbé de l'___, pioneer in sign language
20 With 28-, 48- and 56-Across, riddle whose answer appears in the circled squares
23 "Who ___?" (common riddle ending)
25 Camp seat
26 Largest geological division
27 "Don't wanna"
28 See 20-Across

32 Like frittatas
33 Sun. discourse
34 Year in the reign of Justinian the Great
35 Answers the call, maybe
37 Affluent duo?
39 Fortuneteller
43 Satisfied reactions
45 Suffix with profit
47 Movie featuring Peter O'Toole as Priam
48 See 20-Across
51 Kentucky's Athlete of the Century
53 Goose egg
54 Plugs
55 "Bells ___ Ringing"
56 See 20-Across
60 Like worms
61 Computer unveiled in 1946
62 Cold feet
65 Store drawer
66 See 58-Down
67 Concerning
68 Suit to ___

69 Spin
70 Frequent gift for a PBS donation

DOWN
1 Trucker's place
2 Resort to
3 N.H.L. team at Joe Louis Arena
4 Big party
5 Pulls the plug on
6 Fine metal openwork
7 Reproductive seed
8 Trickled
9 "Odyssey," for one
10 Attach (to)
11 Tuscany city
12 Canines that bite
15 Comparatively noisy
21 Bass ___
22 Bottom-of-letter abbr.
23 One with a sterling service
24 Ancient gift givers
29 How some music is played

30 Monteverdi opera
31 Takes off
36 Stood out
38 Plan for nuptials
40 Musician who created the Windows 95 start-up sound
41 Watch-step connection
42 ___ disease
44 Beamed
46 Avant-garde
48 Changeable on a whim
49 Power tool in woodworking
50 Ukr., once
51 California's Santa ___ Park
52 Kosher
57 MacLachlan of "Desperate Housewives"
58 With 66-Across, Egyptian agricultural area
59 "What ___?" (snippy reply)
63 Knack
64 "Riddle-me-___"

by David J. Kahn

103

ACROSS

1 Part of Poor Richard's Almanack
6 They clear the way
12 Think over, in a way
14 Wearing white after Labor Day, e.g.
15 Rest
16 Border in the court?
17 It might help you take a turn for the better
19 "See ___ care"
20 Bill and Hillary Clinton, e.g.
21 Fast pitch
23 Place to get a C.D.
26 Gaelic tongue
29 Cinnabar, e.g.
30 Emperor under Pope Innocent III
32 Early Surrealist
35 Ten minutes in a laundry, maybe
37 Hangar site
40 Upper armbones
44 Byron's "___ Walks in Beauty"
45 Pay (up)
47 Nutcases
48 Pilgrim to Mecca
51 Fundamental of philosophy
53 First U.S. pres. to travel in a submarine
54 "You'll have to take my word for it"
59 Informal words of concurrence
60 Attribution
62 Strife
63 A Lennon sister
64 Song from "The Music Man" with the lyric "What words could be saner or truer or plainer"
65 Word that can precede the starts of 17-, 35- and 54-Across and 16-Down

DOWN

1 Band score abbr.
2 Frying medium
3 Designate
4 U.F.O. feature, maybe
5 Minimal effort
6 Commanded
7 They are sorry
8 Yellow spring flower
9 Perspective
10 Stable places
11 Abilene-to-San Antonio dir.
13 Unlikely party animal
14 Cry of disgust
16 Low pressure area
18 Good name for a trial lawyer?
19 Abbr. on a film box
22 Tennis call
24 Columnist Maureen
25 Word repeated in a child's taunt
27 For example
28 Kind of rate in a bank: Abbr.
31 Letters on a Rémy Martin bottle
33 Jewish month
34 San ___, Italy
36 Grp. handling insurance forms
37 Wood for oars
38 "Ugh!"
39 Remedy
41 Egg-laying mammal
42 Composer of the opera "Tancredi"
43 Form of the German "to be"
46 7'6" N.B.A. star
49 Titillating

by Michael Shteyman

50 Kindergarten comeback
52 How most computer software is sold
55 No ___ Street
56 Kind of school
57 Salt Lake City daily, briefly, with "the"
58 Learn (of)
59 Year of an Amerigo Vespucci voyage
61 Highest tile value in Scrabble

104

ACROSS

1 Revolutionary James ___, famous for saying "Taxation without representation is tyranny"
5 Elem. sch. class
9 "Look ___" (1975 #1 R & B hit)
13 Main
14 April Fools' Day baby
16 Like one leg of a triathlon
17 ". . . ___ saw Elba"
18 Children's author who wrote "A fly can't bird, but a bird can fly"
19 Cobra's greeting
20 *Undersized bats and gloves, e.g.
23 Accountant's advice
24 Journalist Hamill
25 Cargo compartment
27 Chemical ending
28 Bill Clinton, collegiately
30 *Chophouse order
32 Fixed parts of motors
36 Energy units
37 *Founder of Mesa Petroleum
40 Mystique
41 Dirty campaigner
42 *Alternatives to rope tows
44 Stock (up)
45 Cable channel . . . with a hint to the answers to the five starred clues
48 Start to stammer
49 Not very much
53 J.F.K.'s command
55 *Caucasus capital
58 At a dead end, as a case
59 Ruffles
60 Hostile
61 Sport with masks
62 Serving from a grill
63 Relative of a plum
64 Brand name that sounds like two letters of the alphabet
65 Meddlesome
66 Round up

DOWN

1 "Gonna Let It Shine" singer
2 Diva's headwear
3 Mountaineering aid
4 Circus prop
5 Strategies
6 Actor La Salle
7 Lubricate
8 One often seen with crossed arms
9 "Off the Court" autobiographer
10 Like Romulus and Remus
11 Southern Methodist team, with "the"
12 Accident letters
15 Harvest time: Abbr.
21 Deceive
22 Bumped into
26 "You rang?"
29 Particular
31 Ingredient in some batters
32 Really take off
33 Reveal, in verse
34 Muscat money
35 Makes a very modest living
37 Stretchy attire
38 Hiking hazards
39 ___ the city
40 Part of N.C.A.A.: Abbr.
43 Folk singer's mule
45 Turn on and off
46 Surety poster
47 Didn't split
50 Dagger
51 Like tigers
52 First name in "The Hobbit"

by Elizabeth C. Gorski

54 Momentary
contact
56 Logical
start?
57 Bygone G.M.
cars
58 Mid grade?

105

ACROSS
1 Greta Garbo, by birth
6 Title name after the lyric "What's it all about when you sort it out"
11 Title for a guru
14 Colorful opening course
17 Colorful spread
18 Sparkler
19 "The Dukes of Hazzard" deputy
20 Big spender, maybe
21 Journey
23 Those, to Teodoro
24 Circulating
29 Carnival sights
32 Neighbor of Ivory Coast
33 "A Mighty Fortress ___ God" (hymn)
34 French intimate
37 & 39 Colorful dessert

41 Pointed tool
42 Oscar-nominated Icelandic singer
44 Way down
45 Moon of Saturn
46 Wood carving
47 Sock style
50 Bit of Madison Ave. planning
53 Beat at a hot dog contest
56 Gay Nineties and Roaring Twenties
58 Foofaraw
61 Colorful breakfast food
64 Colorful entree
65 Beverage suffix
66 Place for a swirl
67 www.yahoo.com and others

DOWN
1 Possible cause of heavy breathing
2 Finish line, maybe
3 Means of assessment
4 Place to display trophies
5 Just beat
6 Protection provider
7 Not owners
8 ___-de-lance
9 The Beatles' "___ Life"
10 "___ Wood would saw wood . . ." (part of a classic tongue twister)
11 "Snap out of it!" actions
12 Part of a beach kit
13 What philosophes get
15 Lady's partner
16 Suisse peaks
22 Mall station

24 Taj Mahal's home
25 "Major Barbara" playwright
26 Detective, at times
27 Resting place
28 Harry Kemelman sleuth David Small, e.g.
30 "Well, obviously!"
31 Pitch
33 Obstreperous child's cry
34 Go up against
35 Deal (out)
36 Twosome
38 Spanish eye
40 Fraternity character
43 Game on an 8×8 board
45 Nerd
47 U.S. attack helicopter
48 Like some notepaper
49 Chopin piece
51 Indo-___
52 Curse
54 Not up

by Joseph Crowley

55 Wrest
57 Beer, slangily
58 Throw ___
59 Gambling aids

60 Kind of place
62 Biochemistry abbr.
63 Busy airport time: Abbr.

106

ACROSS
1 Smithereens
5 America's Cup, e.g.
9 It's lowered before a joust
14 Source of misery
15 Volcanic formation
16 Wear
17 Many a Del. registration
18 "Here ___!"
19 Kiboshed
20 PROSE
23 Jeremiah, e.g., in the Bible
24 Potted ornamental
25 Leader of the Autumn Harvest Uprising
28 TORSO
32 1950s–'60s American rocket
35 Hoover Dam's Lake ___
36 University of New Mexico athlete
37 SAP
39 LEAD
42 Car bar
43 Prefix with -drome
44 Turn blue, e.g.
45 GENRES
50 Charlotte-to-Raleigh dir.
51 Yarn producer?
52 "___ is not to . . ."
55 BAIRNS
59 Progeny
62 Hollow, perhaps
63 Dull
64 Targets for weightlifters
65 Itch
66 Well-known maker of two-by-fours
67 Go 50/50 on
68 "Hey, buddy!"
69 Sponsor of early radio's "Five Star Theater"

DOWN
1 Support
2 Shining examples
3 Spasm
4 Snow White's dwarfs, e.g.
5 Nose (out)
6 Fifth-anniversary gift
7 55th-anniversary gift
8 Do cobbling work on
9 Facade
10 You can see through it
11 One of two A.L. teams
12 Wordsworth's "___ to Duty"
13 Obviously chafed
21 March
22 Boll
25 Made farm sounds
26 Cornered
27 "___ Mio"
29 Grant-giving grp.
30 Oomph
31 Moth-eaten
32 ___ worse than death
33 Fifth-century invader of Britain
34 Something a doctor may check
38 Ballot markings
39 School competition
40 It may come after you
41 Organ ___
43 Payments might be in it
46 In position to inherit the throne, say
47 Carried out
48 New Mexico town mentioned in the hit "Route 66"
49 Ripe for a trial lawyer
53 Ruffles
54 Hooks
55 A6 maker
56 Pad
57 TV's Maverick
58 "Out!"
59 Measures of brightness
60 Eat well
61 Dean's companion in Kerouac's "On the Road"

by John Sheehan

107

ACROSS

1 Flicker
6 Dog command
11 Object of some amateur films
14 Aviation name until 1997
15 "Ladies of Leisure" director
16 Comics sound
17 Con man's pay?
19 Afternoon hour in Italy
20 Supply at a changing station
21 Source of wealth
22 Almost white
24 Satan?
28 Full of gusto
31 Vacation destination
32 Blasting
33 Nitwit
35 "The Farmer's ___" (1928 Hitchcock film)
37 Salon acquisition
38 Ingenuous . . . or like 17-, 24-, 50- and 60-Across

41 Joie de vivre
42 Novelist Ferber
44 Seasonal song title opener
45 Heads-up
47 Send back
49 Disturbs the peace, in a way
50 Slapstick staples?
53 "Then what happened?"
54 ___ d'Isère (French skiing locale)
55 Clanton rival
59 Single-stranded molecule
60 Parts of dollhouse dinner table settings?
64 Comprehend
65 Banded stone
66 Snacks
67 Palindromic preposition
68 Ocean explorer's aid
69 Long leg?

DOWN

1 Do some cleaning
2 1930s film dog
3 Polish locale
4 They're easy
5 Bit of work
6 Simple knitting project
7 Went white
8 DDT banner
9 Flight board abbr.
10 Transportation around the Aleutians
11 Jailed
12 Dry season danger
13 1936 Olympics record-breaker
18 Symbol of blackness
23 Symbol of whiteness
25 Singer with the 1992 quintuple-platinum album "Shepherd Moons"
26 Ready to fight
27 Parts of a gym set

28 It may be upped
29 Cartoon beeper
30 Restaurant companion
33 Ear decorations
34 Feverish, say
36 911 responders
39 Eastern dignitary
40 Fit to stand trial
43 Music boosters?
46 Snaps
48 Perfumer's stock in trade
49 Sunny spot for a plant
50 "Beetle Bailey" character
51 Broadway hit that originally opened in London in 1978
52 Cellphone's predecessor
56 Town ESE of Turin
57 Contents of a large, round, flat can
58 Verbal elbow?

by Donna Hoke Kahwaty

61 "Where did ___ wrong?"

62 Bert Bobbsey's twin

63 Midbody muscles

108

ACROSS

1 Crude containers: Abbr.
5 Goddess whose bird was a peacock
9 Water-to-wine town
13 Enemy of la Révolution française
14 Often
15 Southwestern trees
16 Job at a lineup
17 "It's not my fault!"
19 Not giving the police any more information
21 "Beats me"
22 Long line in Rome
24 Suffix meaning "land" in some country names
25 Seek
29 Swank
31 A book title may be in it: Abbr.
32 Hubbub
34 Hunky-dory
38 1961 Del Shannon lyric (and title of this puzzle)
41 Look
42 Factor in a wine review
43 One way to serve ham
44 Rushing group
46 Showing one's age, in a way
47 Fiery
49 Scheherazade's locale
52 Barnard grad, e.g.
54 Double dessert
59 Some crime deterrents
61 Plot again
62 Toots in a restaurant
63 Something that's spun
64 Soul singer Baker
65 Winston Churchill, e.g.
66 River of Flanders
67 "Tell Mama" singer James

DOWN

1 Total chaos
2 Overflow site
3 "WKRP" actress Anderson
4 Help provider
5 Hosted at one's penthouse, say
6 Get together without fanfare?
7 Harry's pal at Hogwarts
8 Ltr. routing aid
9 Frontier sharpshooter
10 Tree-lined promenade
11 "Julius" in Gaius Julius Caesar
12 Between shores, maybe
13 D.M.V. document
18 Cap'n's underling
20 Brit's oath
23 Level
25 Ends
26 Eyelid annoyance
27 Long green
28 Con games
30 Sch. named for a televangelist
32 Cleric's attire
33 Hobbled
35 Out of kilter
36 "The Court Jester" star, 1956
37 Got a load of
39 Program guide abbr.
40 Field part
45 French filmmaker Clair
46 "Hmm, I didn't know that!"
47 Even if, briefly
48 Prelude to a revolution
50 Jobs creation
51 Alarm heeder
52 Deputy: Abbr.
53 Firm member: Abbr.
55 "Ah, for the good old days," e.g.
56 Except

by Nancy Salomon

57 Experiment's yield
58 Waste watchers' org.
60 Eastern priests

109

ACROSS

1 Shorten, say
5 Swindle, in slang
9 Fancy button material
14 Banjoist Fleck
15 "What ___?" (clerk's question)
16 Relatives of English horns
17 Events for some teens
19 Censor
20 Carry out an order
21 Frequently used adverb on Court TV
23 Extremely popular
25 Dog-___
26 Eventually
29 CPR experts
31 Stain collector
34 Kind of officer
35 21, e.g.
36 Subject of many X-Files
37 Bargaining phrase . . . and a hint to this puzzle's theme
41 Call upon
42 Nail, as a gymnastic landing
43 Maximum extent
44 A couple in Mexico?
45 Follower of red or 50
46 Devotes
48 Starts to like, with "to"
49 Like some breakfast cereals
51 It tends to increase with income
55 Places of prayer and reflection
59 "Goody!"
60 Something never shown in bars
62 Struck down
63 "All right already!"
64 Branch headquarters?
65 Warlock, e.g.
66 You can see right through it
67 Gather

DOWN

1 Declines
2 "My stars!"
3 "Would ___?"
4 Fink's activity
5 Bring back
6 Lift
7 Bat material
8 Southwest sight
9 One column in the periodic table
10 More up to the job
11 Not same-sex
12 Stagger
13 Annual athletic award from cable TV
18 Camera feature
22 Free
24 Actual
26 Old war story
27 "I beg to differ"
28 Listings on a to-do list
30 Big truck maker
31 Start of a poker game
32 Poker player's declaration
33 Fights
35 "Come ___!"
38 Food company whose name is spelled out in its advertising jingle
39 Weapons check, in brief
40 Victors of 1865
46 Library area
47 Feature of many a pirate
48 Penned
50 Stage part
51 Reggae musician Peter
52 "Alas!"
53 Microsoft product launched in 2001
54 Sci. course
56 Brave
57 Mimic
58 Drop
61 "South Park" brother

by Mike Nothnagel

110

ACROSS

1 Food that's stuck on a plate
6 Cycle starter
9 Avant-garde composer Brown
14 Where Francis Scott Key saw bombs bursting
15 Site of an annual auto hill climb
17 "Creature From the Black Lagoon," e.g.
19 One trying to stay up while going down
20 Shatner's sci-fi drug
21 Almost bound
24 Overture follower
26 Goes out to sea
30 Attention-getting haircut
32 Suffix with hex-
34 Sundial hour
35 Part of a treaty exchange, for short

36 Affaires d'___
39 Canon rival
41 Gathering of budding agriculturists
44 Cousins of Drama Desk Awards
45 Brim
46 Dye plant
47 Runner of an experiment?
48 Suffix with vapour
50 "Please refrain from personal attacks"
52 "Excuse me"
54 Controversial 1767 act of Parliament
57 Old J.F.K. sight
58 Gray side: Abbr.
60 Separates
62 Some running competitions
69 City of Indiana or Louisiana
70 Severe
71 Big parade organizer
72 Sequel title starter, sometimes
73 Target sport

DOWN

1 Western moniker
2 See 3-Down
3 With 2-Down, what a villain may come to
4 Points
5 "The Greatest Generation" author
6 Not happy at all
7 The N in blasting
8 Mike's partner in candy
9 Salinger girl
10 Give ___ (prod)
11 Rel. title
12 Chou En-___
13 Pull (out), as a narrow victory
16 Some art prints
18 Jefferson site
21 Old wine vessel
22 Bigwig
23 "The Sword in the Stone" author
25 Cry of innocence

27 Two-piece suits?
28 Study involving nature and engineering
29 Wrestler's wear
31 Queens's ___ Stadium
33 Suffix with benz-
37 One in a class by himself
38 Shinzo ___, former Japanese P.M.
40 Call ___ evening
42 Top-rated show of 2002–05
43 Start, with "on"
49 Purse
51 People in a crowd, maybe
53 Longtime "ABC's Wide World of Sports" host
55 Request one's presence at
56 Symbol
59 "The ___ the limit"
61 Bed, slangily

by Patrick Merrell

62 Airline with a crown in its logo
63 "The Jungle Book" python
64 Restaurant with wings
65 Some chess pieces: Abbr.
66 Table stick
67 Season overseas
68 Established

111

ACROSS
1 "That ___ so bad"
6 Hummus holder
10 Relative of Finnish
14 Koran topic
15 ___ Ben Adhem
16 Giant slalom's first Olympic venue
17 Ones with a family connection?
19 Takes root
20 Straight
21 Thrown out
23 It's not forked out
25 Curtain call maker, maybe
26 Slowly or quickly: Abbr.
29 Bayonet, e.g.
31 Not just laugh
35 Clear, in a way
37 Await delivery anxiously
39 Nautical stabilizer
40 Hose hue
41 Former European money
42 It's softer than quartz
43 Rent-___
44 City on Utah Lake
45 Conflagrant
46 Much higher than normal
48 Studious sort, and proud of it
50 Single, for one: Abbr.
51 Belabor, with "on"
53 Soil type
55 Special CD release . . . or a hint to this puzzle's theme
59 Punish by fining
63 Voracious
64 Shrewd bargainers
66 One of a noted nautical trio
67 "I'm working ___!"
68 Lightly pinch
69 On tenterhooks
70 Spell checker's find
71 Relish

DOWN
1 No-loss, no-gain situation
2 Caught in ___
3 Crib component
4 Specifies
5 1980 Bette Midler hit
6 Manhandle
7 Footnote abbr.
8 In pretty good shape
9 Patronage
10 Fail to keep tabs on
11 Kind of prof.
12 Bend at the barre
13 Duck's home
18 Begin
22 Fertility clinic supply
24 Cover (over)
26 Turn ___ ear
27 Bing Crosby's label
28 Like rabies
30 Decimal
32 French military hats
33 Big name in '60s counter-culture
34 The first Mrs. Woodrow Wilson
36 Be very, very sorry
38 Desert mount
41 Hardly a marksman
45 Not taking no for an answer
47 Bit
49 It may come from a crowd
52 Hardy perennial
54 Press
55 Downfall
56 Golden Age poet
57 Deer ___
58 Send sprawling
60 Gym count
61 Bureau add-on?
62 Famed Ferrara family
65 Scrap

1	2	3	4	5		6	7	8	9		10	11	12	13
14						15					16			
17					18						19			
20							21			22				
			23			24		25						
26	27	28		29			30		31			32	33	34
35			36			37		38			39			
40					41						42			
43					44					45				
46				47			48		49			50		
			51			52		53			54			
55	56	57					58		59			60	61	62
63					64			65						
66					67					68				
69					70					71				

by Alan Arbesfeld

112

ACROSS
1 Fix up, informally
6 Where Beetle Bailey can often be found
10 Not toss
14 Province west of Madrid
15 Shape of a mandolin's body
16 Collar's locale
17 =
20 Prime rib cut
21 Big __ (V.I.P.'s)
22 New World flycatchers
23 Infielder's cry
24 "The Cosby Show" boy
25 =
32 One in a chain, often
33 Bonny girl
34 Rapping "Dr."
35 Cousin of Bigfoot
36 Pops
38 Early photo-journalist Jacob
39 ". . . __ quit!"

40 "An Enquiry Concerning Human Under-standing" author
41 Pound parts
42 =
46 Scene stealers
47 Longtime Georgia senator
48 Wise guy
51 "Mighty Aphrodite" co-star Sorvino
52 "The Loco-Motion" singer Little __
55 =
58 Fund-raising letter, basically
59 Scuttled mission
60 University in Peterbor-ough, Ont.
61 "O mighty Caesar! __ thou lie so low?": Shak.
62 Hood catcher
63 Gridiron gain or loss

DOWN
1 Be held in esteem
2 __ so
3 Rear
4 Home of the first capital of the Confederacy: Abbr.
5 Not just a tease
6 Performed prior to the main act
7 Neighbor of Homer, and others
8 Kit __ bar
9 Predict
10 Was familiar with
11 Ice dam site
12 Foil alternative
13 Stockyard divisions
18 Natural flood protection
19 Palm readers, e.g.
23 Year the National University of Mexico was founded

24 Spot
25 Make __ (throw into confusion)
26 Development sites
27 "__ I can help it!"
28 Ancient
29 Taking too much
30 "Vega$" star
31 Odometer button
36 Preparing, as a layout, with "up"
37 People a Frenchman may address, after "mes"
38 Cupid holder?
40 Sheraton rival
41 Foul result
43 It might be idle
44 Tandem
45 Ban alternative
48 Bay Area blues: Abbr.
49 Actor O'Shea
50 Bird classification
51 Start of something big?

by Peter A. Collins

52 At all
53 Market
54 Antenna
holders
56 Quaint tattoo
57 Century 21
competitor

113

ACROSS

1 One left hanging after an election?
5 Janis's hubby in the funnies
9 Sharp pain
13 Dwellers at First Mesa, Ariz.
14 At hand
15 Vacation locale
16 Role in "Troy"
17 The O'Hara spread
18 Land of Ephesus
19 See 61- and 62-Across
22 Not all together
23 Old White House inits.
24 Long-tubed flower
27 Stephen of "Feardot-Com"
29 Kind of adapter
33 Made, as a new trench
34 City on the Alabama River
36 Question from a person just awakened
37 See 61- and 62-Across
40 Like early-morning hours
41 That one and that one
42 Boston team, informally
43 Successor to Claudius I
45 Shock's partner
46 Superlatively collectible
47 ___ es Salaam
49 Car company owned by Volkswagen
50 See 61- and 62-Across
58 "___ kick out of you"
59 False ___
60 Wise to
61 & 62 Clue for 19-, 37- and 50-Across
63 Abba of Israel
64 Title for Miss Spain?: Abbr.
65 Form of "to be" with "vous"
66 Unit of force

DOWN

1 Redden and crack
2 Orange-roofed inn, for short
3 "Be ___"
4 Disposable picnic item
5 Tomfoolery
6 Gain
7 Boris Pasternak heroine
8 Kind of cavity
9 The second of January?
10 Nobel laureate Morrison
11 Take ___ (swing hard in baseball)
12 Jack Kerouac or Allen Ginsberg
15 Unleashes
20 Instructed
21 Cause of a red face
24 Symbol of sovereignty
25 U. S. Grant adversary
26 More curious
27 Kyle ___, "The Terminator" protagonist
28 "Anything ___?"
30 Country claiming a chunk of Antarctica
31 Passages
32 It may be pounded
34 Cause of certain blindness
35 Game venue
38 Midway alternative
39 Authenticated
44 One-named folk singer
46 Moscow moolah
48 Out of town
49 Joined (with)
50 Places for holsters
51 Culture medium

by Richard Chisholm

114

ACROSS

1 Show signs of improvement
11 Second in a series
15 Indication of stress
16 1,575-mile river known to some locals as the Zhayyq
17 "Well, duh!"
18 Hitch
19 Supra
20 Syrup of ___
22 Caustic
23 Sci-fi author McIntyre
25 Bad ___, German resort
26 With eyes open
30 Mr. Levy of 1920s Broadway fame
32 Holders of big pads
33 Marker
34 W.S.J. subjects
35 "It's ___!" ("You're on!")
36 Alt. spelling
37 Slam
38 Dictionary data
39 Minimal change
40 Cloth workers?
42 Big-league
43 Sculptor Oldenburg
44 Dive
46 Game craze of the late 1980s and '90s
49 Direct
51 Island nicknamed the Gathering Place
52 Jump the gun
55 Senior moment?
56 One who's happy when things look black
57 Blunt
58 Undergo a change of habit?

DOWN

1 Olympics item . . . or the winning word in the 1984 National Spelling Bee
2 Civilians eligible to be drafted
3 ___ Line (German/Polish border)
4 Bitter fruit
5 Queues
6 Name on a bottle of Beyond Paradise
7 Sch. staffer
8 French pronoun
9 Suffix with south
10 Sparks a second time
11 Department
12 Greenland colonizer
13 "I did it!"
14 Pianist Templeton
21 Visual PC-to-PC files
23 Appearances
24 Classic Packard model with a numerical name
26 Pompadour, for one
27 Prerecorded
28 Advance
29 Tentlike dwelling with a conical roof
30 Like some electric circuits
31 Be angry as heck
32 "Nothing to it"
38 Hybrid fruit
39 Where cooler heads prevail?
41 Fritz the Cat illustrator
42 Paid (up)
44 Locker room habitués
45 Rain gear brand
46 Maximally
47 Pull down
48 Grand total?
49 Plural suffix with beat or neat

by Henry Hook

50 Kind of pronoun: Abbr.
53 Clause connector
54 Unduly

115

ACROSS

1 Bit of income for the Department of Motor Vehicles
11 Waist products
15 What someone might win after stumping a cultural group?
16 Russian car
17 Greek salad ingredient
18 Seventh-century year
19 Exhausted
20 Body repair sites, briefly
21 Indicated "Just teasing!"
23 Two-timing types
25 Target
26 Where Yankees are found at Shea
31 Dry out
32 They're taken to the cleaners
33 Dude
34 Y.M.C.A. member?: Abbr.
35 Ark contents
36 16 and Seventeen, for short
37 ___ tree
38 Hatch in politics
39 Doesn't quite mash
40 Fan fare?
43 Stinko
44 One-eighties
45 "Jeez!"
47 Amer. capital
48 Flawlessly
52 Corner piece
53 Axiom
56 Snatch, slangily
57 Witness to Anakin Skywalker and Padmé Amidala's secret wedding
58 When tripled, "et cetera"
59 Rod Laver won two

DOWN

1 ___ Mason (asset management firm)
2 "___, dislike it" (start of Marianne Moore's "Poetry")
3 Fictional character who first appeared in "The House Without a Key"
4 Begins
5 Robertson of CNN
6 Controversial 1980s–'90s baseball team owner
7 "A thousand pardons"
8 They're not for you
9 Big-headed sorts, for short
10 Big shoe spec
11 Candidate for the proverbial glue factory
12 Consecutive
13 Frivolous
14 Related
22 Don in the National Radio Hall of Fame
24 City where Cézanne was born
25 Cuisine that may be served with a chork
26 Hornet genus
27 "Everything's cool"
28 Ninth-century founder of the Russian monarchy
29 Id output
30 Put into a 35-Down
31 Smear
35 Waste product
36 Oldtime entertainer
38 Work
39 Skate
41 Start of a little daredevil's declaration
42 Food fish of Australia and New Zealand

by Paula Gamache

45 Binge
46 Ciao, in
   Chile
47 Court
   org.
49 Make ___
   check

50 Little bit
51 Wilson's vice
   pres. ___
   Marshall
54 Sheet
   music
   abbr.

55 Cowboys'
   concerns,
   briefly

116

ACROSS
1 Back-and-forth
6 One at the helm
15 "___ directed"
16 Product identifier
17 Apple storage devices
18 It maintains a proper attitude
19 "Western Star" poet
20 Mount ___, sacred Chinese site
21 Sunder
22 Source of support
23 Fragrant
27 Bbl. fraction
28 ___ rock (radio format)
30 Bills are in it: Abbr.
31 Deal-killing words
33 Bibliographical abbr.
34 Venue of many Richard Petty wins
36 First-class handouts?
38 Herd-thinning menace
42 Semirural, say
44 Time magazine Person of the Year, 2005
45 One working on a board
48 Party in Pretoria: Abbr.
49 Poses in a studio?
50 Photographer Goldin
51 Town on the Long Island Rail Road
54 Sprout
55 Channel blocker
57 Letters before a street name
58 "I'll give you ___ . . ."
60 Colloquial
63 Newswoman Poussaint
64 Logic's counterpart
65 Rich spreads
66 Trunk accumulation
67 Common dog name

DOWN
1 Nitpicking
2 Harshness
3 Relating to babes
4 ___ City, seat of Pasco County, Fla.
5 Right hands: Abbr.
6 1945 film musical with the song "It Might As Well Be Spring"
7 Cutting out?
8 Suffer a loss, slangily
9 Shogunate capital
10 Mouthpiece
11 Scissor
12 Costa del Sol port
13 Unprincipled
14 Green stinger
24 Creme Egg maker
25 Proclaim
26 Underbosses' bosses
29 1990s sitcom
32 Didn't get involved
35 Does, as business
37 Choppers
39 Probe
40 Bring about with some effort
41 Cavalier evaluation?
43 On the sundeck
45 Not yield
46 Corporate shark
47 Seeing the sites
52 Like muesli
53 Diamond protectors
56 Lug
59 Jalopy
61 It was deorbited in 2001
62 "Bel-___" (Maupassant novel)

by Chuck Deodene

117

ACROSS

1 Concerned query
6 Without a leg to stand on?
14 Vermont senator Sanders
15 It's a cinch
16 Pretentious
17 Without a match
18 "Pardon me"
19 Closing bid?
20 Peak
21 McCartney, to fans
24 Horror film that starts in a filthy lavatory
26 Weaken, in a way
29 Monotheistic Syrian
33 Most in need of toning
35 Top-rated, in a way
36 Slant
37 Get all histrionic
38 About 40 degrees, for N.Y.C.
39 Hostel environments
40 Wore out
42 Some lap dogs
44 Result of a new TV series' renewal
46 A.A. discussion topic
48 Appoints as an agent
49 Roast pig side dish
52 Stands
55 Brew choice
56 Afro-Caribbean religion
58 Toeless creature in an Edward Lear verse
60 Engine manufacturer Briggs & ___
61 One with a second helping
62 Super Bowl XX champs
63 Personnel director, at times

DOWN

1 Hoped-for reply to 1-Across
2 Payment is often sent with one
3 Apt to say "So?"
4 Relative of -ish
5 Mauna ___
6 Missile with a mobile launcher
7 Product whose ads featured twins
8 Iroquois' foes
9 Lee Marvin TV oldie
10 Moldovan money
11 He or I, but not you: Abbr.
12 Ward of "Once and Again"
13 Deep river?
14 Sighing a lot, maybe
19 Some Nissans
22 "___ for Alibi"
23 ___ Pendragon, King Arthur's father
25 Call slip?
27 West African currency
28 Ponch player in 1970s–'80s TV
30 Too awful even to fix up, as an apartment
31 Octopus, e.g.
32 Take the cake?
34 Twit
36 Marcel Marceau character
41 Bush league?
43 City connected to the 4.1-mile long Sunshine Skyway Br.
45 Kitchen appliance brand
47 In a sense
49 "Over here"
50 Four-letter word, aptly
51 On

by Henry Hook

118

ACROSS

1 He had a hit with "The Joint Is Jumpin' "
11 Signs of neglect
15 First #1 hit by the Beach Boys
16 Like the sea
17 City on the Trans-continental Railroad
18 Some people have it for life
19 Not do the rite thing?
20 Requests for developers: Abbr.
21 Taylor of "Mystic Pizza"
22 Some cabbage
23 Dwell
24 Much
25 With 52- and 39-Across, gradually
26 Potentate
28 One of a primer pair
29 They're not originals

31 Materials used as inert paint fillers
33 Best people
34 El relative
35 Whole slew of
39 See 25-Across
43 Premium chargers, briefly
44 Like a well-maintained lawn
46 Discrimi-natory leader?
47 What "y" might become
48 Driver on a ranch
49 It's found in a chest
50 Fermentation locations
52 See 25-Across
53 19th-century territorial capital
54 Organs are located in it: Abbr.
55 Block head?
57 Delivery possibility

58 Committed a sports no-no
59 Due and sei
60 Succulent African shrub popular as a bonsai

DOWN

1 Internet Explorer alternative
2 Facial feature, later in life
3 Carpenter, at times
4 They're located on organs
5 Draw to a close
6 It may come after you
7 Hippie happenings
8 African city of 2.5+ million founded by the Portuguese
9 Infinite
10 Food figs.
11 Hanging setting

12 Big name in credit reports
13 Greyhounds may run in it
14 Wilde things?
23 "See ya!"
26 Year of St. Genevieve's death
27 Pitching
28 Fun
30 They're known for head-turning
32 Basketful
35 Fictional doctor
36 "This is no joke!"
37 Letter writing, some say
38 It was first observed in 1846
39 One taken in
40 Like some surgery
41 Group that starred in the 1968 film "Head," with "the"
42 Match-starting cry
45 Establishes

by Barry C. Silk

119

ACROSS

1 News Corporation-owned Web site that's one of the 10 most visited sites in the world
8 Dirt on a person
14 Yellow fliers with large eyespots
15 "Cab," e.g.
16 Abscond
17 What the key of D minor has
18 Sponge
19 Driving distance is a concern in it
21 Dermal opening?
22 Miss Gulch biter
24 Height and such
25 Pet
26 Hostile
28 In advance of
29 Get a handle on?
30 They're played at the track
32 Buries
34 Brass
36 Walled city of the Mideast
37 "Let me live my own life!"
41 Gives a little, say
45 Wedding concern
46 Taper
48 Was sluggish?
49 Old Testament book: Abbr.
50 Reporting to
52 Vapid
53 1980s sitcom title role
54 Flips
56 Hiver's opposite
57 Not-so-good feeling
59 Former field food
61 Terminal timesaver
62 Its value is in creasing
63 Sprint acquisition of 2005
64 Crossword source since 1942: Abbr.

DOWN

1 Slip
2 Poem reader at the 2006 Olympics opening ceremony
3 Gaga
4 With 20-Down, waffle alternative
5 Capping
6 Finishes quickly, in a way
7 Grounds-keeper's charge
8 Family group
9 ___-Neisse Line
10 Abbr. in personal ads
11 Center of Connecticut
12 All thrown together, say
13 Little women
15 Cheering section
20 See 4-Down
23 "Heavens!"
25 1963 Academy Awards host
27 He wrote "It's certain that fine women eat / A crazy salad with their meat"
29 Alb coverer
31 Sharp
33 Meal source
35 Lopsided court result
37 Ones paid to conceive?
38 Cartoon boss working at a quarry
39 Modern rental option
40 Sch. whose colors are "true blue" and gold
42 Cry upon arriving
43 Beau ideal
44 Burial place of many French kings
47 "Way to go, dude!"
50 Bernoulli family birthplace

by David Quarfoot

51 Trouble
54 Raise
55 Not yet
  58-Down
58 See
  55-Down
60 ___ Friday's

120

ACROSS

1 Windshield wipers
10 "Unbeliev-able!"
15 Darwin's home
16 Superrealist sculptor Hanson
17 Zip
18 They stand for something: Abbr.
19 Station info, briefly
20 Checks out
21 1984 hit parody of a 1983 hit song
22 Get moving, with "up"
23 Four-time Vardon Trophy winner
25 Area below the hairline
26 Lock changer?
29 Turn out
31 Narrows: Abbr.
32 Directory data: Abbr.
34 Clam
36 Bluster
40 Hardly humble homes
41 A bit much
43 Call in a calamity
44 No longer doing the job?: Abbr.
45 Bombards with junk
47 Become active
50 Pull out of ___ (produce suddenly)
52 Makes out
54 Fat cat, in England
56 Packs in stacks
58 Short distance
59 "Eight Is Enough" wife
60 Creator of lofty lines
61 Freshening naturally
63 Something to get a kick out of

64 Park gathering place
65 Starters
66 Garb symbolizing youth

DOWN

1 Not as touched
2 Like successful orators
3 James Forrestal was its last cabinet secy.
4 Portions of les années
5 Stat for a reliever
6 Slalom targets
7 Comic Boosler
8 Astronaut Collins and others
9 Toasted triangle topper
10 One of Jon Arbuckle's pets
11 Changsha is its capital
12 "Hang on!"
13 Eager

14 Things that may be shot in stages?
24 "La Reine Margot" novelist
27 ___'acte
28 Ways to go
30 Some shirts
33 Dishes out undaintily
35 Trailer's place
36 South Pacific island
37 Cry before storming out
38 "Lighten up, will ya?!"
39 Hiking aid
42 Hate, say
46 "Tristram Shandy" author
48 Natural
49 In the pink
51 10 kilogauss
53 Relish
55 Disk units
57 Bring to a standstill
59 Mar makeup
62 Letter run

¹	²	³	⁴	⁵	⁶	⁷	⁸	⁹	■	¹⁰	¹¹	¹²	¹³	¹⁴
¹⁵									■	¹⁶				
¹⁷									■	¹⁸				
¹⁹				■	²⁰				■	²¹				
²²			■		²³			²⁴	■	²⁵				
■	²⁶		²⁷	²⁸	■	²⁹			³⁰	■	³¹			
■		■	³²		³³	■	³⁴			³⁵				
³⁶	³⁷	³⁸			³⁹	■	⁴⁰							
⁴¹						⁴²	■	⁴³				■	■	■
⁴⁴			■	⁴⁵			⁴⁶	■	⁴⁷		⁴⁸	⁴⁹	■	
⁵⁰			⁵¹	■	⁵²			⁵³	■		⁵⁴		⁵⁵	
⁵⁶				⁵⁷	■	⁵⁸				■	⁵⁹			
⁶⁰					■	⁶¹			⁶²					
⁶³					■	⁶⁴								
⁶⁵					■	⁶⁶								

by Frederick J. Healy

121

ACROSS
1 Stuck
8 "Not possible"
14 It might go off during a 30-Across
16 "Great taste since 1905" sloganeer
17 Rule broken in leisure?
18 He died soon after escaping from Crete
19 ___ dog
20 Dutch export
22 Van Halen's "Live Without ___"
23 Angle iron
24 TV series whose finale was titled "The Truth," with "The"
26 Unpleasant thing to incur
27 Squadron leader?
28 Swear words?
30 One can be tracked
31 2000 Olympics host
32 Recurring character who dies in the novel "Curtain"
34 Reveals
35 Dusting aid
36 Unesco World Heritage Site on the Arabian Peninsula
37 Scheduled
39 Letters on some college buildings
42 A.L. Central scoreboard abbr.
43 Little tricksters
44 Having good balance
45 Target of milk of magnesia
47 Informal demurral
48 Has a problem on the road
49 College in Claremont, Calif.
51 Tax burden?
53 It might go 7-5
54 Thing with a pressure point?
55 Grinder
56 Butterfly feature

DOWN
1 Totally unemotional type
2 Wheels
3 Things with rings
4 Further out of the woods?
5 Trick
6 One making waves
7 Kids' hideaway
8 Where many prints may be found
9 10-Down div.
10 Org. since 1910
11 Raked over the coals
12 Horse of a certain color
13 Occasions for baskets
15 Clairvoyant
21 Substitute: Abbr.
24 Abscissa
25 Barraged
28 "A Prairie Home Companion" co-star, 2006
29 "Odyssey" high point
30 "Star Wars" order
32 Fruit found among needles
33 Routinely
34 Battle of Put-in-Bay setting
35 16-Across, e.g.
36 General who prevailed over Carthage
38 Big name in ergonomic utensils
39 Settled
40 Shade deeper than heliotrope
41 Sonnet section
44 Flying predators of cold seas

by Mike Nothnagel

46 "O mighty Caesar! ___ thou lie so low?": Shak.

48 Learned

50 "Tutte ___ cor vi sento" (Mozart aria)

52 ___ dog

122

ACROSS

1 Navigation hazard
9 Coolness
15 Way off
16 Special delivery?
17 Married man who had long been a bachelor
18 Many a monthly check writer
19 Missing the point?
21 Car bar
22 W.W. II agcy.
23 Drawer units?
25 ___ Genevieve County, Mo.
26 Take off
29 When repeated, a "Funny Girl" song
30 Utterance when pointing to a woman
31 Chief
32 Famously fussy pair of diners

33 Any of les Trois Mousque-taires
34 Acts on a gut feeling?
35 Gold rush storyteller
36 Hardware store offering
37 In the style of: Suffix
38 Fishing boats
39 Island republic
40 ___ phenomenon (optical illusion)
41 Like most mammals
42 He wrote "A first sign of the beginning of under-standing is the wish to die"
43 Top of some scales
44 Chump
45 Univ. offerings
46 Not having as favorable a prognosis
48 Main, maybe

53 Quiet craft
55 Dangerous places for correspon-dents
56 Bunny backer?
57 Where workers gather
58 Risers meet them
59 QB who was the 1963 N.F.L. M.V.P.

DOWN

1 Five-time U.S. presidential candidate in the early 1900s
2 One making firm decisions
3 Hombre, once
4 Some athletes shoot them
5 Like many an heir apparent
6 Goes under
7 If ever
8 Overdoes it
9 Not out of place
10 Importunes

11 Carnival follower
12 "Che!" title role player, 1969
13 Watch notch
14 Alternative that should be followed
20 Put under?
24 The Chi-___ (1970s R & B group)
26 "Pleasant dreams"
27 Seed-separating gizmo
28 Past prime time?
29 U.S. air-to-air missile
32 Navigation hazard
36 "C'mon, do me this favor"
38 Ordained
42 Post-Taliban Afghan president
45 Kind of scholarship
47 Mrs. Turnblad in "Hairspray"
49 Spanish hors d'oeuvre
50 Competing

by Lynn Lempel

51 Strip
52 Forum
infinitive
54 Commuters'
choices:
Abbr.

123

ACROSS

1 Doesn't sit well
16 Class in which various schools are discussed
17 One way to solve problems
18 Pacer maker: Abbr.
19 Red sky, perhaps
20 "___ dispraise my lord . . .": Juliet
21 Expert in ancient law
24 City on the Natchez Trace
26 Not backing, in the backwoods
27 Lengthens, old-style
31 Retiree's coverage?
32 Basis for a suit
33 "30 Rock" creator
35 What a future American might take: Abbr.
36 Didn't paw
37 ___ grecque
40 Balloon attachment
41 Object in a Monet painting
42 Member of la famille immédiate
45 Floors
46 Frauen, across the border: Abbr.
47 Least spotted
49 Front wheel divergence
51 Hacker's cry of success
52 Something needed for your sake?
56 Gouge, say
57 Day-dreaming, e.g.
62 Completely gone
63 Records of interest to real estate agents

DOWN

1 Distillation location
2 Suffix with cream
3 Encouraging remark
4 Predatory critter
5 Large accounts?
6 Place for jets
7 1968 folk album
8 Bit of moonshine
9 Adolescent outburst
10 Louis Armstrong's "Oh ___ He Ramble"
11 Initials of a noted "Wizard"
12 Go downhill
13 No follower
14 Drive along leisurely
15 Firmly establish
21 Like some shifts
22 Occasional clashers
23 Dakota tongue
25 ___ to be
28 Rather informal?
29 Help set up chairs for?
30 French study, e.g.
34 Take many courses
36 They're against each other
37 Relating to heraldry
38 Place
39 Kind of producer: Abbr.
40 It may contain tear gas
41 Emphatic turndown
42 Curly-haired "Peanuts" character
43 20th-dynasty ruler
44 Lois Lane player Durance and others
48 It may be wrapped in a bun
50 Astrologer with the auto-biography "Answer in the Sky"

by Harvey Estes

53 Iraq's ___ Ali Shrine
54 Grant
55 Business class, briefly

58 Hearing aids, for short
59 Now in
60 R.S.V.P. component
61 D.C. United org.

124

ACROSS
1 Just the pits
16 Classic line of debate?
17 Just a bit, if that
18 Flag holder
19 In shape
20 Means: Abbr.
21 Songwriter Coleman and others
22 Illumination indication
23 Food whose name means "little sash"
28 Many an e-mail attachment
30 Sewn up
37 "The Randi Rhodes Show" network
38 Determine
39 It'll change your mind
40 Drone
41 Dance move
44 Scratch
46 Winner of three consecutive Emmys for "Mission: Impossible"
47 Batman creator Bob

49 Woody Guthrie's "Tom ___"
53 Left-of-center party member
57 "I'll take whatever help I can get"
58 Pro team whose mascot is a blue bird named Blitz

DOWN
1 Thrashers' home in the N.H.L.: Abbr.
2 One just filling up space
3 Second of 24
4 See 52-Down
5 Arm raiser, informally
6 Vote for
7 In need of a sweep
8 Ragged edges, in metalworking
9 Lambs: Lat.
10 Destiny

11 String player?
12 Ottoman officers
13 Simple
14 Toot
15 Some specialize in elec.
21 They may give you a seat
22 Spring river phenomenon
23 Sound-proofing material
24 Converse alternative
25 Yo-yo
26 Requiem title word
27 Alternative to a 23-Across
28 Somewhat, in music
29 Embarrassing way to be caught
31 1856 antislavery novel
32 Insult, on the street
33 Volt-ampere
34 Peculiar: Prefix

35 Relative of -ance
36 Perfect
41 He wrote that government "is but a necessary evil"
42 Gulf of Sidra setting
43 Like the Keystone Kops
44 "The ___ near!"
45 New Hampshire's ___ State College
46 Longfellow's "The Bells of San ___"
47 Rove in politics
48 Old man, in Mannheim
49 Rib
50 Prefix with -hedron
51 In ranks
52 With 4-Down, black magic
54 Raise a stink?
55 Billy's call
56 Logos and the like: Abbr.

by Paula Gamache

125

ACROSS

1 What you might do at the beach
10 Lethargy
15 Early inhabitant
16 Light smoke
17 Choked up
18 This is a test
19 Shaw who led the Gramercy Five
20 Muscleman with a 1980s cartoon series
21 Old-time actress Crabtree
22 Subject of interest in the question "Who are you wearing?"
23 Modern-day monarch, for short
24 Register
25 Brian known for 33-Across music
26 John who succeeded Pierre Trudeau as Canadian P.M.
28 Uris hero

29 Comment after getting something
30 Waves with long wavelengths?
33 See 25-Across
37 "Ash Wednesday" writer
38 Starry-eyed
40 Movie villain voiced by Douglas Rain
41 Miss ___
42 Spell checker?
44 Indian viceroy's authority
47 Damascus V.I.P.
50 Eventful times
51 "Take ___ the River" (Talking Heads hit)
52 Geometric prefix
53 Kip spender
54 Spanish kitties
55 Jerk
56 Doesn't support a conspiracy theory?
58 Deleted part
59 Oslo Accords concern

60 Gear
61 Frank Zappa or Dizzy Gillespie feature

DOWN

1 Forced feeding, as with a tube
2 Moon of Uranus named for a Shakespearean character
3 Like a romantic dinner
4 Big name in pest control
5 Get to
6 Jazz ___
7 Certain switch
8 Available
9 Small in the biggest way?
10 100 to 1, e.g.
11 Actress Nancy of "Sunset Boulevard"
12 Sandwich filler
13 Church piece
14 Old Tory

23 Fundamental energy units
26 "Vincent & ___" (1990 Robert Altman film)
27 Dailies, in the movie biz
29 ___-en-Provence, France
31 Groomed
32 Word before and after "in"
33 Swimming, surfboarding, etc.
34 Uncombed
35 Whitewall, maybe
36 Delays
39 Largest of the ABC islands
43 "The Tao that can be told is not the eternal Tao" philosopher
44 "Touché!" elicitor
45 Not accented
46 Important figure in the Gospels
48 Faulkner's "___ for Emily"

by John Farmer

49 Out

51 1945 conference site for Roosevelt and Churchill

54 One might fight to the last one

57 Sonny's partner in "Dog Day Afternoon"

126

ACROSS

1 Visits
8 French sentry's cry
15 Enter quickly
16 Ethically indifferent
17 "Again . . ."
18 With intensity
19 Four quarters, in France
20 Atlas sect.
22 Yugo-slavian-born court star
23 Chuck
24 Purely physical
26 Show some spunk
27 Court
28 Curl tightly
30 When Hölle freezes over?
31 Pro sports team that moved from New Orleans in 1979
33 Shakes
35 Fat cat
37 Make tracks
40 Concavo-convex lens
44 UV index monitor
45 If it's regular, each of its angles is 144°
47 "Notorious" film studio
48 Memphis's locale
50 Grandparent, frequently
51 One raised on a farm
52 Some jackets
54 Philip of "Kung Fu"
55 Schwar-zenegger title role
56 Outerwear fabric
58 Ding Dong alternative
60 Umm al-Quwain, for one
61 Pro Football Hall-of-Famer-turned-congressman Steve
62 Lured
63 Hides from the enemy, say

DOWN

1 Type of massage
2 Not removed delicately
3 Porthole view
4 The singing voice, informally
5 Old sticker
6 Overseas "-ess"
7 Authenticate, in a way
8 Tiger's-eye, essentially
9 Short family member?
10 "___ in the Morning"
11 Helped someone get a seat
12 Mayo's place
13 1974 Best Actress nominee Perrine
14 Champs ___
21 Approach to arithmetic that emphasizes underlying ideas rather than exact calculations
24 Not generic
25 Daughter of Ferdinand III
28 Greenland's Scoresby Sound is the world's longest
29 Classic American watchmaker
32 Insurance letters
34 Abbr. before many state names
36 "Go easy, please"
37 Had a problem with one's suits?
38 Model
39 Kind of intake
41 Got started, with "up"
42 Locale of the Carpathian Mountains, in part
43 "The New Colossus" and the like
46 Blarneyed
49 When most Capricornios are born

by Barry C. Silk

51 One
beaten
by a
beatnik

53 Not
split

55 No. of
People?

57 A season
abroad

59 Showing
fatigue

127

ACROSS

1 Be an agent of
7 Shock source, sometimes
15 Hawaiian "thank you"
16 Exchange for something you really want?
17 Handle, e.g.
18 Catholic
19 Wrestler Flair
20 They might just squeak by in a basketball game
22 Grooming brand introduced in 1977
24 Runners with hoods
25 Sound from a silencer
28 1965 Sonny Bono hit
31 "Berenice" author, briefly
33 Constellation seen on the flags of Australia, Samoa and Papua New Guinea
35 Club's cover
37 "___ Peak" (1997 Pierce Brosnan film)
38 Parliamentary address?
42 This, in Thüringen
43 Striking figures
46 Regulation targets for Theodore Roosevelt: Abbr.
47 "Deal with it!"
49 Catchers of some ring leaders
50 Hard up
53 Seraglio section
54 Void
57 Second chance
59 Opposite of diminish
60 "Let's have it"
61 Cardinals' gathering place
62 Violent

DOWN

1 Unscrupulous
2 Pantheon heads?
3 Fights with knights
4 Cool, in a way
5 Hockey player Tverdovsky
6 Youngest of the Culkin brothers
7 Gather
8 Scale developer
9 One-room house, typically
10 Skin pics?
11 Truncation indications: Abbr.
12 Skin pic?
13 Agent Gold on HBO's "Entourage"
14 It has pickup lines
21 It has many functions
23 Ancient meeting places
25 Cleaning product that may be useful after a party
26 Spray source
27 Amoco alternative
29 Short, close-fitting jacket
30 To ___
32 Desert Storm reporter
34 Home of Theo. Roosevelt Natl. Park
35 U.S.N. position
36 Eyebrow makeup
39 Speak explosively in anger
40 Dumps
41 Come back
44 Tree with double-toothed leaves and durable wood

by Paula Gamache

45 Bad-
tempered
48 Give a
stemwinder
50 Bygone
magistrate

51 Even ___
52 Lexicog-
raphic
concern
54 "I get it"
responses

55 See, say
56 Turbulent
water stretch
58 Tribe visited
by Lewis
and Clark

128

ACROSS

1 "It's all here" sloganeer, once
4 Frisky one
8 Marie Osmond or Loretta Young
14 "Elijah" or "The Creation"
16 Key on a cash register
17 Drop a few positions, maybe
18 Overprotect
19 Maker of Kiwi Teawi
20 Mystery author Dexter
21 The Pacific Ocean's only island kingdom
22 It was good for Sartre
23 One and only
26 They're staffed with doctors
30 Bad time for a tropical vacation
33 Lawyers with many assts.
34 I.T. firm founded by Ross Perot
35 Wine used to make zabaglione
36 Soviet ___
37 Member of an extended familia
38 Country that won the most medals at the 1980 Winter Olympics
40 Reluctantly accepting
42 First name in cosmonautics
43 Major U.S. Spanish-language daily
44 Rarely written-out Latin phrase
48 "Wozzeck" composer ___ Berg
50 What stare decisis upholds the validity of
52 Red line?
54 Set of guidelines
55 Mrs. Tony Blair
56 Put forward
57 Has trouble sleeping, maybe
58 ___ Ramsay ("The Black Stallion" hero)
59 Sorry

DOWN

1 Continue effortlessly
2 Dog in Disney's "Cinderella"
3 "Paradise Lost" character
4 Ultraloyal employees
5 Passed on by taletellers
6 Not full-bodied
7 Wingtip tip
8 Feeling no better
9 "Man is a ___-using animal": Thomas Carlyle
10 Pass under the basket, maybe
11 Is clueless
12 Stout alternative
13 Drift boat attachment
15 Highest-grossing film of 1986
20 Bridesmaid's accessory
22 Very disagreeable
24 Hear
25 Analytic work
27 Soul singer who is also a coronated king of Ghana
28 New rendering
29 Near the bottom of the drawers?
30 Take one more shot at
31 It may be bid
32 One of the "10 Attic orators"
39 Tate ___ (London art gallery)
41 Team that won the first A.F.L. championship
45 1981 Literature Nobelist Canetti
46 Stocking stuffer
47 Fabric with the same name as a Scottish river

by Patrick Berry

129

ACROSS

1 You can sink your feet into them
12 Bus line?
14 Caribbean cruise port of call
16 Diwali revelers
17 Sprinted, perhaps
18 Home of the Cotopaxi volcano
19 Early film actress Pitts
20 Rolling Stone cover subject
21 Abbr. after an author's name, maybe
22 Marty's mentor in "Back to the Future"
23 Where Japanese shares are bought and sold: Abbr.
25 Mountain
26 Utah's ___ Mountains

28 Comparable to a wet hen
32 Pointed warning?
34 This-and-that recording for a friend or a party
36 Time immemorial
37 Van ___ of "Double Team" and "Double Impact"
39 Some "wax"
40 ___-Bo
42 Beer may be on this
43 Cement layer's work
44 Word before and after "against"
47 Marvel Comics series
49 Profile on a 19¢ stamp
50 Major component of kidney stones
52 Hula-hoop, say

53 Start of a series
55 ___ diet, food plan emphasizing olive oil, fish, fruit, vegetables and red wine
56 Gulf war offensive

DOWN

1 Star performer's reward
2 Got together
3 100, say
4 Classic cars with 389 engines
5 Hotel room option
6 Draw
7 Birds with a name from Greek myth
8 Squirt
9 Title aunt in a 1979 best seller
10 Most affected by pathos
11 Leaves alone, sometimes
12 It's guarded in a soccer game

13 "Copacabana" antagonist
14 Coffee alternative
15 Third-longest river of California
19 Daydreamed, with "out"
22 Pulled off
24 Partner of Coburg, historically
26 Major in astronomy?
27 Site of the King Hussein Mosque
29 Language of India with a palindromic name
30 Home of Lawrence University
31 Accessories for a secretary
33 Go ahead of
35 Dennis the Menace, for one
38 Accepted bad treatment
41 Heat up
43 Like someone who's been fooled before

by Roger Barkan

44 Wickiup,
   for one
45 Self-styled
   "Family
   City U.S.A."
46 Like 1-Across

48 Scrooge
   McDuck,
   notably
49 Sleep: Prefix
51 National
   competitor

52 Swatter's
   target
54 Places
   for
   gurneys,
   for short

130

ACROSS
1 Oblong dessert
12 Compositions
14 Wizards and Magic, e.g.
16 "Heat traps" in houses
17 Suitable for hypertension sufferers
18 Liquid used in canning
19 "The ___ the limit!"
20 Traditional know-how
21 Skull Island denizen, for short
22 Mushy ___ (British dish)
23 Drab and colorless
24 Geom. measure
25 Kind of dish
26 "___ Now" (1968 R & B album)
27 Old masters reside in them
29 Court staff
32 Bully's target, maybe
33 Biblical figure who says to God "Make me understand how I have erred"
36 Takes on
37 Overlook
38 Baker v. ___ (landmark Supreme Court voting rights case)
39 Memo heading
40 Square dance partner
41 Long known for playing football
42 Doesn't stay on topic
44 Gelato sans milk
45 Hiding one's true feelings
47 French-born architect who designed Washington, D.C.
48 1930 novel that takes its title from Shakespeare's "Twelfth Night"

DOWN
1 Bankrupting
2 For the ___
3 Potential heiress
4 Congressional output
5 Grab ahold of
6 It separates the Bering Sea from the Pacific
7 Spreads out
8 Compartmentalized box's contents
9 Two-time football Pro Bowler Leon
10 White sheets
11 Take from a book, say
12 Female prison official
13 "From Russia With Love" org.
14 Sweet, glazed cake
15 "G'bye!"
19 It leaves an impression
22 D.C. players
23 Wilbur Post's "pal"
25 "The Odd Couple" director
26 Is shown
27 Ice cream flavor
28 Lie
29 Early "astronaut"
30 It reveals who's on first
31 Undependable
33 Paleontologist's discovery, maybe
34 Show the ropes to
35 Jeremy ___, 1980s–'90s portrayer of Sherlock Holmes
37 Gets into a single lane, say
38 Stock holder
40 Romance or horror
41 1992 Nicholson title role
43 Highlands weapon
44 Soft rock?
46 Many a retirement gift

by Patrick Berry

131

ACROSS

1 Celebratory cry
9 It can leave you breathless
15 Two-time Nicaraguan president Chamorro
16 Draw successfully
17 County whose seat is Redwood City
18 "Ya got me!"
19 Union in D.C., e.g.
20 Sets up
22 Cleanse
23 Beaucoup de Louises
25 Dismiss as unworthy
26 "Well, I declare!"
27 Three Stooges' actions
29 ___ man
30 San Francisco mayor Newsom
31 Skeleton part
33 Handicap, say

35 "The Da Vinci Code" sequence
39 Sly slur
40 Motor additive?
41 They have five sects. of multiple-choice questions
42 Temp takers
44 ___ Bay (South China Sea inlet)
48 Court interferences
49 Out there
51 Gabrielle's sidekick, in a TV series
52 Place for 42-Across
53 Undercover wear?
55 Prescription notation
56 Bottle
58 Horror cry
60 Religious leader who wrote "Peace With God"
61 Baseball coverings

62 Jennifer Lopez title role
63 Bakes

DOWN

1 Salutation abbreviation
2 Stuff in a bomb
3 Flower named for a German botanist
4 Hackberry relative
5 Pseudologue
6 "Soap" family
7 Breakless, in a way
8 Derogatory term popularized by George H. W. Bush
9 Superman, for one
10 Head makeup
11 Play whose star won the 1990 Best Actor Tony
12 The Wars of the Roses ended in his reign

13 Dwarf
14 Soothing things
21 Prime Minister Nouri al-Maliki, e.g.
24 Salad bar binful
26 France's first minister of culture, 1959–69
28 They can make waves
30 Iona College athletes
32 Stop O.K.'ing
34 Hope offerer: Abbr.
35 They might follow the drill
36 Wobbly
37 Note offering good advice for life?
38 Information holder
43 Help in getting up
45 Come to pass
46 "How dare you!"

by Charles Barasch

47 Treat affectionately

49 Belief in Hinduism

50 "___ have no . . ."

53 Sturdy, twilled cotton fabric

54 "Look Forward in Anger" comedian

57 Word before some animal names

59 Books, for short

132

ACROSS

1 Breakers communicate with them
4 Medevacs, in military slang
9 Shop coat?
13 Gets a move on
15 Officer slain in the Old Testament
16 Ear-relevant
17 Sharply outline
18 Prefix with -hedron
19 Carpenter's groove
20 Avignon infinitive
21 City of canals
23 Roseanne's mom on "Roseanne"
24 Things wheeled in supermarkets?
27 Kind of therapy
29 Cow
30 Judge, e.g.
31 Rock and Roll Hall of Fame inductee known as the White Lady of Soul
36 Tactful
37 Nebulous stuff
43 Words to live by
44 People people
46 Billboard listing
49 Puts together in a hurry
50 Wood smoother
51 Food whose name is Italian for "feathers"
53 Rip off
54 Cry of vehement denial
56 Reservation dwelling
58 Aged Frankfurter?
59 Maestro Masur
60 Make more interesting
61 Future shoot
62 Janitorial tool
63 Big band era standard
64 Kind of ice

DOWN

1 Half of a 1970s–'80s comedy duo
2 Went kaput
3 Opposite of openness
4 Quarrel
5 Treats often taken apart
6 Scuba gear
7 Palestinian group
8 Cadet's topper
9 Plot thickener?
10 Very, very hot
11 Like some highways after construction work
12 Furniture protector
14 What rain might fall in
22 It contains the elastic clause
25 Absorbed
26 Debugging discovery
28 C ration replacer
32 They, in Marseille
33 Thing to be picked
34 Former telecom giant
35 Cop
37 Metal in the points of gold pens
38 EarthLink alternative
39 It's celebrated in late January or early February
40 Socially dominant ones
41 Put a new bottom on, in a way
42 Black & Decker offering
43 Classroom sneeze elicitor
45 Express
47 Country singer McCoy and others
48 Get divorced
49 Grill brand
52 Astronomer's study

by John R. Conrad

55 Motor Up alternative

57 Cleaning product with the slogan "It's that fast"

133

ACROSS

1 Positive
10 Vacuum maintainers
15 Like some fruit bats and petrels
16 Cornrow component
17 Whine
18 Royal jelly consumer
19 Jungian principle
20 Samoan, e.g.
22 Kind of party
23 Top of a stadium
25 Comic character
26 From Niger to Zambia: Abbr.
27 Hacker of the Middle Ages
28 "The Dram Shop" author
29 Squeals
30 Start of a Spanish Christmas greeting
31 Certify

34 Unwelcome discovery on a credit card statement
36 Period to find out more
37 Tough companions?
38 Minor leader?
39 Carving in an Egyptian tomb
41 Relief may follow it
44 Botanist's beard
45 Unproductive
46 Rubberneck
47 Where cell phones don't work
49 Weed-B-Gon maker
50 200 milligrams
51 Popular reference work
54 Match point?
55 "Shoot!"
56 Name on a truck
57 Loser in a casino

DOWN

1 Opportunities to run away from home
2 Gustavo's good
3 Require
4 Female role in "Chicago"
5 "Paint the Sky With Stars" singer
6 Suffix with proto-
7 Abbr. on a key
8 They're back on board
9 City on the Permian Basin
10 Extend awkwardly
11 Sparkle
12 Cousin of a hyena
13 Be what you're not
14 Be a night watchman?
21 Manhattan ave.
23 Sudden impact
24 First home of the University of Nevada

27 Firm assistant, briefly
28 Couple of pizzas?
29 Revelation exclamation
30 Work unit: Abbr.
31 Black-and-white
32 Spent from all the conflict
33 Webbed
34 Generation-to-generation information
35 Poet Seeger
37 Otherworldly one
39 It's appetizing to aphids
40 What ochlophobists fear
41 Big-league promotional event
42 For some time
43 Drinks a toast
45 It's massive and relatively hot
46 ___ Waitz, nine-time New York City Marathon winner

by Barry C. Silk

48 King
Claudius,
e.g.
49 Artist John,
known
as the Cornish
Wonder

52 Malay
Peninsula's
Isthmus of ___
53 Publicity

134

ACROSS

1 "On the other hand . . ."
8 Quaint cry from a caught crook, with "The"
15 Between here and there
16 Hot
17 Go for, as a ball
18 Film director's discovery
19 Powwow place
20 Wrong
22 Town outside Harrisburg
23 Topless?
24 "Le Bon Bock" artist
26 Times on the History Channel?
27 Cusp
28 Sony debut of 1979
30 Swallowed the bait?
31 Spandex and Lurex
33 Hurt
35 Works with
36 "What's the ___?"
37 Seashell hues
40 1940s fashion
44 Smart figures?
45 1938 Daphne du Maurier novel
47 Layer
48 Neighbor of Mex.
50 Ohio city whose name means "hospitality" in Greek
51 Dog
52 High country
54 Popular ISP
55 Slog
56 Wrong
58 Natural gas components
60 "___ Place"
61 Be at rest
62 One who tries
63 Bawls out

DOWN

1 Favorite
2 Backtrack on, as a rug
3 Certain multiscreen cinema
4 Quieted (down)
5 Over-whelming
6 Viscosity symbol, in physics
7 Figure on which royalties are based
8 What to do if you can't beat the suckers
9 Night spot
10 Thomas ___, last royal governor of Massa-chusetts
11 1919 Broadway musical that set a record for most performances up to that time
12 Southwest Arizona's ___ Desert
13 Howl
14 Content
21 Puts one's John Hancock on
24 What X + Y signifies
25 Cassava product
28 Having learned a lesson
29 Mex. is in it
32 Port pusher
34 Hypotheticals
36 How most farm animals behave
37 Very much
38 Zebras, e.g.
39 "___ Daughter," 2003 Judi Hendricks novel
40 Greek philosopher who founded Stoicism
41 High-elevation areas
42 1983 Randy Newman song
43 Ready to be proofed
46 Carrier

by Manny Nosowsky

135

ACROSS

1 Actor whom People magazine erroneously declared dead in 1982
10 Aid in retriever retrieval?
15 Persian's gift
16 Gull-like
17 Basis of "America"
19 "Get ___" (1967 hit for the Esquires)
20 Filmmaker Morris
21 Barrel statistic
22 Turkey dough?
24 "The Christmas Song" co-writer
26 Univ. research grantor
27 Crack
28 Military V.I.P.
30 Slippery as ___
32 Deserve consideration

33 The last novel featuring him was "Stopover: Tokyo"
34 Fugitive's fear
37 "Let's be reasonable . . ."
38 Annular seals
39 Water softener
40 Sensation
41 Cheekbone
42 Syst. of unspoken words
45 Muffin holder
46 He served between Hubert and Gerald
48 First name in college football coaching
50 Pizzeria chain since 1943, informally
52 Val d'___ (French ski resort)
54 "La ___," 1946 Dolores del Rio film

55 Punish publicly, perhaps
58 Way to stand
59 Place for a vacuum
60 Rocker Patty who married John McEnroe
61 Felt suppressed rage

DOWN

1 Land bordered by the Congo
2 Having some replacement parts?
3 Last
4 Line of motor scooters
5 Pier grp.
6 Springiness
7 Implication
8 Home to Rosa Parks Blvd.
9 Bad way for a ship to be driven
10 Govt. probe
11 Plaster
12 Get plastered

13 Not at all fond of
14 Result of cross-fertilization within a population
18 Dartboard material
23 Discards, with "off"
25 Designate
29 Couple's word
31 Home of Silver City: Abbr.
32 Stack on a pallet: Abbr.
33 Melvin of the Orioles
34 Film studio department
35 How some people walk
36 Hammer activator
37 Avalanche setting
39 Something taken before practicing
41 Dough must be squeezed out of them
42 Distinctive director

by Pete Mitchell

43 Light up at a dance?
44 Paged
47 Sticker
49 "Affliction" star, 1998
51 It's splintered

53 Graphic artist Nolde
56 Letter wearer: Abbr.
57 Milkweed part

136

ACROSS

1 Sitcom character with a leather jacket that's now in the Smithsonian
8 The New Yorker cartoonist William
13 Taxing preinitiation period
15 Childish retort
17 Have no dinner companions
18 Make
19 They're numbered in golf
20 Fasten firmly
22 Prefix with lateral
23 One prepared for church: Abbr.
24 Quintillionth: Prefix
25 Thai currency
26 2004 Brad Pitt film
28 Agitate
30 Scream
31 Felicitous
33 1974 Chicago hit

35 2002 sci-fi role for Hayden Christensen
39 Teacher's request of a publisher
40 Capitol Records owner
41 Dancer Limón
42 Moves laboriously
44 New York Cosmos' sports org.
48 Linear, briefly
49 Send a high-tech message
50 Kind of season
51 They, to Thérèse
52 Classic arcade game character who hopped around a pyramid
54 "David ___" (1934 Will Rogers film)
56 Seat of Hillsborough County, N.H.
58 Nintendo game with exercises for mental acuity

60 Treats similar to Mallomars
61 Local election campaign staple
62 Basketball defense
63 Some shorts

DOWN

1 Believer
2 One catching some waves?
3 California air station where Nixon landed after resigning in 1974
4 Glazed dessert
5 Mouse catchers
6 Latin leader?
7 Crown
8 Garment worn over a choli
9 Bygone carnivore
10 "I should ___ die with pity": King Lear
11 Drawing medium

12 Ends one's travels
14 Omaha and Spokane were once in it
16 Competitor in a harness
21 Initial venture
24 Ad directive
25 Player of Dr. Kiley on "Marcus Welby, M.D."
27 Ran on and on
29 Giants are in it: Abbr.
32 Snap
34 Flight
35 Makes contact with
36 Glower?
37 One with a taxing job
38 Avalanche
43 Hollywood crowd?
45 Not stout
46 Ernie Bushmiller comics character
47 Light measures
52 Survey part: Abbr.

by Mike Nothnagel

137

ACROSS

1 Tollbooth option for North-easterners
7 Pennsylvania town that was the longtime home of Rolling Rock beer
14 Ogle
15 Plans named for a Delaware senator
16 One concerned with school activities?
18 Comment after "So"
19 Itself, in a legal phrase
20 Dating concern
21 Martini go-with?
22 Approve
24 BusinessWeek topic: Abbr.
26 N.F.L.'er or N.B.A.'er
27 Mathematician seen on a Swiss 10-franc note
29 Lounging terrace
31 "The Last of the Plainsmen" novelist
32 Judge's declaration
33 Yes-men
37 Worn rocks
38 Cold evidence
39 "Blade Runner" actress Young
40 Give an invitation for
41 A challenger might go after one
42 Cheer starter
45 Word with time or tone
46 Plays first
48 Steel guitar sound
50 With 9-Down, albeit, poetically
52 Length of a kids' fun run, briefly
53 Kind of wind
54 Disneyland attraction since 1955
57 Sweethearts
58 It may sit near a jack
59 "After you"
60 Deck reply

DOWN

1 College in south central New York
2 Extremist
3 Be wiped out
4 Easter baby, maybe
5 Birthplace of the first giant panda in North America to survive to adulthood
6 Abbr. on many Québec road signs
7 Slacker
8 Bearer of scales and plates
9 See 50-Across
10 Capital on the Daugava River
11 Fresh
12 Link between DNA strands
13 Round fig.
15 Collector of bizarre facts
17 Books with many cross references?
23 Cause for some fluff filling
25 Suave, and then some
28 Addict's bugbear
30 Former Japanese P.M. Shinzo ___
32 "Crypto-nomicon" novelist Stephenson
33 Some coll. seniors take it
34 Have as a boss
35 The orange variety is black
36 One with the force: Abbr.
37 Maker of a wake on a lake
39 Source of strength
41 Showed anxiety
42 Flint, e.g.
43 Tomorrow
44 Cool

by Mike Nothnagel

138

ACROSS

1 Energy source
11 Troy Aikman, John Elway and others, in brief
15 Home of the National Automobile Museum
16 Self-styled world salsa capital
17 First lady who was once a prominent radio actress
18 Catch
19 1899 gold rush site
20 Tick off
22 Bull Halsey's org.
23 Rap sheet abbr.
24 Machu Picchu, for one
25 Swell
27 Certain campus Greeks
30 Ages
31 X maker, at times

32 Two Ralph Waldo Emerson collections
34 Political payoff, perhaps
36 Word with speed or fire
38 ___ P. Halliburton, founder of the Halliburton company
39 Pops
43 Sandinista's foe
47 TV chef Deen
48 JetBlue competitor
50 1994 Peace Nobelist
51 "The Beverly Hillbillies" star
52 Gambler's option
54 Spots
55 Trawler equipment
56 "Gulliver's Travels," e.g.
58 Remain
59 With 4-Down, longtime jazz record label

61 One who deals in futures
63 High places
64 Construction equipment
65 Break
66 Angels

DOWN

1 Pineapple, e.g.
2 Takes back
3 Brutes
4 See 59-Across
5 ___ roll
6 Object of a miracle of Jesus
7 Pennsylvania, e.g.
8 En estos lugares se habla español
9 "Oklahoma!" girl
10 "You ___?"
11 D.J.'s, at times
12 "Survivor" setting, 2004
13 Drub
14 Gentleman of Verona
21 Wrap

26 Dawn-of-mammals epoch
28 Tell
29 Modern dwellers of ancient Ebla
33 ___ Hill
35 Protective agcy. since 1974
37 Place with cages
39 Where drinks aren't on you
40 Singer with the 1975 #1 hit "Lady Marmalade"
41 Scraps
42 Turns in
44 Tramp
45 Highlands relative of an elk
46 Maintains
49 Some hogs
53 Villa ___
57 "Sorry to intrude . . ."
58 Winner of Wimbledon for five consecutive years
60 Store sign abbr.
62 Yardbird

by Nancy Joline

139

ACROSS

1 1971 hit with the lyric "He danced for those at minstrel shows"
12 Big shot? Hardly!
15 Film in which Ford was president
16 1998 Tony winner for Best Play
17 Clowns
18 Agatha Christie's "___ M?"
19 Flower with a bulb
20 Have insomnia
22 Tough guys
26 Group on Miles Davis's "Birth of the Cool," e.g.
27 Boxer's training equipment
30 Playwright Connelly who won a Pulitzer for "The Green Pastures"

31 Torah's beginning?
32 Grammy winner Blige
34 Like arctic winters
35 Least interesting
37 Issue
39 Curved nail
40 Seen enough
42 Launch of 1986
43 Title boy in a 1964 Disney film
44 McIntosh cousins
46 Improves
48 Most of Mauritania
49 Makes obsolete
51 "The X-Files" fodder
55 A, in Aix
56 Oscar winner between Tom Hanks and Geoffrey Rush
60 Victoria in London, e.g.: Abbr.
61 Subject of "The Double Helix"

62 Id follower
63 Protected areas

DOWN

1 Google heading
2 Bring to a boil
3 Crow
4 In the distant past
5 ___ A. Bank, menswear retailer
6 Constellation near Norma
7 Big ATM maker
8 Topic in oil exploration
9 Tiffany who made Tiffany lamps
10 Relative of -trix
11 Body type
12 Girl group with the 1986 #1 hit "Venus"
13 "Buy now," e.g.
14 Emergency equipment
21 Creation of Genesis 2:22
23 Some pitchers

24 Stern School degs.
25 Author of "The Sot-Weed Factor"
27 Dome site
28 Supreme rulers
29 Malice aforethought
33 Film knights
34 Misanthrope
36 Given (out)
38 Gold digger's destination
41 Skater dude's exclamation
45 Wall treatment
47 Erstwhile Vegas hotel
48 After-dinner request
50 Brown with a blue pencil
52 Pan, for one
53 Give a body check?
54 Meets
57 Ultimate outcome
58 One of the Khans
59 "___ who?"

by Randolph Ross

140

ACROSS

1 White-bearded, red-capped patriarch
10 G.I.'s sod
15 One with spin control?
16 Famous last word
17 Lexington Center centerpiece
18 Open
19 Concert equipment
20 Substantial bill
22 Toshiba competitor
23 Place for a swing
24 Recording standard
25 Club alternative
27 He came out of retirement in 1980
28 Doom
29 Decca rival
30 Flooded
32 Set right
33 Symbol of contrasting principles
34 Alongside, nautically
37 Floods
38 Eye site
40 Stretch
41 Slip acknowledgment
42 Form letters?
43 Org. whose logo is a torch
46 Lead seeker: Abbr.
47 Seminoles' sch.
48 See
49 Bill of Rights subj.
50 Churn
52 Doctor's orders
54 Crimson and white school, for short
55 Setting of van Gogh's "Bedroom"
57 Wally Schirra commanded it in 1968
59 All-natural abode
60 Car-jacking aids
61 Garish glowers
62 Plain

DOWN

1 Marine menace
2 Sagacity
3 Put spirit into, with "up"
4 Hooded menaces
5 Pop of Jamaica
6 The Elite Eight are associated with it
7 Piece of silver
8 Silver State city
9 One who's made a pledge
10 Subject of some sightings
11 Hindu trinity member
12 About three grains
13 Corridor to be kept clear
14 Quartet in a string quartet
21 Subject of some sightings
24 Change course
26 A little after, timewise
31 Hero of several Clancy novels
32 Good sign?
34 Environmental awareness topic
35 Cry when you think you've got it?
36 Cactuslike tree of the Southwest
39 Show a thing or two
40 Modena misters
43 They may keep the show going
44 Words on a heart
45 Philosopher Pascal
51 Oil magnate Hess
53 Capital where tala are spent
54 Staten Isl., e.g.
56 Emergency letters
58 Fried

by David Quarfoot and Katy Swalwell

141

ACROSS

1 Called for
10 Not get along
15 Common bank deposit?
16 Slow in scoring
17 1976–85 sitcom setting
18 Zealous
19 Philologists' work, for short
20 Rd. designer, e.g.
21 Begin energetically
22 Feed
24 Where things may be neatly ordered?
25 Doesn't belt it out
27 Unsettled sort
28 Lash with a whip
29 Source of political support
33 "Happy Days Are Here Again" composer
34 Three-time 1990s French Open winner

35 Israeli opera conductor Daniel
36 Encore setting
38 ___ Diamond, author of the 1998 Pulitzer-winning book "Guns, Germs, and Steel"
39 They may be done in a salon
40 Results of some glances
41 Onsets
44 Fast-food chain known for its floats
45 Distress call
46 Some shooters, briefly
47 Where to find "Rome"
50 Lead-in to phobia
51 Drop off
53 Filibustered, say
54 Clumsy

55 "Why, what ___ am I!" (Hamlet soliloquy line)
56 Some Mozart works

DOWN

1 Pitcher who was the 1995 N.L. Rookie of the Year
2 Guarded weapon
3 They may accompany fevers
4 Part of a long and winding road?
5 It's usually spun first
6 Performs awfully
7 1980s–'90s N.B.A. star Danny
8 Many a camper, informally
9 "___ out!"
10 Butcher's need
11 Display at a golf tournament

12 Provocation result
13 Draft holder
14 They frequently become locked
21 Shock aftermath
23 Open competitors, often
24 Kind of rack
25 Good secret-keeper
26 Unilever brand
27 7 and 11, in a casino
29 Storm sounds
30 Game sticker?
31 Look
32 Far left and far right
34 Perform superbly
37 Tropical reptiles
38 Star of TV's "The Fugitive"
40 King of pop
41 "Ten North Frederick" novelist
42 Duke of Cornwall's wife

by Victor Fleming

43 Massey of film
44 Take in, e.g.
46 Loudness unit
48 Well around Trevi Fountain?
49 Goes (for)
51 They're found in a mess
52 Big Apple-bound luggage tag code

142

ACROSS
1 Liniment ingredient
11 Certain copier
15 Presidents Adams, Fillmore and Taft
16 ". . . on the head of ___?"
17 Rap
18 "The Man Who Fell to Earth" director
19 Make a scene?
20 Put down some chips?
21 Minute buzzer
22 Detail on some tickets
24 Its banks are lined with nearly 200 palaces
26 Cousin of -trix
27 "Giuliani: Nasty Man" author
28 Booster of a rock band
29 Tackle box item
31 Ici ___ (here and there, to Thérèse)
32 "In the," in Italy
33 Nostalgia elicitor
36 Imprecise
38 Alma mater of Albert Sabin and Jonas Salk: Abbr.
39 You may get into it while shopping
43 Rx specification
44 Sinusitis studier's specialty: Abbr.
45 100 centimes, in Haiti
47 Like the Chrysler Building
51 Nightspots where the attraction is simply a gas
53 Characteristic quality
54 Direct
55 Makes a raucous noise
57 Project wrap-up?
58 Rolls roller
59 National Historic Landmark in Manhattan
61 Quarter division
62 Apropos
63 Pablo Neruda's "___ to Common Things"
64 Big name in Dakota history

DOWN
1 Parish leader
2 Its ads once showed hammers inside the head
3 One of a protective pair
4 Org. addressing class conflict
5 Occupiers of top spots
6 Like a bad spray-on tan
7 Score direction: Abbr.
8 Scottish cereal staple
9 Snarled
10 "Saving Private Ryan" craft, for short
11 Musical character who sings "My Favorite Things"
12 Player in a shirt pocket
13 Anticlimactic court outcomes
14 Lemony meringue concoction
21 Celtic Kevin with a retired jersey #32
23 Bank offering, briefly
25 Seventh-century year
30 It can help you keep your balance
33 Not many
34 Keen of vision
35 Like some airport shopping
37 Novus ___ seclorum (Great Seal phrase)
40 It goes on and on
41 Drinking fountain
42 Syllables to skip by
43 Willful state?
46 Character on trial in "A Passage to India"
48 People person?

by Brad Wilber

49 Mint-family plant with bright-colored leaves and blue flowers

50 Goon's last words

52 Unlikely prom kings

56 "___ Ching" (classic book of Chinese poetry)

59 U.S.M.C. E-2

60 Ear: Prefix

143

ACROSS

1 Vegetable oil, e.g.
6 College major, briefly
10 Fog
14 Up
15 "Got it"
16 It's often marked with a number
17 Knee problem
19 Very small serving
20 ". . . __ faith turn to despair": Romeo
21 Capital, usually
23 Leon who won both a Pulitzer and a National Book Award in 1963
24 Smith, e.g.
25 Symbols of freshness
27 Rogers Hornsby's nickname, with "the"
31 Senior ctr.?
33 Garage alternative
34 Before analysis, after "a"
35 Hangers-on
37 Select groups
38 Other drivers (never you, of course)
39 Following group
40 Character lineup
41 It's been put on before
42 Ammunition carrier on wheels
44 Windfall
46 Target of a rabbit punch
49 Like Y, e.g.
52 __ francese
53 Crown
54 Soft, high-fiber dish
56 Red-bellied trout
57 Topic lead-in
58 Beehive division
59 Firm fear
60 "Saint Joan" playwright
61 Fisherman's basket

DOWN

1 Maker of a historic touchdown
2 Iota
3 Feature of many a big do
4 Neighbor of Monterey Park, briefly
5 Atlas info: Abbr.
6 Filling stations?
7 Had a causerie
8 The sacred bull Apis was his embodiment
9 They're proscribed
10 Jaunty
11 Botanist's angle
12 Fusilli alternative
13 Form of the French "to be"
18 #1 best sellers
22 Apes
26 "Right?"
28 Some clichéd writing
29 Some matériel
30 H.S. subject
31 Do something emotionally to
32 Word preceding various colors
34 Beat
36 They have nagging questions
37 It has valuable questions
39 Game derived from 500 rummy
42 Light carriage with a folding top
43 Even
45 Mexican uncle?
47 Part of the earth's outer layer
48 Oil holder
49 Halite, chemically
50 Be reminiscent of
51 Present occasion, informally
55 Multiple of LXX

by Dana Motley

144

ACROSS
1 Sleuthing aid
11 Early education
15 Hammer wielder
16 Bangkok currency
17 YouTube phenomenon
18 ___ witness
19 Suffix with polymer
20 Walk-on parts?
21 Safari hazard
23 "Rhapsodie norvégienne" composer
24 Co-creator of Hulk and Thor
25 Napoleon, e.g.
28 Allergist's procedure
29 Lexicon listing
30 Relative of homespun
31 Century-ending Middle Ages year
32 Modern organizers, briefly
33 Judge, e.g.
34 Skittish wildlife
35 Record finish?
36 Fail to be
37 Food also called mostaccioli
38 Fictional Pulitzer-winning journalist in a 2006 film
40 Didn't fizzle
41 Aquatinting acid
42 Succeed
43 Grinders
44 One might be kidding
45 U.S.C.G. rank
48 "Madama Butterfly" wear
49 Much-anticipated Paris debut of 1992
52 Colleague of 38-Across
53 Place for trophies at an awards luncheon
54 Concert venues
55 1971 Elton John song

DOWN
1 Kind of bean
2 See 51-Down
3 Plot segment
4 Where folks go off and on: Abbr.
5 "View From the Summit" memoirist
6 Swell
7 ___ López de Loyola, founder of the Society of Jesus
8 People may get them before going to coll.
9 Part of a giggle
10 Hockey Hall-of-Famer Bryan
11 Not in the picture
12 Archer's post
13 Action thriller staple
14 Homey's acceptance
22 Innards of some clocks
23 Posts: Abbr.
24 Earth-shattering activity?
25 Casbah fugitive of French film
26 Noted diary words
27 Alternative to a rip cord
28 Coarse type
30 ___ Canal (connector of lakes Ontario and Huron)
33 It intersects the nave
34 Secretary, e.g.
36 Garden no-no, now
37 One of six pieces by Bach
39 Daisy variety
40 Like some questions
42 Vertiginous
44 Wink accompanier
45 "Power Lunch" channel
46 Legendary kicker
47 Legal hearing

by Brad Wilber

50 Sch. in Kingston
51 With 2-Down, seat of Costilla County, Colo.

145

ACROSS

1 Billionaire sports entrepreneur who heads HDNet
10 Like some seasonal helpers
15 Within the next few minutes, potentially
16 Some piano players
17 Case made for a shooter
18 Agitated
19 Real-estate ad statistic
20 Its motto is "All for our country": Abbr.
22 Go over
23 Orchestra section
25 Dr. Seuss's "Too Many ___"
27 Consumer protection grp.
28 Yokohama "yes"
30 Marathon runner Gebrselassie

32 It served the Mid-Atlantic until 1976
39 Classic laugh-inducing parlor game with writing or illustrations
40 Move on after a humiliating defeat
41 Claimed
42 Vintner's prefix
43 Kind of engr.
44 Member of a popular college frat
47 Parliament rival
52 Shot one on
54 Name for Quantum Computer Services since '89
55 Heavyweights compete in it
56 An over-abundance
58 "You said it!"
62 Sent regrets, say
63 Help get settled
64 Priceless instrument
65 What green might ripen into

DOWN

1 Bird remarkable for its longevity
2 Breakout maker
3 Far Eastern bowlful
4 Manipulate, in a way
5 France's Saint-___-l'École
6 She played Martha in Broadway's "Who's Afraid of Virginia Woolf?"
7 One hanging around at Red Lobster?
8 Range option
9 Ben-Gurion setting
10 Stumble
11 "Happy Birthday" playwright
12 About-faces
13 Nervous
14 Band with the highest first-week album sales in music history

21 It'll get you somewhere
24 Some religious funda-mentalists
25 Cook's words
26 Old settings for many out-of-tune pianos
29 Connecticut city on the Naugatuck
31 Factory seconds: Abbr.
32 Sport, for short
33 Foreignness
34 Old Spice alternative
35 Court stuff
36 Bus spec.
37 "The Mischievous Dog" author
38 ___ Peres (St. Louis suburb)
43 "Lady for a Day" director, 1933
45 One who's waited upon
46 Ecuador's southernmost coastal province

by Brendan Emmett Quigley

48 Provide an invitation for
49 Kind of cycle
50 Mug, e.g.
51 Cut
53 Firm part: Abbr.

57 Arms race plan: Abbr.
59 Takeaway game
60 Hot spot?
61 Gridiron datum

146

ACROSS

1 Small suit
7 Cheese with a greenish tint
14 "The Outsiders" author
15 Band seen at parties
16 Available if needed
17 Aircraft for the Red Baron
18 Without reservation
19 "The Blessed Damozel" poet
20 "Mr. ___," 1983 comedy
21 Military classification
23 Result of a day at the beach?
24 "Infidel" author Ayaan Hirsi ___
25 ___ Island
26 Object of Oliver Twist's request for "more"
27 Semimonthly ocean occurrence
29 Somewhat
30 "___ and Janis" (comic strip)
31 Linguist Okrand who created the Klingon language
32 It's "heavier freight for the shipper than it is for the consignee": Augustus Thomas
35 Poem whose first, third and seventh lines are identical
39 Ready to explode
40 Garçon's counterpart
41 Application file extension
42 Big seller of smoothies
43 Economist who wrote "The Theory of the Leisure Class"
44 ___-Hulk (Marvel Comics character)
45 Goshen raceway's length
47 It's cleared for a debriefing
49 In a despicable way
50 Play a flute
51 Details
52 Book before Job
53 Future hunters
54 Does a landscaper's job

DOWN

1 Troupe leader
2 Camera obscura feature
3 Laudations
4 Biblio-graphical abbr.
5 National chain of everything-costs-the-same stores
6 Eloise of Kay Thompson books, e.g.
7 Made an effort
8 Become evident
9 Enlivens, with "up"
10 Figure seen in a store window
11 Pan American Games participant
12 Refined
13 Author of the 2006 best seller "Culture Warrior"
15 Big step
22 Disturbance
26 Typically green tube
28 Gaffe at a social gathering, in modern lingo
29 Often-unanswered missive
31 Tough's partner
32 Seemed particularly relevant
33 Pan's realm
34 Putting aside temporarily

by Patrick Berry

35 Hearty entree
36 Country of
two million
surrounded
by a single
other country

37 Let the
air out,
say
38 Betrays
unsteadiness
40 Guys

43 See
46 Universal
remote
button
48 Breaks
down

147

ACROSS

1 Classic sports lineup
11 All in favor
15 Antipathy
16 Not be fair?
17 "I hear ya!"
18 Regard impolitely
19 Low square
20 Work period
21 Intelligence problem
22 Winter fall, in Falkirk
23 Fortune 500 company founded in 1995
24 It's often administered orally
25 Needle holders
27 Power system
28 Birthplace of Evel Knievel and Martha Raye
29 Dill herb
30 "Follow the Fleet" co-star, 1936
32 Precursor to a historical "party"

34 Winner of four Oscars for musical scores
38 "Seems that way"
42 One-named singer with the 1960s Velvet Underground
43 Decision maker
46 Calls in a field
47 Proof word
48 Home of Gannon University
49 "I'll Be Doggone" singer, 1965
50 Lovelace who was called "The Enchantress of Numbers"
51 Cossacks' leader
52 Take the top off
54 Wild
55 Break
56 Enterprise
58 Natural healer
59 Decision maker

60 Revolutionary War general Thomas
61 Big name in foot care

DOWN

1 Dietary danger
2 Like some charms
3 Range, e.g.
4 Old character
5 Company keepers: Abbr.
6 Calendario units
7 Ribbons
8 Check
9 Preceder of many hockey games
10 Like a snood, commonly
11 Some dance honorees
12 Cousin of goulash
13 Like some old-fashioned lamps
14 Cold response?

26 1959 #1 hit for Lloyd Price
27 Track take
28 Cold response?
31 Corp. capital raisers
33 Breaking need
35 It's found in eggs
36 Like some streams in winter
37 "Isn't anyone interested?"
39 Like many supermarket lines?
40 Greet
41 Producer of some beads
43 It can give people flight reservations
44 Legendary Christian martyr
45 It's open for discussion
49 "Life Is Beautiful" hero
53 Spare change?

by Barry C. Silk

54 Buckling
down
57 Org. with
its own
insurance
agency

148

ACROSS

1 Blockbuster alternative
8 Material for drainage lines
15 Just as anyone can be
16 What some bombs release
17 Early filmmaking brothers Auguste and Louis ___
18 What a cause might turn into
19 Noted 1915 West Point grad.
20 Bond type whose first purchaser was F.D.R.
22 Atkins diet no-no
23 "No god but God" author ___ Aslan
25 ___ Malfoy, bully in Harry Potter books
26 German city where Napoleon defeated the Prussians
27 States

29 Org. with a Council on Ethical and Judicial Affairs
30 Pitch problems?
31 May day events, perhaps
33 Big name in coffee makers
35 Ruffles
37 "Oh, I give up!"
41 Rot
43 Minus sign equivalent
44 Fractional currency
47 A sucker, for short
49 Layered dessert
50 Reunion gatherers
51 Apollo's birthplace
53 Be reminiscent of
54 Part of "the many," in Greek
55 Scull part
57 Printed
58 Noted Art Deco building in the Big Apple, with "the"

60 Dinar spender
62 Some
63 1962 hit with the lyric "Like the samba sound, my heart begins to pound"
64 Shop tool with pulleys
65 Has at a spread

DOWN

1 Annual sports event with seven rounds
2 Brandy
3 Mountain, e.g.
4 What many workers look forward to: Abbr.
5 Refuse
6 "The East ___" (1960s Chinese anthem)
7 Nissan model
8 Track warm-up leaders
9 Back of a leaf
10 "Red, White & ___" (2005 rock album)
11 On the plus side?: Abbr.

12 Deadly 2003 hurricane that hit North Carolina
13 It's far from a metropolis
14 Figure skater Sokolova and others
21 Foot type
24 Totally covered by
26 Miss No-Name
28 Relative of a cutter
30 Black, say
32 Hub NW of LAX
34 Buddy, in slang
36 Plant used as an herbal remedy for headaches
38 Rallying slogans
39 "Who'd a thunk it?!"
40 Paper that calls itself "America's Finest News Source"
42 Dialectal contraction
44 Brokerage giant

by Brendan Emmett Quigley and David Quarfoot

45 Zoological cavity
46 Criticize harshly and repeatedly
48 Like some books
51 Friend of Porky
52 "Pardon me," in Parma
55 Dropping sound
56 Tae ___ do
59 Bomb not bursting in air?
61 Bart Simpson's grandpa

149

ACROSS

1 When
9 Slip covers?
15 She was executed in 1917
16 100 centésimos
17 "Nonsense!"
19 Pentax Spotmatic, e.g., in brief
20 Boy in the comic strip "Rose Is Rose"
21 Parents
22 Parts of many jam sessions
25 Minute
27 African evergreen shrub
29 Vlasic varieties
30 Get ready to grill
33 Like VCRs in the 1970s
36 Delicacy
39 One-striper: Abbr.
40 Stuck with no way out
41 Kitchen pieces
43 Animal visitor to Paris in a classic children's book
44 Cornmeal concoction
47 One that takes a picture?
49 Crosses
50 Lead, e.g.
52 Engraved message?: Abbr.
55 "I'm not volunteering!"
59 Ring of anatomy
60 Boring people
61 On notice
62 "Tonka" star, 1958

DOWN

1 Withdrawal figs.
2 Joke writer for many Kennedy campaign speeches
3 Astrological set
4 Some husk contents
5 Understanding responses
6 Pusher
7 Botanical appendages
8 Fries, say
9 A telly may get it
10 Old Olympics award
11 Scarlett O'Hara's mother and others
12 W.W. II vessel
13 Cascades
14 Flip
18 Comment before turning in
23 Director of the Associated Press, 1900–35
24 Scale succession
26 Nicholas Gage title character
27 More
28 Tout's opposite
29 45-Down performers
31 How some hats are worn
32 Drawing, e.g.
33 Start of some countdowns
34 "Piece of My Heart" singer Franklin
35 Result of regular use
37 "Sin City" actress, 2005
38 Stagecoach puller
41 Body band
42 Flat part
44 17-Across, quaintly
45 See 29-Down
46 Parfait part
47 It's a big part of life
48 Do some tune-up work on
51 Aurora producer
53 2002 Literature Nobelist Kertész
54 Capital of Colombia
56 Land of "20,000 Leagues Under the Sea"
57 Dutch traveler's choice
58 Figure in the Sunni/Shia split

by Robert H. Wolfe

150

ACROSS

1 Mad magazine feature
9 Spherical bacteria
14 Weekly since 1865
16 Financial V.I.P.
17 Martin of Hollywood
18 Quaint contraction
19 Puts in
20 Admits
22 Falls apart
23 Not quite up yet
24 Pick apart
25 1990s N.F.L. running back Curtis ___
26 ___ Paradise of Kerouac's "On the Road"
27 Keep in order
29 Ones needing fulfillment?
30 Locale for most of the New York Marathon
32 Kind of state

33 Rest stops?
36 Dobby or Winky, in Harry Potter
39 Solo
40 Hum follower?
41 "Pinocchio" character voiced by Mel Blanc
42 "That hurts!"
43 Played out
45 Rialto Bridge sight
46 One use for anise
48 Risqué
49 Not broadside
50 Mountain climber's need
52 Jaguar maker
53 When Hamlet first sees a ghost
54 Band active from 1995 to 2002
55 Providers of peer review?

DOWN

1 Figure in many jokes
2 Troop group
3 Arabs who are not in OPEC
4 Some sweaters
5 Smelling things
6 London's Covent Garden and others: Abbr.
7 Dicks
8 Daredevil's creed
9 Home of "The NFL Today"
10 Bishop Museum setting
11 Small sunfish
12 Help for a secret agent
13 Cantillates
15 1995 political book subtitled "Leader of the Second American Revolution"
21 When the kids are out

23 Old drive-in fare
26 "Happy Days" catchphrase
28 The General ___, "The Dukes of Hazzard" auto
30 Beyond oblivious
31 Turned
32 Half of a 1960s R & B duo
33 Source of lecithin
34 Chooses
35 Long Island Journal
36 Current events around Christmas
37 Round steak, e.g.
38 Kind of crystals
41 Wine order
44 Rounds: Abbr.
45 Addition sign
47 It's hard to walk on
48 Rise by the shore

by Mark Diehl

51 "The Partridge Family" actress

151

ACROSS
1. Interest of Miss Marple
5. Blow-drying problem
15. Liner's locale
16. Slipping frequencies
17. Spot
18. Steering system components
19. "___ the glad waters of the dark blue sea": Byron
20. James Bond was kicked out of it
21. Eric of "Lucky You"
22. Contortionist's inspiration?
24. Aquavit flavorer
27. Risible
28. Paris fashion house since 1956
29. Seed's exterior
30. Off by a mile
34. 1990s Indian P.M.
35. Where some addresses come from
36. Massenet's "Le ___ de Lahore"
37. Setting of Camus's "The Fall"
40. One yawning
42. Sign at some booths
43. Marina accommodations
44. Notoriety
47. Hansom cab accessory
48. Massive star
49. Half of doce
50. Something often smelled
51. Factor in a home's market value
55. Do groundbreaking work?
56. Carried by currents, in a way
57. Winetaster's concern
58. Serenity
59. Forum infinitive

DOWN
1. Shakespearean character who introduced the phrase "salad days"
2. Tattoo remover
3. Coffeehouse menu subheading
4. 1959 #1 Frankie Avalon hit
5. Tested, as a load
6. Documentarian Morris
7. Elvis follower
8. Lot
9. Richard Gere title role of 2000
10. Basso Berberian
11. Sports champ depicted in "Cinderella Man," 2005
12. Counselor-___
13. Davis of "Cutthroat Island"
14. Theme
20. Fitch who co-founded Abercrombie & Fitch
23. Indication of disapproval
24. Novelist Potok
25. Tony winner for "Guys and Dolls," 1951
26. Detail on some tickets
28. Material used in making saunas
30. "Pink Shoe Laces" singer Stevens
31. "Elijah" and others
32. Bridle parts
33. Piercing glance
35. Coventry park sight
38. It's raised after a payment is collected
39. Disney doe
40. Pinches
41. Part of a laugh
43. Temporary property holder
44. Konica Minolta competitor

by Brad Wilber

45 Elicit
46 Chick
playing a
piano
47 Isn't quite
neutral

49 Toxin
fighters
52 Symbol of
industry
53 "Be more . . ."
sloganeer

54 "Some Words
With a
Mummy"
penner
55 Honourary
title: Abbr.

152

ACROSS

1 African city with famed botanical gardens
8 Riddle ender
15 Yosemite setting
16 Still oblivious
17 It has a fast, easy gait
19 Things you enjoy doing
20 Having new tournament rankings
21 Marxist quality?
29 Dish with tomato sauce
36 Area of W.W. II fighting
37 Like Dacron
38 Pros
39 Football helmet features
47 One working for a flat fee?
54 Has an accommo- dating spirit
55 Island just north of the Equator
56 Advances

57 Activity of an organism in response to light, e.g.
58 Puts away

DOWN

1 Spanish 101 verb
2 Wedding invitee
3 Wedding rentals
4 __ Davis, first African- American to win the Heisman Trophy
5 Music symbol
6 Set (in)
7 "Ah, Wilderness!" mother
8 PBS station behind Charlie Rose
9 British general in the American Revolution
10 "I'll raise the preparation of __": Mark Antony
11 Square in a steam room
12 Bids

13 A runner might enter it
14 Some flawed mdse.
18 Spot from which you might see a bomb headed your way
22 Recipe details: Abbr.
23 Cadbury Schweppes brand
24 Composition of some French chains
25 Drink preference
26 Editorial cartoonist Hulme
27 Antique gun
28 Harvard Science Center architect José Luis __
29 Dry, in Durango
30 Reverse movement, of a sort
31 Cézanne's "Boy in __ Vest"

32 Longtime "All Things Considered" host Adams
33 Itself, in a Latin legal phrase
34 Not secret
35 Compact
40 Things hypothesized by Democritus
41 Move shoots, say
42 Flaky Turkish confection
43 Some moldings
44 Canine line
45 Follow
46 Way down
47 Popular U.S. board game since 1959
48 He played Bob in "La Bamba," 1987
49 It goes on and on and on
50 Former
51 They're big in Hollywood

by Brendan Emmett Quigley

52 Rest stop
sight
53 "___
Hombres"
(ZZ Top
record)

153

ACROSS

1 Backup
6 Squirts
10 Size in a lingerie shop
14 Music maker "played" by the wind
16 Basse-Normandie department
17 Stereotypical nerd
18 2004–06 poet laureate Kooser and others
19 Boards
20 Fluffy, perhaps
22 Tears
24 Trainee
25 Zodiac symbol
28 ___ Britannica
29 Navajo handicrafts
31 Car rental company founder Warren
33 Country with coups d'état in 2000 and 2006
35 Airline purchased by T.W.A. in 1986
36 Cellist who debuted at London's Wigmore Hall at age 16
39 Invite to one's penthouse suite
40 Robed dignitary
41 Fen bender
42 Availed
44 It lands at Landvetter
46 Holders of shoulders: Abbr.
47 Ancient Greek sculptor famous for his athletes in bronze
48 Inclusive pronoun
50 Cautious people stay on it
52 Shakespearean scholar Edmond
56 Problem ending
57 Expensive choice for a commuter
59 Big name in contact lens cleaners
60 "Madame Butterfly," updated
61 Peer on a stage
62 Being tossed, maybe
63 Statistical calculations

DOWN

1 Tio ___ (sherry brand)
2 Crazy
3 Set down
4 Bronc rival
5 Wrongful slammer sentence, say
6 Appreciation abbreviation
7 Curses
8 Palm smartphone
9 Smart
10 Fashionable resort area
11 Piñata decoration
12 Not put off
13 Raid victim
15 Instant success?
21 Indian lute
23 Like Shakespeare's Prospero, e.g.
25 Javanese chiefs
26 Salt halter
27 It'll knock you out after you knock it back
29 1996 Golden Globe winner for "Truman"
30 Variety listings
32 Like some diamonds
34 Lord of fiction
37 Beehives, e.g.
38 He wrote "In the country of the blind the one-eyed man is king"
43 Knot
45 Gomer Pyle expletive

by Karen M. Tracey

48 Where the Fulda flows
49 Cartoonist Segar
50 Pioneering puppeteer
51 Place of honor
53 Grammy-winning merengue singer Tañón
54 Rialto sign
55 Coastal avifauna
58 Fed. property overseer

154

ACROSS

1 "That may be true, but . . ."
11 ". . . there are evils ___ to darken all his goodness": Shak.
15 Visit
16 ___ Lemaris, early love of Superman
17 When a procrastinator tends to something
18 Exultant cry
19 Advance further?
20 Comic Boosler
22 Place of refuse
26 Tons of fun
27 It's built for a trial
31 Shot putters' supplies?
33 Player of June in "Henry & June"
34 Title locale of five 1980s films: Abbr.
36 Russian peasant wear
38 Chic
40 No-nonsense cry
41 King's second
43 Diamond, e.g.
44 Like petty offs.
45 She had brief roles as Phyllis on "Rhoda" and Rhoda on "Dr. Kildare"
47 Prize cup, maybe
48 Jazz pianist who played with Satchmo
50 Address south of the border
52 They're thick
54 Feast
59 Ones going head to head
60 Magazine that hands out annual Independent Press Awards
64 Part of a rebel name
65 Little redhead
66 "Buona ___!"
67 Puppet glue-ons

DOWN

1 Alexis, e.g.
2 Improve
3 Green's concern: Abbr.
4 Italian tenor ___ Schipa
5 Routine responses?
6 Soap actress Kristen and others
7 Money machine mfr.
8 Knock around
9 Pier grp.
10 Roy Rogers's surname at birth
11 Son of Elam whose name means "God the Lord"
12 Response to "I had no idea!"
13 Northeastern city named for a Penobscot chief
14 One concerned with the nose
21 Some of those who "hail the new" in "Deck the Halls"
23 Arrow of Light earner's program
24 Nostalgia elicitor
25 Cry "nyah, nyah!"
27 Engagement breakers?
28 Outlaw band member
29 Insignificant sort
30 Saki story whose title character is a hyena
32 Clammed up
35 Felix, e.g.
37 Bête noire
39 Modern provider of fast service, briefly
42 Nugget holder
46 Light reddish-brown
49 God commanded him to marry a harlot
51 Like some instruments
53 Like some instruments: Abbr.

by Myles Callum

55 "What's Going On" singer, 1971

56 What you may call it when you're wiped out

57 New Wave singer Lovich

58 Shore scavengers

61 Governing creative principle

62 Vietnam's ___ Dinh Diem

63 It's most useful when cracked

155

ACROSS

1 Adoption option: Abbr.
6 Settled down securely
12 They're often unpaid
14 Do further work on a bird?
15 Construction material
17 Applies polish to?
18 Some sit on pads
19 Parcel part
20 Face with stone
21 It may be usurious: Abbr.
22 Waite ___, Hall-of-Fame Yankees pitcher
23 Hospital supplies
24 Feature of some classical architecture
26 Fragrant heartwood
27 James Bay native
29 Five atoms in a ulexite molecule
31 Face attack
35 Writ introduction?
36 1988 tennis Grand Slam winner
37 Actress Pataky
38 Cockney greeting
40 Relatives of pollocks
44 It might consist of a 19-Across
45 Become full
46 High-tech surveillance acronym
48 Soapstone, say
49 "You betcha, Bartolomé!"
50 "___ Work" (George F. Will best seller)
51 Early
54 Some bygone roadsters
55 Blue Angels member, e.g.
56 Fluish, perhaps
57 Less like a yo-yo

DOWN

1 Some poles
2 Fight
3 Relatively fresh
4 Water fleas, barnacles, etc.
5 Lee of Hollywood
6 Grant
7 Filter holders, briefly
8 1932 Garbo title role
9 Give shades to in advance
10 Who's a critic?
11 Strikes
12 Certain rose creator
13 Banjolike Japanese instrument
14 Leaf part
16 Auto option
25 Julie Harris's "East of Eden" role
28 Machination
30 So as to avoid getting shot
31 Eastwood played him in five films
32 Out
33 Thighs may be displayed in it
34 Thighs may be displayed in it
35 Water polo teams, e.g.
39 Conductor Segerstam and novelist Enger
41 As yet uncollected for
42 It rises in the Black Forest
43 Graduated
47 Galley countermand
49 Sharp rival
52 Old washday choice
53 The Platters' "___ Mine"

by Jim Page

156

ACROSS

1 Whole ___
8 Place on a Monopoly board
15 What goes around
16 Gain or loss
17 Line from a scam artist
18 Tablets site
19 Where the African Union is head-quartered
21 Headache intensifiers
22 Patient status
23 Slicer locale
24 Little sucker?
25 Dept. store stock
27 Fictional salesman of '80s ads
31 Shrink
34 It's hard to fail
35 Grammy category
36 Biographical subject of the Best Picture of 1936
39 A driver might dip into it
40 Farm housing
41 Place for a clown
42 Tap type
44 He beat Botvinnik in 1960
45 Unlikely to break the ice
46 Firm wheel: Abbr.
48 Per ___
52 1988 chart-topping country album
54 Resident of Chinese highlands
56 Hero's welcome
58 Jambalaya
59 Relief pitcher Armando
60 Went over
61 Substitute for some snack foods
62 McDonald's mascot before Ronald

DOWN

1 Misses at fiestas: Abbr.
2 Group of 6-Down
3 Exercise of a sort
4 Best Supporting Actress of 1997
5 Some defenders: Abbr.
6 See 2-Down
7 Relative of a loon
8 Mutualism
9 Cry before disappearing
10 Univ. class
11 Sportswear company whose logo is three parallel stripes
12 Like a well-kept lawn
13 Science fiction author Greg
14 Number of wives of Enrique VIII
20 Mideastern news source
24 Sex therapist's suggestion
26 Smart
28 One held in an orbit
29 ___ Corporation (jewelry retail giant)
30 Hair salon option
31 Corp. bigwigs
32 Jambalaya
33 Monkshood
34 Co-star of Broadway's "Fanny"
37 Indefinitely large
38 Like many a road map
43 Clarifying words
44 Pump alternative
47 Boeing personnel: Abbr.
49 On the outs (with)
50 Virtual meeting of a sort
51 Patrick with a Tony
52 Cyborg's beginning?

by Karen M. Tracey

53 First name in motorcycling
54 It may follow convention
55 Oft-framed piece
57 Cousin of TV

157

ACROSS

1 First
16 Dante characters?
17 The "she" in the lyric "And when she passes, I smile"
18 Relinquish
19 Central square, maybe
20 50 Cent cover
21 First word of "Shrek"
22 Its capital is Porto-Novo
24 "Lo, here ___, / Never to rise again": "Hamlet"
25 ___ Digital Shorts (late-night comic bits)
26 One way to work
27 Drawing of the heart?
29 See 58-Down
30 Discoverer of the law of quadratic reciprocity
32 Disparage
34 Sideshow staple
37 Strong aversion
38 With 55-Across, $MgSO_4 \cdot 7H_2O$
40 Afternoon ora
43 Stop: Abbr.
44 Amber, for example
45 Capital of New Zealand: Abbr.
47 Food eaten with gravy
49 Mallow family members
51 "Vogliatemi ___" (aria from "Madama Butterfly")
52 The Green Hornet's real first name
54 Some stipend recipients, for short
55 See 38-Across
56 Interdisciplinary college major
59 Patch alternative
60 Last

DOWN

1 Galas
2 Saint-___-du-Mont, church containing the remains of the patron saint of Paris
3 Place for some prospects
4 Hardy one?
5 Break
6 Place for a stirrup
7 They may take a few yrs. to mature
8 Villain in the book of Esther
9 Brought out
10 NE for SW, e.g.
11 Jazz trumpeter/composer Jones
12 "Trip to ___" (1968 Susan Sontag book)
13 "Over the Rainbow" vocalist Ray
14 Be extant
15 Like some disappearances
22 Chihuahua fare
23 Chromosome home
26 Wampum
28 Gatorade choice
31 Olympics theme composer Arnaud
32 Person on the left?: Abbr.
33 Bolt measures: Abbr.
35 Charity carnival feature
36 Higher calling?
39 Former Mercury model
40 L.A.'s ___ Tower, tallest building in the West
41 Nickname on "Cheers"
42 Not together
44 Headache
46 Bring down
48 Leather band
50 Eastern royal
51 ___-Württemberg (Stuttgart's state)

by Byron Walden

158

ACROSS

1 Claimed as one's own
8 Paper binder
15 Sandlot game
16 Draft pick
17 Looking ragged
18 Lined with trees
19 Rock guitarist born David Evans
20 Mike Brady of "The Brady Bunch," e.g.
21 Half a nursery-rhyme spider's description: Var.
22 Longtime "What's My Line?" panelist
23 "Go jump in the lake!"
25 Begin, as an enterprise
26 1947 semi-documentary-style crime drama
27 Aces
29 Communist federation: Abbr.
30 Common site of archaeological remains
31 They mean nothing
35 Red stain in a lab
37 Dance in a pit
41 Running wild
43 "It's true!"
45 Carrying on
46 First name in electrical engineering
47 Run-in
49 Made happy
50 Bigger and stronger
51 Class struggles?
52 Sanctions
53 Pro performer
54 Others
55 Expose and destroy

DOWN

1 Guinness Book weather record category
2 Former home of the N.F.L.'s Rams
3 Cooling-off period
4 Spoils
5 Immobile in winter
6 Not wait for an invitation
7 Eye sore
8 Bath and others
9 Carnegie Mellon athletes
10 King of Belgium
11 Races
12 Pantries
13 "___ and Franklin," 1976 biopic
14 Makes flush
24 Drum accompanying a pipe
25 The ___ Marbles
28 Island said to be the home of Homer's tomb
31 "Again?!"
32 With no time to lose
33 Celebrity chef
34 Scoundrel
35 Young members of a convocation
36 Melville's Ishmael, e.g.
37 Comes through successfully
38 Bristol Cream ingredient
39 Guide feature?
40 Control tower equipment
42 Purrer
44 Links with
48 Once, long ago
49 Woodwind instrument: Abbr.

by Manny Nosowsky

159

ACROSS
1 Faux pa?
11 Fortifies
15 Helpful figures?
16 Not yours, in Tours
17 Retinue
18 One given a staff position?
19 Enough for everyone to have seconds
20 Options for salting away, briefly
21 They're taken out in an alley
22 Purveyor of hot stuff
24 Med. specialty
25 Target of some antibiotics
27 2002 French Open winner Albert
28 Opposite of ephemeral
30 "Moesha" actress Wilson and others

32 Jump provider: Abbr.
33 G.P.S. fig.
34 1920 Summer Olympics site
38 Something often looked for on a rainy day
42 ___-Meal (vacuum food storage system)
43 ___ la Plata
45 One photocopier tray: Abbr.
46 DC figure
48 De ___ (Dallas suburb)
49 Reply to "That so?"
50 Libretto accompaniment
53 French painter of Napoleonic scenes
54 Little shooter
55 Shaker formula
56 Became adjusted

57 Whack
58 Something to crack

DOWN
1 Stir-fry vegetable
2 Calling
3 Dove's desire
4 Tool parts for bending and shaping
5 Rite aid?
6 He's a doll
7 Special-___ (football players used only in specific situations)
8 French novelist d'Urfé
9 Chaos
10 Ready to be used again
11 Italian for "sleeves"
12 Love lover
13 Blandness
14 Breaks in the heat?
23 Scaling aid
25 Abalone
26 The first one ruled 1547–84

29 How a mob acts
31 15th-century prince of Wallachia
34 Gives out
35 Uncommitted
36 Dessert Calvin doesn't like in "Calvin and Hobbes"
37 Train, say
38 Specially
39 Almost at
40 Not au naturel
41 Weave a raised design into
44 Peaceful
47 Snack cake brand since 1967
48 Cashew family member
51 It can leave you red-faced
52 "Futurama" creator Groening

by Raymond C. Young

160

ACROSS
1 Player in three 1970s Pro Bowls
9 Dispersion devices
15 Infernal
16 Any of six popes
17 It's heard at many a wedding
18 San Francisco neighborhood, with "the"
19 Basketball analyst Elmore
20 Former Shea players
22 Neighbor of Isr., once
23 Threaded holder
25 "Christ's Entry Into Brussels in 1889" painter
26 Snow on an album cover
27 Sigmoid curves
29 Trough site
30 "Please," to Franz

31 Swiss multinational
33 Didn't just nosh
35 Kind of carriage
37 Molotov cocktail, e.g.
40 Shucks, so to speak
44 Mets manager Minaya and others
45 One along an autobahn?
47 Aunt who sings part of "The Farmer and the Cowman"
48 High ones may produce a roar
49 Cape wearer's field
51 Focus provider?
52 Canyon, e.g.
53 Columbus, e.g.
55 Educ. Testing Service offering
56 "Not right now"

58 Picasso mistress and subject
60 Where Antonio and Shylock litigate
61 Ingress
62 Tequila brand with a red sombrero bottle top
63 Levied

DOWN
1 Waldenbooks alternative
2 It's sweet, it's said
3 Ways of access
4 Lower, in a way
5 Tombstone, e.g.
6 Fresh face at a firm
7 Easterners
8 "Hey!?"
9 Edsel model
10 Intake optima: Abbr.
11 Return address abbr.?
12 Orient

13 Plant of the arrowroot family
14 View coral reefs, maybe
21 Not false
24 Mountaineering aids
26 Word in a documentary's credits
28 Folks guilty of disorderly conduct
30 "Goin' to Chicago Blues" composer
32 Ranch extension?
34 "Of the," in Oviedo
36 Campaign staple
37 Not hold something against
38 Select for a case
39 Runaway
41 Advertisers' output
42 Cookout setting
43 In sequence
46 Curtain fabrics

by Victor Fleming

49 One of the
Gospels, in
a Spanish
Bible
50 Cadbury
Adams
brand

53 Minute:
Prefix
54 Thin
57 RNA is a
topic in it
59 Family
V.I.P.'s

161

ACROSS

1 Magellan, e.g.
11 Three-time Gold Glove winner ___ Otis
15 Enthusiastic welcome
16 Undergo ecdysis
17 Imparts artfully
18 "Put your wallet away"
19 Word with age or weight
20 Surveillance setup
22 Bricklike
25 Idolized artist in Ouida's "A Dog of Flanders"
26 Bad combustion
29 Sorority letters
31 Shatt al Arab port
32 Put away
33 Many a Degas portrait
35 Skipper, to Barbie
36 La Grande Jatte, e.g.
37 Zolaesque imputation
38 Duct opening
39 Outboard motor inventor Evinrude
40 Release a bulletin?
41 TV role for Bamboo Harvester
42 Attack
44 Basketball court's three-point line, e.g.
45 Rumble in the Jungle setting
46 Whizzes
48 One who's more than attentive
50 Its flag depicts a plow, shovel and pick
52 Contend (with), in the country
56 St. ___ (Cornwall resort town)
57 Doctor, at times
60 Fröbe who played Goldfinger
61 Cosmopolitan alternative
62 ". . . maybe more, maybe less"
63 Supporters of roads

DOWN

1 Some Muslims
2 Shut (up)
3 Dictionary word before a variant spelling
4 Mount
5 Eternal
6 Toss
7 "V for Vendetta" actor, 2006
8 ___-Tab (PC window-switching shortcut)
9 Gained popular acceptance
10 Quaint note opener
11 Simple life?
12 Casa dei Bambini school founder
13 Show tune sung by a stevedore named Joe
14 Relinquishes control
21 Tula moolah
23 Track wager
24 Toss
26 Words to leave by
27 Did a dog trick
28 Aids in closing deals
30 Lath cover
33 It may lack stars
34 Northwest Terr. native
37 Pre-election group
41 Zabaglione ingredient
43 Decides one will
45 Hound
47 Sassers
49 Result of a handshake, maybe
51 Pick ___ (pettifog)
53 Record label for Sam & Dave and Booker T. & the MG's

by Todd McClary

54 Sourdough's dream
55 Period pieces?
58 ___ crusade
59 Dude

162

ACROSS

1 Where to find the Mercury line and the Girdle of Venus
5 Small wonders
15 Novel that ends "By noon, the island had gone down in the horizon; and all before us was the wide Pacific"
16 Dirt
17 Frill
18 Alley oops
19 Historical succession
20 Millet, for one
21 Antarctica's Prince ___ Mountains
22 Many G's
23 D-Ray, e.g.
24 Word with building or burial
25 Uncouth
27 Title for Camilla
30 Shade of red
31 Writer who was a source for Verdi's "Rigoletto"
32 Be profligate, in a way
38 Like Pompeii, once
39 Kind of service
40 1961 film also known as "The Job"
44 Numbered 31-Down
45 Bourbon order
46 Proofs of purchase, often: Abbr.
47 Part of the Dept. of Justice
48 Predecessor of the boliviano
49 "Tout le monde en ___" ("Everyone's talking about it": Fr.)
51 With 54-Across, black magic
52 It can keep ballfields dry
54 See 51-Across
55 Lots to offer
56 Invite letters
57 Bank holdings?
58 Like porridge

DOWN

1 Controversial study
2 Title city in a 1983 George Strait hit
3 Ordinance
4 TV tavern
5 Check for credibility, in modern lingo
6 Hardened
7 Polaris or Procyon
8 Furry tree-dweller of the Amazon
9 The river Pison flowed from it
10 Austrian article
11 Squelch
12 Unpleasant way to catch one's spouse
13 They're found by the C's
14 Does the math
23 Bowls
26 Good bud
27 Result of too many rusty nails on the road?
28 Melees
29 Some Microsoft employees
31 See 44-Across: Abbr.
33 "Weeds" channel, briefly
34 Line struck through by a winner
35 Aral Sea feeder
36 Starchy bite
37 Beats narrowly and unexpectedly
40 Somewhat
41 Sobieski of "Joan of Arc"
42 He wrote "The heart has its reasons which reason knows nothing of"
43 Most-nominated Best Actor (eight times) never to win an Oscar

by Byron Walden

44 Burning the midnight oil
46 Built up
49 Uptown
50 Lola in "Damn Yankees," e.g.
51 Actress Maryam
53 Plugged in

163

ACROSS

1 Landscaper's aid
7 Woodcutter's aid
15 First in line
16 Woman who's just too cool?
17 Food brand with a sun in its logo
18 1978 Stephen King novel made into a miniseries
19 Fisherman's supply
20 They may come from the wings
21 Defibrillator users, for short
22 [Just like that!]
23 Follow
25 Falls at the hands of
27 Acted impulsively
31 Passed-down strands
33 Offer courses for
34 Kind of furniture
35 Money maker
37 Breakfast fare
38 Three-star officer: Abbr.
39 Perfect
42 Satisfied
43 Composer Frederick
44 Turgite or limonite
46 Delaware, the ___ State
48 Slight progress, after "from"
51 Bologna oils
54 Son of Leah
55 Grimalkin
56 Where many people may lie
58 Schubert works
59 Place to order rolls
60 Store, in a way
61 Further evidence
62 It might ask "What comes next?"

DOWN

1 Does a job on
2 Marsh denizen
3 Like some T-shirts and eggs
4 Returning to an old beat
5 Persians, e.g.
6 It might let off some steam
7 Place
8 Want in the worst way
9 Minute to the max
10 Administration ctrs.
11 It contains the auricle
12 Printer's amount
13 Thrilled
14 Breaks off
20 Run
23 The first one gets you going
24 It's near Fort Bliss
26 Shakespearean opener
28 Wicker work
29 Resin source
30 Exactly
31 Computer exec Michael
32 It has ports in Port.
36 Residence of some Indians
37 Provide money for
39 Went for
40 Words from the wise
41 Actress Anderson
45 Least known
47 Out
49 J.D.'s of the future
50 Uniform part, maybe
51 Architectural projection
52 Sauce thickener
53 Nonsense
55 Roulette play
57 Brief connection?
58 Floral offering

by Joe DiPietro

164

ACROSS

1 Extra-curricular activity traditionally for men
9 Measure of reflected light
15 Digitalis source
16 Manage adversity
17 Fresh
18 Kind of case
19 Fix at a farrier's
20 Confident affirmation
22 "Princess Caraboo" star, 1994
23 Set
24 Is peaked
25 Opera heroine with the aria "Einsam in trüben Tagen"
26 Singer Stubbs of the Four Tops
27 Murphy of "To Hell and Back"
28 Valium, generically
31 Place for buttercups
32 Overdo it at the gym
35 Withstands
37 Tognazzi of "La Cage aux Folles"
38 Opera that opens on Christmas Eve
40 Best Actor nominee for "Affliction," 1998
42 Life sci.
43 Captain of Stubb and Flask
47 Old World duck
48 Split
49 Ready
50 County holding part of Yosemite National Park
52 Old-fashioned letter opener: Abbr.
53 Less likely to fly?
54 Complex component
56 Having a hint
57 Paramount
58 Bigots
59 Not fleshed out

DOWN

1 Jet pilot's concern
2 Owner of Maybelline
3 Has substance
4 Einsteins
5 Awards for some campaigns
6 Set apart
7 A.C.C. member
8 Hold
9 Arabic name that means "servant of God"
10 He wrote "There was an old man of Thermopylae / Who never did anything properly . . ."
11 River craft
12 Author of "The Greedy Bastard Diary: A Comic Tour of America"
13 President who claimed to be a voodoo priest
14 Pirates' domain
21 Loose
23 Shameless hussies
26 Newswoman Logan
27 Band switch
29 Princess loved by Heracles
30 "Earth's Children" series author Jean
32 Colt handler
33 Extreme bovarism
34 Accepting
36 Ogrelike
39 Brother and husband of Tethys
41 Qualm
44 Greet cattily
45 Hindu drink of immortality
46 German astronomer who was the first to measure the distance to a star

by Karen M. Tracey

48 Wades
through
49 Precipice, say
51 ___ review
52 Remote
option
55 Puma prey

165

ACROSS

1 Fix . . . or damage
7 Deltiologist's purchase
15 Connected
16 U.S. city whose name is pronounced differently from its foreign namesake
17 Got around
18 "Two Years Before the Mast" star, 1946
19 Green marker?
20 Silver holder
22 Broke down
23 Year in the papacy of St. Pius I
24 Part of Bach's oeuvre
26 "Hänsel und Gretel" composer
28 See 53-Down
31 Literary name with a dieresis
32 Prince in an L. Frank Baum "Oz" book
33 Nerve
34 "Saturday ___," 1976 Earth, Wind & Fire hit
35 Something often laid at a window
36 1971 documentary about Ravi Shankar
37 Decamps
38 Part of I.L.G.W.U.: Abbr.
39 Like best buds
40 & 41 Go out nicely
43 Distinction
44 "Judge ___, . . ."
45 Western ___
48 A pinch, maybe
49 52-Across, for example
50 Sour orange, in French cuisine
52 White 49-Across
54 Intro to an unvarnished opinion
55 Cutthroat
56 Like centurions, typically
57 Benders

DOWN

1 Marked difference
2 Coupling device?
3 Jump-started
4 Interject
5 Runs through
6 Charm
7 Groundwork?
8 Standard offering of old
9 European two-seater
10 Pacific Coast evergreen
11 Super Bowl XLI winners
12 "___ Full of Sky" (2004 Terry Pratchett novel)
13 Coaster, e.g.
14 Georgia Tech football coaching great Bobby
21 Many an 11-Down fan
25 "Farewell, ___," 1965 top 10 Joan Baez album
27 Chiffon creations
28 It might singe a knight, in legend
29 Sizable, as a hamburger patty
30 Candlenut and buckeye
33 :D, in an e-mail
35 Sweep the competition
39 1967 Peter Fonda film written by Jack Nicholson
41 Gag rule, of a sort
42 Scoring leaders?
43 Savannah bounder
45 Waist products
46 Muscovite, for one
47 Richard of "The 300 Spartans"

by Byron Walden

51 Pip location
53 With
28-Across,
___ Caraïbes
(Guadeloupe
setting)

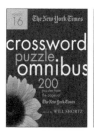

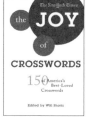

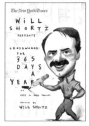
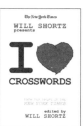

1

```
G A R B . B R O W . A P P L E
O R E O . O E N O . F R I E S
H A C K Y S A C K . L A P S E
O B E . A C R E . L A N E S .
M I S S Y O U . H E C K L E R
E A S Y . P L U G . S I N K .
. . N A G . A B U T . N E O .
. H I C K O R Y S M O K E D .
R O D . A L O T . E G O . . .
A L E S . D R O P . L A W S .
H O C K N E Y . R O M A N I A
. G L E A N . R I S E . G P S
B R A I N . H U C K A B E E S
E A R N A . A S E A . B L U E
A M E S S . T E R R . S A P S
```

2

```
W I S P . C R I P E S . T I M
A L O E . D E N A L I . O N E
F I F T H C O L U M N . P A L
T E T R A . . E L I . V I L E
. . T O I L E T A R T I C L E
T R O L L E D . . A V A . . .
I O U . S A G E S . A L I B I
L O C H . P A P E R . S N U B
E T H A N . R A D I O . T R I
. . I F S . . G O P H E R S .
S C A R L E T L E T T E R . .
M A N Y . R O E . . I S L A M
I N N . B E S T P I C T U R E
T O E . U N C O O L . O D I E
H E X . B E A N I E . N E A T
```

3

```
B O S C . P I G S T Y . G R A S
A N K A . E N A M O R . L A S T
D R I V I N G M I S S D A I S Y
M E T . S T O U T S . A N S E L
O P T . M A T T E . E N C O R E
V O I C E D . . C L I E N T S .
E R S E . P A T O I S . . . . .
. T H E B L A C K D A H L I A .
. . R O D E O S . . E S P N . .
V A S S A L S . . T R O U P E .
A R E T H A . M E D I A . P E T
S C R A M . P O L I T Y . P A Z
T H E N A M E O F T H E R O S E
L I N D . O N S I T E . U S E R
Y E A S . S T E N O S . N E R O
```

4

```
P A T T I . R I F F . A S E A
A V I A N . O M A R . P A T S
J A L F R E D P R U F R O C K
A L L T I M E . G O O P . . .
M O E . T O S S . O N A I R
A N D I E . A W E D . U R I .
. . P I L S N E R . U L A N .
. J J O N A H J A M E S O N .
P I E D . L E O T A R D . . .
A M T . B A A S . R A F T S
Z I P P O . F E A R . R I P .
. L O F T . . S E R R A T E .
J D A N F O R T H Q U A Y L E
L A N D . O B O E . S T E E D
O D E S . N I P S . T E D D Y
```

5

```
L I T U P . M A S T . F A N S
A R O S E . O K R A . O V A L
G E N E R A T I O N . R O S A
E N G . . W O N . L E E W A Y
R E A C T O R . H I T S . . .
. . A W L . P A N A T E L A .
T E T R A . L I V E S A L I E
A T O B . S E X E S . T I E R
M A J O R E D I N . P I A N O
S T O N E A G E . R E O . . .
. . A S H E . S E A N C E S .
B L O T T O . A P E . O V O .
R A V I . R E V E L A T I O N
O R E O . S P I N . S A N K A
W A R N . E A S T . P O S E R
```

6

```
A D D S . . D O W N . B O B S
D I R T . M A C H O . L A R K
U V E A . A C H E S . O K A Y
L A W R E N C E W E L K . L K
T N T . L I A R . J E E R A T
. H U L A . G O D . A C E .
R T E S . C L A M B I S Q U E
A R L E S . O S E . N A U R U
F A I R A M O U N T . H E A P
T I N . L E T . H I L L . .
S L E E T S . F L E D . W P A
. L I T T L E B O P E E P .
M A U I . I R A T E . A L A S
R A Z Z . Z E R O S . A C R E
S H I A . O X E N . R H Y S .
```

7

```
S T O I C . N E A R . C O A T
H O N D A . U R G E . O A T H
E A T I N G C R O W . I S E E
A D O . C U L . G R A N T E E
. . R E N E E . I R E . . .
. T A L K I N G T U R K E Y
J O E Y S . C O E N . A R E
E R T E . C A R T S . I S I N
E A R . T O N Y . A M E N S
P L A Y I N G P O S S U M .
. . A N D . T R E S S . . .
D E F R A U D . G A I . B A A
O V E R . C R Y I N G W O L F
C A T O . T I M E . N O R M A
K N E W . S P A S . S W E A R
```

8

```
W A G S . A D D U P . E L S E
I D E A . L O O S E . N O U N
G O L D F I N G E R . O W E D
. . . D I S S . . R U S T S
L A M E N T . S H R U G . .
E R A S E . S T E E L H E A D
T O R T . E T E R N E . R H O
H U T . C L A R E T S . R O W
A S H . A D L I B S . B A R N
L E A D B E L L Y . S E N S E
. . V E R S E . G O A D E D
A C T O R . . E L A N . . .
R O A R . S I L V E R B A C K
A L G A . P R E E N . A L O E
B A S K . Y E A R N . G A N G
```

9

```
B E T . E F F U S E . M A Y S
U Z I . F O R A L L . A L O E
N R C . F L O R I D A K E Y S
T A K E A I M . M E D I C O S
. . E N C A M P . S O N . . .
T A R G E T . I N T L . J A S
A S T A . E D G E . P L U N K
S T A G E . O P T . H I N D I
T O P E R . D E S I . O K I E
E R E . O D O N . M I N D E D
. . A D O . S I M M E R . . .
S I N C E R E . S E A L A N T
T H I R D S T R I N G . W A R
L O C I . A T E A S E . E M I
O P E D . L A S H E S . R E X
```

10

```
D O U S E . A L F . P I Q U E
I D S A Y . L E A . L A U R A
S I E V E . L A W . A M I S S
H E R E S J O H N N Y . P A Y
. . . H O W . A M C . . . . .
P A C M A N . R E L E A S E D
A C R I D . G O L D . S U M O
T H E R E S N O I . I N T E A M
R E M I . M A M A . O L D I E
I D E N T I T Y . S T E E L S
. . . G O T . V I A . . . . .
S A M . W H E R E S W A L D O
O C E A N . Z E N . H O A R D
A L I B I . R E A . I N B A D
P U R S E . A L L . T E S T S
```

11

```
A V O N . I D L E . O R A T E
P A C O . T R A M . B O X E R
A C C T . C A V E . S U E D E
C H U R C H W A R D E N . . .
H E R E I . . Y E S D E A R
E L S . V I D A . E S T A T E
. . D I C I E R . R U I N
. P E R C U S S I O N I S T
H I K E . H O T T I P . . .
B L E A T S . P E O N . E T H
O L D M A I D . E R N I E
. . B I C Y C L E R I D E R
A S S O C . I R O N . G O R E
M I C A H . N E R O . E R O S
I S I T I . G E E S . L A D Y
```

12

```
D U S K . P O E M S . U S S R
A S I A . I N D I A . S O H O
D O G B R E E D E R . U F O S
E C H O E R . A N I M A T E S
. . . B I R D . . A L P . . .
L E A . N E U M A N N . A C T
U N C L E . F A T E . S L A W
N O T E S O F T H E S C A L E
A C I D . B E T E . T I T L E
R H O . S I L E N C E . E S T
. . N I T . . S H A H . . .
D O D D E R E D . E M I N E M
A H O Y . S M I L E Y F A C E
M I L L . V I N E S . I D O L
P O L L . P R O X Y . S A N D
```

13

Y	O	G	A	■	A	T	T	I	C	■	D	O	C	K
E	A	S	T	■	B	U	R	R	O	■	O	T	O	E
S	T	A	L	E	B	R	E	A	D	■	O	T	B	S
■	■	A	R	E	N	A	■	■	A	D	A	R	E	■
E	W	I	N	G	■	S	T	E	A	L	A	W	A	Y
L	A	O	T	S	E	■	■	A	D	I	D	A	S	■
A	N	T	I	■	A	G	A	T	E	S	■	■	■	■
L	E	A	S	T	R	E	S	I	S	T	A	N	C	E
■	■	■	U	N	S	E	N	T	■	I	C	E	T	■
■	P	H	O	N	E	S	■	E	R	R	A	N	T	■
S	L	A	T	E	R	O	O	F	■	E	L	A	T	E
N	A	M	E	D	■	■	I	R	A	N	I	■	■	■
I	T	L	L	■	T	A	L	E	S	O	F	W	O	E
P	E	E	L	■	S	L	E	E	T	■	T	I	L	L
E	S	T	O	■	K	I	D	D	O	■	S	T	E	M

14

H	E	R	D	■	P	E	D	A	L	■	A	C	M	E
M	A	U	I	■	A	N	N	I	E	■	F	L	A	X
O	R	G	A	N	T	R	A	N	S	P	L	A	N	T
■	■	Z	E	R	O	■	T	S	E	■	S	H	E	■
C	H	I	■	W	O	N	T	■	E	G	G	S	O	N
A	U	S	T	E	N	■	W	I	N	■	M	A	L	T
B	E	A	U	S	■	F	O	R	E	■	I	C	E	S
■	■	A	N	T	I	O	X	I	D	A	N	T	■	■
L	A	C	E	■	N	I	T	S	■	V	O	I	C	E
I	B	A	R	■	F	E	W	■	C	A	R	O	L	S
T	A	S	S	E	L	■	O	R	A	L	■	N	I	P
E	L	I	■	O	A	T	■	E	N	O	S	■	■	■
R	O	M	A	N	T	I	C	F	A	N	T	A	S	Y
A	N	O	N	■	E	M	A	I	L	■	A	N	T	S
L	E	V	Y	■	D	E	N	T	S	■	N	O	E	L

15

S	A	L	E	M	■	U	S	E	R	■	E	M	M	A
O	B	A	M	A	■	P	A	G	E	■	R	E	A	L
L	I	T	T	L	E	P	I	G	S	■	O	N	C	E
E	D	T	■	A	P	E	D	■	P	I	T	I	E	S
S	E	E	S	R	E	D	■	D	I	D	I	N	■	■
■	■	E	K	E	■	T	I	T	I	C	A	C	A	■
A	M	B	L	E	■	T	R	E	E	■	■	T	A	R
B	I	L	L	Y	G	O	A	T	S	G	R	U	F	F
E	L	I	■	■	R	O	C	S	■	L	O	B	E	S
D	O	N	T	W	A	L	K	■	M	I	A	■	■	■
■	■	D	R	A	T	S	■	S	A	T	D	O	W	N
H	O	M	A	G	E	■	N	A	R	C	■	M	A	O
A	V	I	D	■	F	R	E	N	C	H	H	E	N	S
L	A	C	E	■	U	N	I	T	■	E	A	G	L	E
F	L	E	D	■	L	A	N	A	■	S	T	A	Y	S

16

A	L	A	S	■	D	A	I	L	Y	■	J	O	T	S
G	O	R	P	■	E	R	N	I	E	■	E	V	E	L
A	L	I	I	■	C	O	S	T	S	■	S	E	X	Y
P	L	A	C	E	I	N	T	H	E	S	U	N	■	■
E	S	S	E	X	■	■	O	S	U	■	M	A	T	■
■	■	■	A	B	C	S	■	■	N	E	I	G	H	■
O	P	S	■	M	O	R	N	I	N	G	S	T	A	R
C	U	T	E	■	N	A	I	V	E	■	E	T	T	E
T	R	A	D	I	N	G	P	O	S	T	■	S	E	W
A	S	T	A	B	■	S	R	T	A	■	■	■	■	■
L	E	I	■	E	O	S	■	■	■	F	L	A	M	E
■	■	S	I	G	N	O	T	H	E	T	I	M	E	S
H	A	T	S	■	T	U	R	O	W	■	M	U	T	T
Q	T	I	P	■	A	S	O	N	E	■	I	S	E	E
S	A	C	S	■	P	A	P	E	R	■	T	E	S	S

17

E	X	C	E	L	■	S	E	L	M	A	■	B	B	C
L	E	O	X	I	■	A	R	O	A	R	■	A	O	L
F	R	E	E	Z	E	F	R	A	M	E	■	N	A	E
■	■	C	A	R	E	■	M	A	N	D	A	T	E	■
T	O	F	U	■	A	S	H	■	B	A	I	N	E	S
U	N	I	T	A	S	■	A	S	E	■	V	A	L	E
B	A	R	E	S	■	O	T	T	A	W	A	S	■	■
E	N	S	■	T	O	S	P	A	R	E	■	P	J	S
■	T	R	A	N	S	I	T	■	N	O	L	I	E	■
P	O	S	E	■	N	O	N	■	S	T	R	I	V	E
O	C	T	A	V	O	■	S	S	W	■	I	T	E	M
P	A	R	R	O	T	S	■	C	A	T	O	■	■	■
P	S	I	■	T	I	N	P	A	N	A	L	L	E	Y
E	E	K	■	E	C	A	R	D	■	L	E	A	V	E
D	Y	E	■	R	E	P	O	S	■	C	S	P	A	N

18

W	I	V	E	S	■	F	A	C	T	■	B	I	K	E
E	M	I	L	E	■	I	N	O	R	■	U	K	E	S
S	M	A	L	L	■	D	I	M	E	■	R	E	N	T
L	U	C	I	L	L	E	S	B	A	L	L	■	■	■
E	N	O	S	■	O	L	E	A	T	E	■	T	A	U
Y	O	M	■	S	C	I	■	T	Y	C	O	O	N	S
■	■	S	P	A	T	E	■	■	T	I	L	D	E	■
■	S	A	L	L	Y	S	F	I	E	L	D	■	■	■
S	N	A	F	U	■	■	P	A	R	R	Y	■	■	■
P	O	W	E	R	P	C	■	C	A	N	■	G	A	M
A	D	S	■	G	R	A	V	E	N	■	A	R	N	O
■	■	■	N	E	I	L	S	D	I	A	M	O	N	D
L	E	G	O	■	O	L	I	O	■	L	O	U	I	E
I	R	I	S	■	R	A	G	U	■	M	U	S	E	S
Z	A	N	Y	■	I	S	N	T	■	A	R	E	S	T

19

S	A	L	U	D	■	C	R	A	N	E	■	D	E	B
A	B	A	S	E	■	O	I	L	E	R	■	U	N	O
L	O	B	S	T	E	R	P	O	T	S	■	P	E	P
T	O	O	T	■	V	A	S	E	S	■	H	O	S	E
■	■	R	E	B	E	L	■	■	S	I	N	C	E	■
N	O	D	E	A	L	■	B	A	C	K	S	T	O	P
O	R	A	L	S	■	S	A	M	E	A	S	■	■	■
W	R	Y	■	S	U	N	S	P	O	T	■	B	R	O
■	■	D	E	F	I	E	S	■	I	B	E	A	M	■
T	A	N	K	T	O	P	S	■	I	N	L	A	W	S
O	V	E	N	S	■	■	E	G	G	O	N	■	■	■
D	E	W	Y	■	P	E	D	R	O	■	O	P	I	E
A	N	A	■	N	E	W	Y	O	R	K	P	O	S	T
T	U	G	■	B	R	E	E	D	■	F	E	L	L	A
E	E	E	■	C	U	R	S	E	■	C	R	E	E	L

20

O	L	D	S	■	C	O	M	A	■	C	O	O	L	S
R	I	O	T	■	U	S	E	D	■	A	L	C	O	A
S	A	G	E	B	R	U	S	H	■	N	E	E	D	Y
O	R	G	A	N	■	S	O	Y	A	■	A	G	E	■
■	■	M	A	H	I	■	C	O	S	T	N	E	R	■
S	E	S	S	I	O	N	S	■	U	T	E	S	■	■
E	M	T	■	W	N	W	■	R	A	S	P	E	D	■
L	I	R	A	■	T	O	U	G	H	■	T	R	U	E
F	R	I	S	C	O	■	N	R	A	■	A	R	A	■
■	■	P	I	A	F	■	G	U	I	L	T	Y	O	F
O	C	T	A	V	I	A	■	B	R	I	O	■	■	■
P	O	E	■	E	X	P	O	■	L	U	C	I	A	■
A	M	A	N	A	■	H	O	N	E	Y	C	O	M	B
R	E	S	E	T	■	I	Z	O	D	■	A	L	A	I
T	R	E	E	S	■	D	E	M	S	■	N	E	X	T

21

M	A	M	M	A	L	■	Y	E	S	M	A	A	M
E	R	I	T	R	E	A	■	A	R	R	E	A	R	S
S	E	A	S	T	A	R	■	C	A	T	N	A	P	S
■	■	■	I	O	N	S	■	H	O	A	D	■	■
A	L	A	N	I	S	■	A	T	F	■	E	T	C
C	O	L	A	S	■	P	B	S	■	D	R	O	O	P
C	O	L	I	■	A	I	D	■	C	O	S	E	L	L
E	N	E	■	O	C	T	O	P	U	S	■	R	O	E
N	I	G	G	L	E	■	M	O	P	■	T	I	N	A
T	E	R	R	A	■	J	E	D	■	S	I	N	E	S
■	S	O	O	■	T	I	N	■	S	I	N	G	L	E
■	■	W	O	R	N	■	T	H	E	Y	■	■
R	O	A	D	T	A	X	■	B	A	R	T	A	B	S
P	R	A	I	R	I	E	■	A	R	R	I	E	R	E
M	A	R	M	O	T	S	■	I	A	M	S	A	M

22

C	A	R	A	T	S	■	C	H	E	■	C	R	A	B
O	N	E	C	U	P	■	H	A	L	■	L	A	N	A
S	T	U	C	C	O	W	A	L	L	■	A	M	E	N
A	S	P	■	S	T	I	F	F	A	R	M	■	I	N	G
■	■	F	O	S	S	E	■	O	U	S	T	S	■
J	A	S	O	N	■	■	C	O	O	P	■	■
A	L	I	E	■	S	P	E	E	D	S	■	G	U	Y
W	O	R	S	E	C	O	N	D	I	T	I	O	N	S
S	T	E	■	G	O	T	T	E	N	■	R	I	D	E
■	■	C	A	T	S	■	■	D	O	N	O	R
S	W	O	R	D	■	A	S	P	E	N	■	■
T	I	M	E	S	T	A	B	L	E	S	■	F	A	A
E	L	I	A	■	B	E	F	O	R	E	H	A	N	D
A	C	T	S	■	A	R	A	■	E	R	M	I	N	E
D	O	S	E	■	R	O	B	■	S	T	O	R	E	S

23

S	C	A	T	■	A	D	A	M	S	■	A	C	H	E
H	A	R	E	■	R	E	B	U	T	■	S	H	O	T
I	R	O	N	■	E	L	E	N	A	■	P	A	T	S
P	A	S	S	F	A	I	L	C	L	A	S	S	■	■
S	T	E	E	R	■	■	H	E	S	■	E	S	S
■	■	S	E	P	I	A	■	■	S	W	A	T	H
A	G	A	■	Y	E	S	N	O	A	N	S	W	E	R
T	U	T	U	■	T	A	T	A	R	■	W	A	V	E
O	N	O	F	F	S	W	I	T	C	H	■	Y	E	W
M	I	N	O	R	■	■	C	H	O	I	R	■	■
S	T	E	■	A	L	E	■	■	R	O	L	E	S
■	■	T	R	U	E	F	A	L	S	E	T	E	S	T
C	L	I	O	■	A	L	L	A	H	■	A	P	S	O
H	A	M	S	■	F	A	T	S	O	■	T	E	E	N
E	Y	E	S	■	S	T	A	T	E	■	E	R	N	E

24

A	D	A	M	S	■	H	A	M	S	■	M	R	E	D
R	E	N	E	W	■	O	M	A	N	■	Y	O	Y	O
M	A	N	N	A	■	F	A	T	E	■	B	O	R	N
■	L	A	D	Y	O	F	T	H	E	L	A	K	E	■
■	■	■	B	R	A	■	■	Z	E	D	■	■
M	A	C	R	A	E	■	D	I	E	D	■	P	G	A
E	T	H	I	C	■	S	O	F	A	■	N	O	R	M
C	H	I	C	K	E	N	O	F	T	H	E	S	E	A
C	O	M	E	■	T	O	N	Y	■	E	A	S	E	S
A	S	P	■	H	O	W	E	■	C	A	T	E	R	S
■	■	E	M	U	■	■	B	E	D	■	■
■	G	E	M	O	F	T	H	E	O	C	E	A	N	■
N	O	R	A	■	F	O	A	L	■	A	R	I	E	S
A	N	T	I	■	E	A	R	L	■	S	O	L	V	E
P	E	E	L	■	E	D	D	Y	■	E	S	S	E	X

25

```
S U B S . S L I D . S T A M P
O G R E . T E R I . N E P A L
F L A T B R O K E . E M O T E
T I S S U E . S T R A P P E D
. . . S T E M . O D E . . .
N C A A . T A P A S . R A V E
A U D I O . R A D I O . N I T
F E E L I N G T H E P I N C H
T I P . L O O I E . E V I A N
A N T S . S T O R M . E E R O
. . . P H I . E A C H . . .
I N T H E R E D . P E A R L S
H O S E R . T A P P E D O U T
O P A R T . C R E E . I O T A
P E R E Z . H E R D . T M E N
```

26

```
O W I N G . I C U . . P O T S
R O D E O . R I N D . O M E N
A V E R S . O R Z O . L E N O
L E A D P E N C I L . I G O R
. . . E X S . P E A S A N T
D O U B L E T S . D U H . . .
E D N A . C O O P . F J O R D
N O T S . S N A R L . O U S E
G R O S S . E P E E . K I T E
. . . G A P . S C A R E S U P
V A C U O U S . L S U . . .
A G R I . M I N U T E M A I D
L O O T . P L O D . F A R S I
I N C A . S O R E . U N C L E
D Y E R . S A D . L O S E S
```

27

```
H O F F A . S K I . V I B E S
A B D U L . P A L . U S U R P
G I A N T B I L L . L A I N E
. . . N O I R E . A C A C I A
E B A Y . C O L T P A C K E R
D A L L A S . R I N . . .
I B E A M . S E A S . M A Y O
C A R D I N A L C H A R G E R
T R O Y . O U S T . L O R N E
. . . X I N . E T C E T C
C H I E F S A I N T . T E A K
R O N N I E . L O T T O . . .
A W F U L . S U P E R B O W L
S T O R E . O V A . A E R I E
S O R E S . B U R . P R E G O
```

28

```
A T M O . R A T E D . B O O M
B R I S . A G A P E . E R M A
C U S S . D E N I M . A D E N
. S H O W I N G C O N C E R N
A T M . O U T . . I H A T E
L E A S E S . J O E S . L A D
P E S T . . V A R L E T . .
. . H O L D I N G F I R M .
. . P A U L E Y . . E A T S
A L T . N E A T . I B E R I A
S O U S A . . S N O . I N D
P A R T I N G C O M P A N Y .
E T N A . O M A N I . R A T S
C H I N . M E G A N . T R I O
T E N D . S N E R D . Y A M S
```

29

L	O	F	T		E	B	O	L	A		O	M	S	K
I	D	I	O		N	O	R	A	D		M	U	N	I
F	I	V	E	S	T	A	R	G	E	N	E	R	A	L
T	E	E	T	E	R				A	L	A	I	N	
		C	O	E		F	I	V	E	B	E	L	L	S
S	T	E	T	S		A	F	I	R	S	T			
H	A	N	O	I		T	S	A	R		G	A	D	
E	X	T	E	N	T			S	I	C	I	L	Y	
D	I	S		G	U	L	F		N	O	M	D	E	
		T	A	I	P	E	I		P	U	M	A	S	
T	A	K	E	S	F	I	V	E		O	N	E		
O	D	E	T	S				A	R	T	F	U	L	
Q	U	A	R	T	E	R	P	A	S	T	F	I	V	E
U	L	N	A		R	A	B	B	I		O	V	E	N
E	T	E	S		A	T	S	E	A		R	E	A	D

30

A	C	M	E		R	A	N	O	N		F	U	R	Y
B	I	A	S		I	R	A	T	E		O	N	E	A
C	O	C	A		P	A	N	I	C		C	A	P	P
		H	U	M	P	B	A	C	K	W	A	I	L	
A	V	E		A	L	I			O	L	D	E	R	
B	A	T	T	L	E	C	R	E	A	K		E	T	E
A	L	E	U	T			E	R	G		I	D	E	A
		F	A	R	M	G	R	O	A	N				
S	E	C	T		A	A	A		R	C	P	T	S	
O	A	R		B	E	L	L	A	N	D	H	O	W	L
P	R	O	S	Y			T	O	E		B	O	Y	
	M	A	K	E	S	A	B	O	O	B	O	O		
H	A	T	E		E	L	A	N	D		A	X	L	E
E	R	I	E		R	U	R	A	L		H	E	E	L
S	K	A	T		A	M	B	L	E		U	S	A	F

31

S	T	A	G	E		T	A	N	G	O		H	I	T
A	R	I	E	S		I	C	E	A	X		U	F	O
C	U	R	T	A	I	N	C	A	L	L		M	O	P
			B	U	S	H			I	N	A	R	T	
B	A	B	Y		B	A	T	H	S	P	O	N	G	E
U	N	O		A	N	T	E	U	P		D	C	O	N
G	O	B	A	D			A	N	A		S	O	T	S
		B	L	O	O	D	S	T	R	E	A	M		
J	A	Y	E		M	I	I		S	T	E	R	N	
I	L	K	A		N	O	N	F	A	T		D	A	B
G	U	N	S	L	I	N	G	E	R		S	Y	N	C
S	M	I	T	E				I	M	A	C			
A	N	G		T	H	I	N	G	S	D	R	A	W	N
W	A	H		B	A	C	O	N		Z	A	I	R	E
S	E	T		E	D	I	T	S		E	M	M	Y	S

32

F	U	M	E		S	E	M	I		B	A	S	I	N
U	N	I	V		A	X	E	D		A	C	H	O	O
S	I	D	E		L	I	M	E		S	T	E	W	S
S	T	A	N	D	A	T	E	A	S	E		D	A	Y
Y	E	S	S	I	R			S	A	M	B	A		
			O	B	I	E	S		P	A	R	T	E	D
I	C	U		S	E	V	E	N		N	E	E	D	Y
L	A	P	D		D	A	T	E	S		W	A	G	E
S	M	A	R	T		C	O	A	L	S		R	E	D
A	E	N	E	A	S			F	R	I	T	O		
		D	I	X	O	N		M	O	P	T	O	P	
B	A	A		F	L	O	R	I	D	A	T	E	C	H
A	S	T	R	O		W	A	C	O		S	R	T	A
S	T	E	E	R		A	N	E	W		I	R	E	S
H	I	M	O	M		Y	A	R	N		N	A	T	E

33

S	E	Z		U	T	T	E	R		R	A	N	D	B
I	L	E		N	O	O	S	E		A	D	O	R	E
T	I	R	E	S	O	M	E	W	I	N	D	B	A	G
A	H	O	L	E			I	N	S			I	T	S
T	U	S	K	E	D	W	A	R	T	H	O	G		
		S	N	O	O	Z	E		O	L	D	I	E	
J	A	M			L	E	O		P	R	I	E	S	T
P	R	O	M	P	T	S		P	E	T	N	A	M	E
E	M	B	E	R	S		R	E	T			L	E	S
G	E	S	S	O		H	E	A	R	S	T			
		C	A	P	E	A	F	R	I	K	A	N	E	R
E	R	E		O	T	T			E	L	E	N	A	
D	A	N	I	S	H	P	H	Y	S	I	C	I	S	T
G	R	E	T	A		I	M	E	A	N		G	U	T
E	A	S	E	L		N	O	N	O	S		H	E	Y

34

S	A	M	I	A	M		A	L	A			T	A	O
A	G	E	N	D	A		W	E	N	T	S	O	L	O
P	E	R	S	O	N	A	L	I	T	Y	Q	U	I	Z
S	E	E			I	F	S			P	U	T	T	Y
			I	S	L	A		S	P	E	E			
P	R	O	Q	U	A	R	T	E	R	B	A	C	K	
L	A	P	S	E			O	R	O		L	A	N	A
E	N	E		D	A	R	K	A	G	E		P	E	T
A	U	R	A		C	O	Y			S	H	R	E	W
	P	A	T	C	H	W	O	R	K	Q	U	I	L	T
			O	L	E	S		S	A	S	H			
M	T	I	D	A			O	V	I			E	E	E
M	I	N	D	Y	O	U	R	P	S	A	N	D	Q	S
E	M	I	S	S	A	R	Y			E	V	E	N	U	P
S	E	T			K	I	X			R	E	T	A	I	N

35

J	E	D		S	T	A	M	O	S		M	O	J	O
A	M	A		I	M	P	O	S	E		A	W	O	L
B	A	N	A	N	A	B	O	A	T		K	N	E	E
B	I	G	T	E	N			S	K	A	T	E		
E	L	I	A			M	E	A	T	W	A	G	O	N
D	S	T		P	E	A			O	F	U	S	E	
			R	E	D	R	O	S	E		A	N	U	T
		T	U	R	N	I	P	T	R	U	C	K		
A	R	A	B		A	S	T	A	I	R	E			
H	I	R	E	D			R	E	N		P	G	A	
A	P	P	L	E	C	A	R	T		P	I	E	R	
			B	L	I	G	E		D	I	A	N	N	E
V	E	T	O		G	R	A	V	Y	T	R	A	I	N
A	V	O	W		A	E	R	I	E	S		T	E	A
L	E	N	S		R	E	S	E	D	A		A	S	S

36

D	U	M	B		I	R	I	S		Z	O	N	E	D
I	B	E	T		N	A	S	A		S	M	I	L	E
N	O	N	E	E	D	T	O	T	H	A	N	K	M	E
G	A	L	A	X	Y			C	O	Z	I	E	S	T
S	T	O	M	P		J	O	H	N	S				.
			A	L	A	R	M		A	S	T	E	R	
G	L	A	D	T	O	B	E	O	F		H	O	P	I
N	U	D	I	S	M			U	S	E	R	I	D	
A	L	E	C		A	S	S	I	S	T	A	N	C	E
T	U	N	E	D		A	R	O	S	E				
			R	A	Y	O	N		L	A	S	T	S	
T	E	A	S	E	T	S		C	L	I	Q	U	E	
I	T	W	A	S	M	Y	P	L	E	A	S	U	R	E
P	A	R	I	S		E	V	E	N		L	A	N	D
S	L	Y	L	Y		S	C	O	T		E	B	A	Y

37

38

39

40

41

I	C	O	N		T	A	P	E		B	R	A	N	
N	A	N	U		I	M	A	X		A	U	R	A	S
S	T	E	M		N	I	N	C	O	M	P	O	O	P
		S	O	Y		S	E	R		E	M	M	A	
L	O	C	K	E		B	I	R	D	B	R	A	I	N
A	M	O	U	R		R	E	P	E	A	T			
P	I	L	L		P	O	S	T	A	L		D	J	S
S	T	E	L	L	A			L	E	D	O	U	T	
E	S	S		A	R	E	T	E	S		U	N	D	O
		E	L	O	P	E	R		S	M	E	A	R	
D	I	N	G	A	L	I	N	G		O	B	E	S	E
A	G	O	G		E	T	D		A	L	B			
N	O	O	D	L	E	H	E	A	D		E	S	P	Y
S	O	N	Y	S		E	R	M	A		L	O	G	O
	N	E	E	D		T	S	A	R		L	U	A	U

42

F	L	A	S	K		A	W	E		B	E	E	P	S
L	A	C	T	I		T	H	E		U	L	T	R	A
A	V	E	R	T		O	I	L		Z	O	N	E	S
B	A	D	A	B	I	N	G		E	Z	P	A	S	S
		W	A	D	E		O	N	C	E				
	F	U	H	G	E	D	A	B	O	U	D	I	T	
H	A	R	A	S	S		B	E	S	T		S	A	G
A	N	A	T		B	A	Y		I	L	S	A		
I	N	N		S	P	E	C		K	A	R	A	T	S
Y	O	U	T	A	L	K	I	N	T	O	M	E		
		P	A	C	T		C	O	I	N				
B	A	D	D	I	E		M	O	B	S	C	E	N	E
O	C	E	A	N		B	A	N		K	A	R	E	N
E	L	A	T	E		U	Z	I		E	G	G	E	D
R	U	L	E	D		S	E	C		T	E	S	T	S

43

G	A	B	S		C	A	V	S		R	A	H	A	L
A	L	L	A		A	L	E	C		O	R	O	N	O
R	E	A	M		V	E	E	R		M	I	L	N	E
T	R	I	P	L	E	S	P	A	C	E		Y	A	W
H	O	R	R	O	R		M	I	R	A	C	L	E	
	A	G	N	E	W		R	O	A	R				
P	E	P	S	I		L	A	I	C		H	O	C	K
A	L	A		C	O	O	L	C	A	T		S	H	E
W	I	T	H		P	I	K	E		H	O	S	E	A
	T	A	U	T		S	T	A	R	T				
O	L	Y	M	P	I	C		P	O	T	P	I	E	
S	O	C		S	C	H	O	O	L	B	O	A	R	D
C	O	A	T	I		A	R	G	O		M	B	A	S
A	S	K	E	D		M	A	R	M		A	L	T	E
R	E	E	C	E		P	L	E	B		N	O	E	L

44

E	S	P	E	R	A	N	T	O		W	A	T	C	H
C	O	U	T	U	R	I	E	R		A	N	G	L	E
H	O	T	C	R	O	S	S	B	U	N	N	I	E	S
O	N	T		M	I	S		D	E	A	L			
		P	D	A		D	E	A	L		S	T	U	F	F	S
H	I	G	H	E	S	T	B	I	D	D	I	E	S	
A	N	O	D	E		A	E	R	O	S		N	A	G
H	I	S	S		A	L	I	E	N		A	L	B	A
N	N	E		O	P	E	N	S		A	B	A	L	L
	K	E	E	P	I	N	G	T	A	B	B	I	E	S
		D	U	C	T		F	E	E					
A	W	H	I	L	E		A	I	L		M	M	E	
W	H	I	T	E	S	O	X	F	A	N	N	I	E	S
L	A	Y	O	N		C	L	A	M	B	A	K	E	S
S	M	A	R	T		T	E	T	E	A	T	E	T	E

45

R	I	C		N	A	D	I	A		S	I	L	L
E	N	O	W		I	S	I	N	G		A	S	E	A
C	A	S	A	B	L	A	N	C	A		X	R	A	Y
I	N	T	R	A			A	T	T		A	D	S	
T	E	A	M	M	A	T	E		H	O	P	E	R	
E	R	S	T		N	A	S		A	N	A	L	O	G
			O	C	T	E	T	S		S	M	I	L	E
C	A	R		H	I	B	A	C	H	I		S	E	E
I	R	E	N	E		O	T	O	O	L	E			
A	T	D	A	W	N		E	R	R		M	A	I	L
	O	S	H	E	A		S	E	A	H	O	R	S	E
K	F	C		D	I	X			A	T	E	I	N	
A	W	A	Y		A	T	B	O	T	H	E	N	D	S
R	A	R	E		D	R	O	N	E		D	A	R	E
T	R	E	S		S	A	X	O	N			S	O	S

46

T	O	T	A	L		E	L	L		I	D	A	H	O
A	E	R	I	E		F	E	E		G	I	V	E	R
B	R	I	D	G	E	F	I	N	A	N	C	I	N	G
		P	A	S	T	E		S	L	I	T			
P	O	L			C	T	R		I	T	A	S	C	A
O	V	E	R	T	H	E	E	D	G	E		T	O	D
D	A	C	H	A			N	A	H		E	R	A	S
	T	R	O	U	B	L	E	D	T	I	M	E	S	
B	I	O	S		R	A	W			D	I	E	T	S
R	O	W		W	A	T	E	R	F	I	L	T	E	R
A	N	N	I	E	S		D	O	A		L	D	S	
			N	T	S	B		G	I	N	Z	A		
S	O	N	G	B	Y	P	A	U	L	S	I	M	O	N
K	O	A	L	A		O	W	E		E	M	P	T	Y
A	F	T	E	R		E	L	S		C	A	S	T	E

47

T	A	B	O	O		G	A	M	E		B	A	I	T
A	L	L	A	H		I	B	A	R		O	N	C	E
O	P	A	H	S		J	E	S	T		S	T	I	R
		C	U	T	T	O	T	H	E	Q	U	I	C	K
E	L	K		O	D	E			U	N	C	L	E	
S	I	T	U	P	S		G	A	L	A		S	E	L
P	A	I	R		P	R	O	O	F	S				
	R	E	L	I	G	I	O	U	S	F	A	S	T	
		S	N	A	P	A	T			L	I	O	N	
I	M	P		E	D	E	N		T	I	E	D	O	N
N	A	A	C	P			P	O	D		E	N	E	
J	O	N	A	T	H	A	N	S	W	I	F	T		
O	R	E	S		A	R	I	A		D	A	R	T	S
K	I	L	T		W	E	N	T		I	R	I	S	H
E	S	S	E		N	A	E	S		T	E	P	E	E

48

E	L	I	A		A	B	B	E		D	R	A	W
M	A	R	C		T	R	A	C	T		E	A	C	H
I	M	A	C		P	E	T	R	I		S	P	R	Y
T	E	Q	U	I	L	A	S	U	N	R	I	S	E	
			R	N	A			G	A	G				
R	E	D	S	K	Y	A	T	M	O	R	N	I	N	G
A	R	I	E	S		G	E	O	D	E		T	O	R
T	A	M		B	O	N	U	S			A	T	E	
E	T	A		B	A	R	O	N		F	A	L	S	E
D	O	G	D	A	Y	A	F	T	E	R	N	O	O	N
	A	L	A				A	A	A				
	A	F	T	E	R	T	H	E	S	U	N	S	E	T
A	X	I	S		E	R	A	S	E		I	O	W	A
M	E	N	U		A	U	R	A	L		A	H	E	M
A	D	E	N			E	M	U	S		S	O	R	E

49

```
A T O Z . R E H A B S . E W E
D A V E . E D E N I C . X E R
I C E S . G A M E K E E P E R
N O R T H A M P T O N M A . .
. . . S O L E . . E A R E D
A R E . W E S T P O I N T N Y
L A P S E . . R A W . A N T E
O T I C . J O Y C E . T E R P
N I C O . I D O . . A E R E O
S O U T H B E N D I N . S E T
O N R I O . . E N D S . . .
. E A S T L A N S I N G M I .
P L A N E T A R I A . A E O N
A Y N . R O T T E N . F L U X
Y E S . S P H E R E . U S E S
```

50

```
P E R E Z . D Y E R . F I S T
A L A M O . E A V E . I N C H
S L I P O F T H E T O N G U E
T A N . . E E O . . V I O L S
. W I N D S O R C A S T L E .
K E E N E S T . O A T . S S S
G R A T E . . J O N E S . . .
B A R R . K N O T S . I C O N
. . . O W L E T . . A T O N E
A S P . O E R . U N W A X E D
S Q U A R E D A N C E R S . .
K U R T S . . T S O . W E E
F I S H E R M A N S W H A R F
O R E O . D O R A . H O I S T
R E D S . S N I P . A G N E S
```

51

```
R O C . S N A R L . T E N A M
C L U . P I X I E . U V U L A
C D E . A C E O F S P A D E S
O P T S T O . . T E A . E X T
L A I C . . J S B A C H . . .
A L P H A M A L E . . O U S T
. . . E R I T U . W A S T E S
L E A D E R O F T H E P A C K
A R O U S E . F I O R I . . .
W A L L . D E N M O T H E R .
. . E M B O D Y . . A O N E
A K A . O R G . . M I L T I E
M A R L B O R O M A N . K G B
E N L A I . U T I L E . E M O
S T O O L . N O D O Z . Y A K
```

52

```
E D W A R D . Q T R . H A S P
Q U A K E R . W Y O . I T A L
U L T I M A T E P U R P O S E
A L T O . W I R E T A P P E D
L Y S . C E N T . E G O . . .
. . F O R . Y A M . S K I P
A U D E N . . K H A N . I S R
U S I N G O N E S N O O D L E
L S D . O N B Y . . V J D A Y
D R O P . T A B . S A S . . .
. . A V A . O L E S . H B O
E X A C E R B A T E . H E A P
Z O N I N G O R D I N A N C E
R U I N . E N D . N I M R O D
A T N O . T D S . G A M I N S
```

53

```
F L A K ■ A B R A M ■ V E R B S
L A M A ■ B L A M E ■ E M A I L
O R I N ■ B U Y E R S G U I D E
P V T S C R E E N I N G ■ N E D
S A Y A H ■ ■ ■ T O I L E ■ ■ ■
■ ■ ■ N A M E I T ■ W E E D E D
A R E ■ C A R P O O L ■ F O R E
M A J M O T I O N P I C T U R E
O N E A ■ I N D I A N A ■ T S P
K I C K I N ■ S O L E M N ■ ■ ■
■ ■ ■ T O N E S ■ ■ ■ P O L K A
P O I ■ G E N A D M I S S I O N
S M O K E S I G N A L ■ H E A D
A N N E S ■ P R A N K ■ O G L E
T I S N T ■ E A S E S ■ W E A R
```

54

```
N E A L ■ E S T O P S ■ D A M
T R I O ■ B O O H O O ■ E T A
H O L D S B A R R E D ■ T H E
■ S E G O ■ K N O T ■ D E L ■
T I R E O F ■ B R A I N E R ■
G O O D N I K ■ Y V E T T E ■
I N N ■ R I N G ■ O G E E S ■
■ ■ ■ J U S T S A Y N O ■ ■ ■
■ Y E T I S ■ S A F E ■ M O P
■ A D O N I S ■ F L Y Z O N E
■ H I T G A M E ■ L E A N E R
■ T A O ■ A M M O ■ A P I T ■
O I L ■ G R E A T S H A K E S
V O L ■ A M E L I A ■ T E R I
A N Y ■ L Y R I C S ■ A R M S
```

55

```
C H A L K S ■ E P E E ■ C A T
L A D I E S ■ U R N S ■ A L E
A S I A N S ■ L O V E L I F E
S T E I N ■ R E N O ■ E R I N
H O U S E P A R T Y ■ G O E S
■ ■ ■ E L E V ■ O S H A ■ ■ ■
S T L ■ ■ N E E ■ ■ U T I C A
T W O K I N D S O F B O A T S
S I X A M ■ ■ P L O ■ ■ N R A
■ ■ ■ N A P S ■ A C E S ■ ■ ■
B O O S ■ I C E F I S H I N G
L P G A ■ P H I S ■ C U T I E
A I R S P E E D ■ M O T I V E
N N E ■ A T M E ■ I R I S E S
D E S ■ Y S E R ■ A T N I N E
```

56

```
W A S P S ■ W K R P ■ M S R P ■
A G O R A ■ O L I O ■ O T O E ■
X A X E S ■ L U G S ■ O P A L ■
■ ■ ★ S O F T H E T R A D E ■ ■
I M A M ■ P E E T ■ R E ★ S ■ ■
Q U E E N E D ■ S U E D ■ J I F
T U R N E D ■ ★ I S E ■ ■ ■ ■ ■
E M O T E ■ S O D A ■ P I N E ■
S U B S ■ R A R E ■ V E N T I ■
T U E ■ H A T ★ ■ H O A X E S ■
■ ■ ■ K I W I ■ T E N C E N T ■
■ ■ D C I V ■ R O A M ■ E D D Y
■ ■ J E A N E K I R K P A ★ ■ ■
■ A I R S ■ A C T E ■ N I E C E
■ N O D E ■ O A H U ■ D E L L A
■ E N ★ Y ■ S L O P ■ A S S E T
```

57

L	I	M	E		L	A	M	B		R	I	O	T	S
A	S	E	C		A	L	O	E		E	R	R	O	R
T	A	L	C		T	E	R	R	A	F	I	R	M	A
H	A	B	E	A	S	C	O	R	P	U	S			
		I	A	M	S				S	A	S	H	E	S
J	O	N	G		B	U	L	B		L	I	E	N	S
A	R	O	N		A	B	O	V	O		N	E	N	E
P	A	D	U	A		J	U	D	O		E	R	S	T
A	T	O	M	I	C			S	H	A	Q			
N	E	Z		M	U	S	H			R	U	S	T	S
	A	L	E	A	I	A	C	T	A	E	S	T		
S	E	M	P	E	R	I	D	E	M		N	E	A	R
E	P	E	E	S		N	E	R	O		O	T	R	A
W	A	R	D	S		T	R	O	N		N	O	S	Y

58

T	O	R	M	E		D	I	C	E		C	L	U	B
O	P	I	U	M		I	M	A	X		R	O	S	E
M	I	S	S	I	L	E	U	N	I	V	E	R	S	E
S	E	E	K		O	D	S		T	A	V	E	R	N
		O	O	O			A	F	T	A				
T	E	X	T	I	L	E	M	E	S	S	A	G	E	
R	I	D		T	E	E	N	I	E		S	O	U	P
O	B	E	Y	S		S	A	N		E	E	R	I	E
T	I	N	A		A	L	M	O	N	D		T	O	E
C	A	S	T	I	L	E	I	R	O	N	P	A	N	
			I	N	K	Y			V	A	R			
C	O	N	T	R	A		I	O	U		O	S	S	O
H	O	S	T	I	L	E	C	O	M	P	U	T	E	R
O	N	E	L		I	H	O	P		A	S	Y	E	T
P	A	C	E		S	S	N	S		S	T	E	P	S

59

C	L	A	M	P		A	R	M	O	R		I	S	H
R	A	D	I	I		L	E	A	V	E		C	P	A
E	Z	O	N	T	H	E		E	Y	E	S		S	I	N
M	A	R	I	S	A		F	O	R	E	S	T	E	D
E	R	N	O		H	M	S		K	N	U	R	L	S
		N	C	A	A		T	I	T	L	E			
B	A	S	S	O		I	D	O	L		K	E	E	N
U	S	A		Q	P	D	O	L	L	S		T	O	E
S	P	C	A		R	E	E	L		T	A	S	S	O
	O	L	D	E	N		E	D	E	N				
F	U	N	G	U	S		A	D	O		A	L	S	O
L	I	T	A	N	I	E	S		E	R	R	A	T	A
E	N	E		C	D	C	H	A	R	A	C	T	E	R
S	T	S		A	I	R	E	D		T	H	I	N	E
H	A	T		N	O	U	N	S		S	Y	N	O	D

60

S	C	A	L	P		A	M	A	S	S		T	D	S
O	M	N	I	A		L	A	C	T	O		H	O	T
F	O	U	R	T	E	E	N	R	E	D		E	R	Y
A	N	T	I	T	A	X		E	N	A	B	L	E	R
			I	C	E	S			A	M	M	O		
O	L	A	F		H	I	T	M	E	A	G	A	I	N
R	O	S	I	E			A	I	D	S				
D	O	U	B	L	E	O	R	N	O	T	H	I	N	G
			L	E	N	D			A	U	D	I	O	
I	L	L	T	A	K	E	O	N	E		M	O	T	O
M	E	A	N			M	E	T	A					
P	A	T	T	E	R	S		S	C	R	A	P	E	R
E	S	E		R	O	L	L	T	H	E	D	I	C	E
D	E	N		A	D	U	E	L		N	I	E	C	E
E	S	T		S	E	E	M	E		A	N	S	E	L

61

O	L	I	V	E	R		O	K	L	A	H	O	M	A
M	I	N	O	S	O		S	P	A	M	A	L	O	T
A	V	A	L	O	N		L	A	V	A	L	I	E	R
R	E	N	T			C	O	X	E	S		N	S	A
R	U	E		T	R	A		D	S	C				
	P	R	O	V	E	R	B	S			H	A	I	R
		C	A	B	A	R	E	T		A	N	N	E	
E	C	R	U		E	V	I	T	A		L	Y	N	X
P	H	I	L		C	A	N	D	I	D	E			
A	I	D	A		N	E	O	N	A	T	A	L		
	R	S	A		C	L	O	W	N	S		N	A	T
D	E	N		C	L	O	W	N			F	A	M	E
O	V	E	R	R	I	D	E		J	O	R	D	A	N
C	A	R	O	U	S	E	L		F	R	I	E	Z	E
S	H	O	W	B	O	A	T		K	I	S	M	E	T

62

B	A	H		F	A	L	L		C	A	T	N	I	P
O	R	U		A	S	E	A		A	I	R	A	C	E
A	I	M		C	H	I	C	K	F	L	I	C	K	S
R	A	B	B	I		S	E	N	T		F	R	E	T
		L	E	A	S		E	A	R	L	E	S	S	
J	O	E	Y	L	A	W	R	E	N	C	E			
A	M	P		S	A	H	I	B		A	R	N	A	Z
M	A	I	M		B	I	G	O	T		S	E	R	B
S	N	E	R	D		S	O	N	I	C		R	N	A
			C	O	L	T	R	E	V	O	L	V	E	R
A	L	C	O	H	O	L			O	M	O	O		
L	I	E	F		Q	E	I	I		E	X	U	R	B
C	A	L	F	M	U	S	C	L	E	S		S	O	O
O	R	T	E	G	A		K	I	R	I		L	A	C
A	S	S	E	R	T		Y	A	R	N		Y	M	A

63

C	R	A	G		U	B	O	L	T		F	A	Z	E
R	U	L	E		S	A	T	I	E		E	X	E	C
A	M	E	N		A	L	I	N	E		L	E	N	O
B	O	X	O	F	F	I	C	E	H	I	T			
B	R	I	A	R			A	E	R	I	A	L	S	
E	S	S		A	R	M	W	R	E	S	T	L	E	R
			F	I	O	N	A			C	O	M	O	
	H	O	L	D	O	N	T	I	G	H	T			
A	J	A	R			D	E	R	R	Y				
S	U	I	T	S	T	O	A	T	E	E		S	E	C
S	T	R	I	K	E	R			A	P	P	L	Y	
		F	I	N	I	S	H	S	T	R	O	N	G	
F	I	J	I		N	O	H	I	T		A	K	I	N
O	K	I	E		I	L	I	K	E		N	E	N	E
B	E	G	S		S	E	V	E	R		K	N	O	T

64

B	A	L	E		S	P	E	A	R		S	C	R	A	P
A	L	A	N		A	I	S	L	E		T	R	A	S	H
S	O	R	T		F	E	T	A	L		A	O	R	T	A
I	F	V	E	G	E	T	A	R	I	A	N	S	E	A	T
S	T	A	R	E			M	E	L	D	S				
			O	S	L	O		D	L	I		M	O	O	
E	V	E	L		W	A	I	L		O	S	W	A	L	D
V	E	G	E	T	A	B	L	E	S	W	H	A	T	D	O
I	S	A	I	A	H		S	A	K	E		D	E	E	R
L	T	D		L	I	P		F	I	D	O				
			M	E	L	O	N			W	A	L	E	S	
H	U	M	A	N	I	T	A	R	I	A	N	S	E	A	T
E	V	E	N	T		A	B	O	M	B		P	A	G	E
L	E	A	S	E		T	O	T	A	L		I	S	L	E
P	A	L	E	D		O	B	E	S	E		C	H	E	R

65

```
T I L T   A B O V E   F I J I
O D O R   B O R A X   L O O N
M A G I   A R E N T   O W E N
◊ S O N E S N O S E   W A Y S
    K L E E     N Y E
S C R E E D   U N D E R M Y ◊
O R A T E   G R E E N   I A N
R U N S   N A I A D   A L L A
E S C   P E N A L   M U L T I
◊ T H R O U G H   R E D E A L
    H E R     Z I T I
Q U A Y   O P P O S A B L E ◊
T R I M   S A O N E   L A T S
I D L E   I N N E R   E C R U
P U S S   S E E D S   S E E P
```

66

```
S P A T   M I K A D O   A G R
U R N S   G U N N E R   R O E
B O O K E M D A N N O   M E G
P R I E S T   V I A   S O S A
L A N D S   N E E D A L I F T
O T T   O V A   A R A R A T
T E S T   W I N G   O P E R A
    I T S F O R Y O U
S A U D I   S W E E   P I C A
E L N I N O   E N D   N O M
L I K E A R O C K   E L T O N
F E N D   S R O   O L E O L E
I N O   P I C K U P L I N E S
S E W   I N H E R E   L E S T
H E N   T O S S I N   A R T Y
```

67

```
S W A M   B O O M   S A B L E
O H I O   I S L E   T U T U S
D I D O   S L A T   E D E N S
  M A N W H O F E L L I N T O
    S H O     I L O
D S C   O P S   B L A T A N T
U P H O L S T E R Y   A M I R
N A I V E   E T A   S P I N E
E S N E   M A C H I N E N O W
S M A R T E D   E G O   O S S
    S R I     I R E
F U L L Y R E C O V E R E D
A L O E S   W O K E   E L A N
I N S E T   E C R U   C L I O
R A S P S   S O A P   T A S S
```

68

```
S O L A R A   F A T S   A S S
T H E F O G   I B E T   D R E
E D E R L E   R O N A   O I L
P A R O L E R E V E R S A L
P R E P S   I M E T   O N A N
E N D O   A S A   S U N N Y
    P A R E N T S T R I K E
A L P   B T U   S H A   E A T
C I R C U S P A T E N T
A F O O T   T R A   A L E R
P E D I   W A W A   S P I N E
  B U F F A L O P A W I N G S
D O C   I G O R   D O O G I E
R A E   E E N S   D O C E N T
Y T D   F R E T   S P A R E S
```

69

D	I	D	S	O	■	B	A	T	H	■	■	F	T	D
O	M	I	T	S	■	E	R	R	E	D	■	R	O	O
P	A	R	I	S	H	H	O	U	S	E	■	E	R	N
A	C	E	R	■	O	E	D	S	■	L	A	S	S	O
■	■	■	F	A	R	M	■	S	E	T	S	H	O	T
I	N	P	R	I	S	O	N	■	L	A	S	H	■	■
L	L	O	Y	D	■	T	E	S	S	■	T	E	N	D
E	E	L	■	A	S	H	H	E	A	P	■	R	O	E
T	R	I	S	■	A	S	I	T	■	A	M	B	L	E
■	■	S	H	U	N	■	S	U	N	V	I	S	O	R
S	C	H	O	L	A	R	■	P	O	E	T	■	■	■
I	N	H	O	T	■	A	S	S	N	■	C	Z	A	R
T	O	A	■	R	O	S	H	H	A	S	H	A	N	A
A	T	M	■	A	R	T	O	O	■	M	U	Z	A	K
R	E	S	■	■	Y	A	W	P	■	A	M	U	S	E

70

T	O	S	C	A	■	S	C	R	I	P	■	M	O	N
G	R	I	L	L	■	T	E	A	R	S	■	C	E	E
I	D	G	I	V	E	Y	O	U	M	Y	■	E	D	T
■	I	N	M	A	N	■	■	L	A	C	O	N	I	C
O	N	E	A	■	O	P	S	■	■	H	A	R	P	O
M	A	R	X	■	S	E	U	S	S	■	S	O	U	S
E	L	S	E	S	■	S	N	A	G	S	■	E	S	T
■	■	■	S	E	A	T	B	U	T	I	M	■	■	■
A	C	T	■	P	A	L	E	D	■	N	O	A	H	S
N	O	R	M	■	S	E	L	I	G	■	B	R	O	S
C	H	I	C	O	■	■	T	S	O	■	I	M	U	S
H	A	V	A	R	T	I	■	■	W	A	L	E	D	■
O	B	I	■	S	I	T	T	I	N	G	I	N	I	T
R	I	A	■	O	V	E	N	S	■	E	Z	I	N	E
S	T	L	■	N	O	R	T	H	■	R	E	A	I	M

71

S	O	L	O	N	G	■	G	O	T	T	A	R	U	N
T	R	I	B	A	L	■	O	K	A	Y	B	Y	M	E
R	A	M	O	N	A	■	P	I	C	K	I	E	S	T
A	T	P	E	A	C	E	■	E	K	E	D	■	■	■
T	O	E	■	■	E	E	R	■	■	E	B	B	S	■
A	R	R	A	Y	■	L	O	B	B	Y	■	E	Y	E
■	■	■	L	O	A	■	S	A	Y	O	N	A	R	A
F	A	M	O	U	S	L	A	S	T	W	O	R	D	S
A	U	R	E	V	O	I	R	■	E	L	L	■	■	■
I	R	E	■	E	N	D	I	T	■	S	O	B	E	R
L	A	D	S	■	■	O	A	K	■	■	A	V	E	■
■	■	■	A	D	D	S	■	S	A	T	I	R	E	S
H	A	S	B	E	E	N	S	■	B	I	S	T	R	O
I	S	U	R	E	C	A	N	■	O	N	E	A	L	L
T	I	M	E	T	O	G	O	■	B	Y	E	B	Y	E

72

O	R	C	A	S	■	R	A	P	■	W	E	A	V	E
N	E	A	T	O	■	I	K	E	■	O	L	L	I	E
E	L	B	O	W	■	V	I	N	E	R	I	P	E	N
T	A	B	L	E	T	E	N	N	I	S	■	■	■	■
W	I	E	L	D	E	R	■	■	R	E	A	D	E	R
O	D	D	■	■	T	R	I	K	E	■	G	I	V	E
■	■	■	D	R	A	N	O	■	Q	U	A	I	L	■
■	A	R	E	N	A	F	O	O	T	B	A	L	L	■
P	R	A	D	A	■	T	I	L	E	S	■	■	■	■
O	C	T	A	■	A	S	L	A	N	■	■	D	I	E
T	H	E	M	O	B	■	■	I	T	S	S	A	F	E
■	■	■	F	I	E	L	D	H	O	C	K	E	Y	■
B	U	B	B	L	E	G	U	M	■	P	R	O	V	O
O	H	A	R	A	■	A	L	A	■	H	A	T	E	R
P	S	H	A	W	■	D	U	N	■	S	P	A	R	E

73

```
C H O P . F O N Z . . C E L S
L I N A . U L E E S . U F O S
O A S T . R A T A T A T T A T
S T E R O L . L O V E . . .
E A T I N . S M O K E . L O U
S L S . E S T A T E S . E O N
. . G U L A G . . . E N Z O
H A P P Y B I R T H D A Y .
S E M S . . C A S E S . .
O L E . O N D A T E S . F E W
C L X . K O O L S . S T A R E
. S E C S . . S O B E R S
D I R T Y H A R R Y . I R A S
E V E L . E G G O N . R O T O
N E M O . . E S O S . D E A N
```

74

```
B O E R . A S S T D A . P T A
A R C O . H O O R A H . O O P
S A L A M A N D E R S . I T T
S C A R A B . O S E . O N A N
E L I E L . D I S M A N T L E
T E R R A C E . E L . I T E S
S S S . Y E A H . G O O D S
. . M I D D L E M A N . . .
S T R A D . S P A M . . T A S
T H E M E S . R E S C A L E
P E R M A N E N T . P O R T A
A S E A . A L A . B U N T E D
U P A . K I L I M A N J A R O
L O D . O L I V I A . O R E G
S T S . A S S E S S . B E D S
```

75

```
(T)H E . J A I . . I M P A C(T)
O I L W E L L . A R E A M A P
Y E S I S E E . M A N L E S S
. . N S C . (T)S Q U A R E
P A I G E . (T)O(T) . S C I
A N N E . (T)E N E(T) . E N D E
L A N D(T)A X . L O(T) . D I A
A C E(T)I C . P A(T)I O S
D I R . (T)I S . N O(T)M A N Y
E N C E . (T)A R O(T) . O N N O
. I V E . (T)U(T) . E B S E N
. C R O S S A(T) . E L I
L O C K S I N . B U E L L E R
A L L E A R S . A L G E B R A
(T)I E D Y E . D A Y . O A(T)
```

76

```
G T O S . U R S A . A B H O R
A O U T . R O A M . T R O V E
G O T O P L A N B . P A T E S
A T O L L . D E U C E . D R E
. . F E A S T . S R A . O D A
D U G . T H E C H I C A G O L
O N A L E A S H . P E W . . .
S O S A . T I C . . O S A Y
. . K E V . L O I S L A N E
S L E E V E L E S S T . L O S
T I N . I R A . T R E S S
E E C . L A N C E . N E A T O
A L O N E . D E L I O R D E R
M O R E Y . I L L S . T I M E
S W E D E . S T O P . A P P S
```

77

A	T	A	D	■	S	P	A	T	■	A	T	T	A	R
L	A	M	E	■	T	O	R	O	■	N	A	U	R	U
I	D	O	L	■	A	L	A	N	■	G	O	R	E	D
T	A	K	I	N	G	A	B	Y	T	E	■	N	A	Y
■	■	■	V	E	E	R	■	■	A	L	A	S	■	■
W	I	P	E	R	S	■	R	E	P	O	R	T	S	■
H	O	A	R	D	■	D	I	V	E	■	M	Y	T	H
I	N	C	■	S	L	I	V	E	R	S	■	L	E	E
P	I	K	E	■	A	M	E	N	■	O	P	E	R	A
■	C	O	A	S	T	E	R	■	N	U	R	S	E	D
■	■	F	R	A	T	■	■	P	I	S	A	■	■	■
I	L	L	■	N	E	V	E	R	S	A	Y	D	Y	E
R	A	Y	E	D	■	A	X	I	S	■	I	R	O	N
A	R	E	N	A	■	L	I	M	A	■	N	A	U	T
N	A	S	A	L	■	E	T	O	N	■	G	Y	R	O

78

W	H	E	W	■	E	C	O	L	■	O	S	K	A	R
R	O	A	R	■	N	O	R	A	■	P	U	N	N	Y
Y	E	T	I	■	D	R	E	W	■	E	M	O	T	E
■	■	■	T	U	R	N	O	N	A	N	A	X	I	S
I	T	S	T	R	U	E	■	■	B	E	T	■	■	■
T	U	N	E	I	N	T	O	M	O	R	R	O	W	■
N	S	Y	N	C	■	■	R	E	M	■	A	B	E	D
O	K	D	■	H	E	Y	B	A	B	Y	■	L	I	E
W	E	E	P	■	P	O	I	■	■	A	L	I	G	N
■	D	R	O	P	O	U	T	O	F	S	I	G	H	T
■	■	■	P	A	C	■	■	T	O	I	L	E	T	S
T	I	M	O	T	H	Y	L	E	A	R	Y	■	■	■
O	L	I	V	E	■	M	I	L	L	■	P	E	W	S
S	I	R	E	N	■	C	O	L	E	■	A	V	I	S
H	E	A	R	T	■	A	N	O	D	■	D	A	Z	E

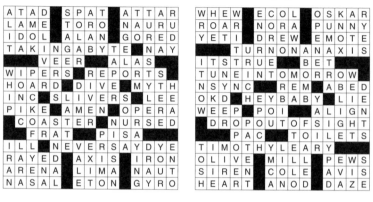

79

B	A	S	T	E	■	S	W	A	B	■	A	B	E	D
A	T	E	U	P	■	H	A	L	O	■	S	A	S	E
N	O	D	E	S	■	A	D	E	N	■	C	R	A	W
A	M	A	■	I	T	R	I	E	D	T	O	B	U	Y
N	I	K	O	L	A	I	■	■	A	R	T	■	■	■
A	C	A	M	O	U	F	L	A	G	E	S	U	I	T
■	■	■	A	N	T	■	A	M	E	X	■	T	O	E
F	E	A	R	■	■	S	P	Y	■	■	C	E	N	T
O	A	F	■	S	H	O	E	■	G	S	A	■	■	■
B	U	T	I	C	O	U	L	D	N	T	F	I	N	D
■	■	■	S	A	L	■	■	C	A	R	E	F	O	R
O	N	E	A	N	Y	W	H	E	R	E	■	T	M	I
S	E	R	A	■	C	O	I	L	■	T	E	H	E	E
L	A	I	C	■	O	R	E	L	■	C	L	E	A	R
O	R	E	S	■	W	E	D	S	■	H	I	N	T	S

80

P	I	S	A	■	A	T	B	A	T	■	A	T	A	D
I	D	E	S	■	C	O	R	P	S	■	R	A	B	E
T	I	C	K	L	E	P	I	N	K	■	I	C	U	S
T	E	T	E	A	T	E	T	E	■	L	A	H	T	I
■	■	■	D	Y	A	D	■	A	M	I	N	O	■	■
A	R	T	I	S	T	■	■	T	I	N	M	A	N	■
L	I	O	N	■	E	X	X	O	N	■	A	E	R	O
L	A	E	■	■	O	X	X	■	■	T	E	N	■	■
O	T	T	S	■	B	O	X	O	F	■	R	E	N	E
T	A	H	I	T	I	■	■	L	E	E	R	A	T	■
■	■	■	E	R	I	C	A	■	B	A	W	L	■	■
H	I	L	L	S	■	S	T	A	G	E	A	C	T	S
O	H	I	O	■	C	H	I	L	D	S	P	L	A	Y
J	O	N	I	■	S	E	L	M	A	■	S	A	L	S
O	P	E	N	■	A	N	T	S	Y	■	E	M	I	T

81

R	O	I	L	■	F	A	B	L	E	■	T	S	A	R
O	R	C	A	■	O	B	O	E	S	■	U	P	T	O
O	N	E	W	H	O	C	A	N	T	■	B	E	A	M
F	O	R	M	A	T	■	■	S	E	P	■	E	R	A
■	■	■	A	I	R	■	R	E	E	L	E	D	I	N
C	H	A	N	G	E	H	I	S	M	I	N	D	■	■
A	I	L	■	■	S	A	P	■	■	N	O	E	L	S
S	E	L	E	C	T	S	■	A	B	Y	S	M	A	L
E	D	D	I	E	■	■	A	P	E	■	■	O	N	O
■	■	A	N	D	W	O	N	T	C	H	A	N	G	E
B	I	Y	E	A	R	L	Y	■	L	E	M	■	■	■
I	L	L	■	■	R	I	D	■	■	O	R	A	T	E	S
B	I	O	S	■	T	H	E	S	U	B	J	E	C	T
L	A	N	K	■	H	A	T	E	D	■	O	T	O	E
E	D	G	Y	■	E	T	O	N	S	■	R	E	N	T

82

T	R	I	O	■	S	C	A	B	■	A	T	E	A	M
I	O	N	A	■	M	A	G	I	■	D	R	A	M	A
M	O	T	H	■	I	N	R	E	■	H	E	R	O	N
■	F	O	U	N	T	A	I	N	P	E	N	N	Y	■
■	■	■	O	E	D	■	N	E	R	D	■	■	■	■
B	U	R	R	O	■	A	F	I	R	E	■	C	B	S
A	S	I	A	N	S	■	L	A	I	■	H	A	I	L
B	A	S	K	E	T	B	A	L	L	F	A	N	N	Y
A	G	E	E	■	A	A	R	■	S	I	L	A	G	E
R	E	N	■	O	G	L	E	D	■	C	O	L	O	R
■	■	■	O	N	E	L	■	O	O	H	■	■	■	■
■	H	O	T	C	R	O	S	S	B	U	N	N	Y	■
P	A	S	T	A	■	O	K	I	E	■	E	A	V	E
E	T	H	E	L	■	N	U	N	S	■	A	P	E	X
P	E	A	R	L	■	S	A	G	E	■	T	E	S	T

83

*	C	O	R	N	E	R	S	■	C	A	M	E	R	*
T	O	P	S	I	D	E	S	■	H	O	U	S	E	D
O	U	T	T	H	E	R	E	■	O	N	U	S	E	S
T	R	I	■	I	N	E	■	I	C	E	M	E	N	■
H	A	M	E	L	■	A	M	O	K	■	U	N	T	O
A	G	A	R	■	E	D	I	T	■	D	U	C	E	S
T	E	L	L	E	R	■	M	A	T	E	■	E	R	S
■	■	■	E	N	D	R	E	S	U	L	T	■	■	■
M	C	S	■	D	E	U	T	■	S	L	A	L	O	M
R	A	T	S	O	■	M	I	C	H	■	R	O	N	I
I	M	A	C	■	B	O	C	A	■	D	O	W	E	L
■	P	R	A	Y	E	R	■	R	T	E	■	M	A	I
S	A	L	M	A	N	■	P	I	E	C	H	A	R	T
T	R	I	P	L	E	■	C	O	N	C	E	R	T	I
*	I	T	I	E	S	■	T	U	T	A	N	K	H	*

84

■	A	W	A	R	D	S	■	R	E	W	A	S	H	■
S	N	O	W	P	E	A	■	I	N	E	R	T	I	A
A	D	U	L	T	F	I	L	M	R	A	T	I	N	G
F	A	N	■	S	O	L	O	M	O	N	■	M	T	A
E	N	D	O	■	G	O	R	E	N	■	R	U	S	S
S	T	U	N	T	■	R	A	D	■	S	I	L	A	S
T	E	P	E	E	S	■	X	■	W	A	P	I	T	I
■	■	■	R	E	X	■	X	E	S	■	■	■	■	■
A	L	D	I	N	E	■	X	■	T	H	E	L	M	A
S	E	U	S	S	■	S	Y	D	■	A	R	E	A	S
H	O	S	T	■	P	A	L	O	S	■	A	G	E	S
A	N	T	■	S	I	L	E	N	T	B	■	A	W	E
R	O	M	A	N	N	U	M	E	R	A	L	T	E	N
P	R	O	D	U	C	T	■	E	E	R	I	E	S	T
■	A	P	O	G	E	E	■	S	P	I	N	E	T	■

* = Amen

85

E	R	A	S	■	S	L	O	E	■	A	L	E	T	A
L	O	S	E	A	T	U	R	N	■	B	E	S	O	T
M	U	S	T	S	A	V	E	V	A	S	T	S	U	M
S	E	N	S	O	R	■	S	I	D	E	B	E	T	S
■	■	■	N	E	O	■	E	R	N	E	■	■	■	■
P	A	G	E	G	A	W	K	S	A	T	■	W	H	O
E	D	A	M	■	T	E	A	■	W	E	A	R	O	N
T	A	M	M	I	■	N	Y	C	■	E	L	I	S	T
I	G	U	E	S	S	■	A	A	H	■	O	N	E	A
T	E	T	■	T	A	S	K	W	A	G	E	G	A	P
■	■	S	H	U	T	■	S	S	R	■	■	■	■	■
F	R	O	M	A	T	O	Z	■	B	I	G	T	E	N
A	E	R	A	T	E	P	I	P	E	T	A	R	E	A
S	P	A	R	S	■	I	N	S	E	S	S	I	O	N
T	O	N	T	O	■	N	E	I	N	■	P	O	C	O

86

S	P	A	R	■	I	N	F	O	■	■	M	I	C	A
C	A	N	I	■	P	O	E	M	■	M	C	C	O	Y
A	R	G	O	■	A	M	I	E	■	O	N	I	O	N
P	I	S	T	O	N	E	N	G	I	N	E	■	■	■
E	S	T	A	T	E	■	■	A	R	R	I	V	A	L
■	■	■	C	O	M	E	S	■	O	O	L	A	L	A
B	R	E	T	E	A	S	T	O	N	E	L	L	I	S
Y	E	A	■	■	■	P	E	N	■	■	■	L	E	I
F	I	R	S	T	O	N	E	T	O	B	L	I	N	K
A	N	N	E	A	L	■	P	O	L	I	O	■	■	■
R	E	S	E	L	L	S	■	■	D	A	W	N	E	D
■	■	■	H	E	A	R	T	O	F	S	T	O	N	E
R	A	V	E	N	■	T	O	D	O	■	I	T	A	L
E	X	E	R	T	■	A	F	I	G	■	D	I	C	E
P	E	T	E	■	S	U	E	Y	■	■	E	N	T	S

87

A	V	O	W	■	A	M	E	N	D	■	G	A	W	K
V	I	D	I	■	L	E	R	O	I	■	A	G	E	E
E	V	E	L	■	T	S	A	R	S	■	P	U	N	Y
R	O	A	D	T	E	S	T	■	G	R	E	A	T	S
■	■	■	I	M	R	E	■	D	U	O	■	■	■	■
E	V	A	D	E	■	D	A	Y	I	N	■	V	I	M
L	I	N	E	N	S	■	P	A	S	A	D	E	N	A
U	S	D	A	■	M	A	L	D	E	■	A	R	T	I
D	O	N	S	H	U	L	A	■	S	E	R	V	E	D
E	R	O	■	A	R	E	N	A	■	A	K	E	R	S
■	■	■	K	F	C	■	M	A	S	H	■	■	■	■
A	P	O	G	E	E	■	R	U	P	T	U	R	E	D
C	O	O	L	■	T	H	E	S	E	■	M	A	Z	E
M	O	P	E	■	T	U	N	E	R	■	O	K	R	A
E	L	S	E	■	E	N	T	R	Y	■	R	E	A	L

88

■	L	I	L	A	C	S	■	T	I	E	■	P	A	K
D	E	V	I	L	L	E	■	I	N	A	■	I	C	E
I	T	A	L	I	A	N	■	A	T	R	O	P	H	Y
C	N	N	■	Q	U	A	D	■	A	L	B	E	E	S
T	O	T	R	U	S	T	I	S	G	O	O	D	■	■
■	■	■	H	O	E	■	G	I	L	B	E	R	T	S
C	A	P	E	T	■	D	I	X	I	E	■	E	A	U
H	I	R	E	■	N	O	T	T	O	■	D	A	R	N
A	D	A	■	J	O	N	A	H	■	P	U	M	P	S
R	A	T	I	O	N	A	L	■	O	R	E	■	■	■
■	■	■	T	R	U	S	T	I	S	B	E	T	T	E	R
A	S	L	A	N	T	■	S	E	E	S	■	H	R	E
S	T	E	N	C	I	L	■	P	R	O	V	E	R	B
T	O	O	■	E	C	O	■	T	O	R	E	R	O	S
O	W	N	■	S	K	Y	■	A	N	T	L	E	R	■

89

F	R	A	U		B	A	K	E	D		C	O	L	E
R	E	V	S		O	X	I	D	E		A	V	I	V
E	G	O	S		R	E	T	I	E		F	A	Z	E
N	A	W		I	N	S	E	C	R	E	T			
C	L	E	A	N				T	E	N	A	B	L	E
H	E	R	C	U	L	E	S			O	N	I	O	N
			E	R	O	S	I	V	E			O	N	T
	S	I	D	E	S	P	L	I	T	T	I	N	G	
U	P	S		E	N	A	C	T	E	D				
R	I	N	G	S			S	E	A	L	E	D	U	P
I	N	T	E	N	S	E				L	A	Y	T	O
			T	O	P	S	T	O	R	Y		N	E	T
M	E	A	L		I	T	A	K	E		S	A	R	A
R	E	D	O		F	E	T	I	D		S	M	U	T
S	L	A	W		F	R	I	E	S		S	O	S	O

90

G	A	B	O	R		C	H	I	P		A	R	A	B
A	G	R	E	E		O	A	T	H		M	E	G	R
G	E	O	R	G	E	C	L	O	O		O	N	L	Y
A	D	A		A	S	O	F		N	E	S	T	E	A
		D	E	L	T	A		M	E	W		S	T	N
G	R	A	C	I	E		L	A	Y	E	R			
R	E	X	H	A	R	R	I	S		R	E	H	A	B
A	V	E	O		S	A	M	O	A		T	E	L	E
Y	E	S	E	S		B	E	N	S	T	I	L	L	E
			S	A	P	I	D		S	I	M	P	E	R
O	V	A		G	A	D		K	I	T	E	D		
R	E	G	I	O	N		P	I	S	A		E	S	P
B	R	A	N		F	A	L	L	I	N	G	S	T	A
E	N	I	D		R	A	U	L		I	N	K	E	R
D	E	N	Y		Y	A	M	S		C	U	S	P	S

91

P	A	N	G		A	B	O	M	B	S		S	E	A
A	M	O	R		R	E	B	A	L	E		A	X	L
Y	U	R	I	G	A	G	A	R	I	N		T	I	E
E	S	T	E	E	M		M	I	N	D	S	E	T	S
R	E	E	V	E		S	A	N	I	B	E	L		
			E	R	S	T			A	L	L	A	H	
B	A	S	S		A	R	E	S		C	L	I	V	E
A	M	P		S	P	U	T	N	I	K		T	O	W
R	O	A	S	T		T	A	O	S		S	E	W	N
D	I	C	T	A			R	H	E	E				
		E	A	R	H	A	R	T		L	A	S	S	O
F	E	R	N	D	A	L	E		S	I	L	T	E	D
E	R	A		A	L	A	N	S	H	E	P	A	R	D
T	I	C		T	E	N	D	T	O		U	R	G	E
A	C	E		E	N	D	S	U	P		P	E	E	R

92

D	O	T	E	D	U		S	M	E	E		D	O	M
A	V	O	W	A	L		H	I	L	L		E	N	O
P	A	R	E	N	T	H	E	S	E	S		N	E	V
			R	A	R	E		S	E	E	P	A	G	E
P	A	T			A	L	P	O			O	L	I	O
I	M	A	M	S		P	O	U	N	D	S	I	G	N
P	E	L	O	T	A		T	R	O	U	T			
E	X	C	L	A	M	A	T	I	O	N	M	A	R	K
			I	R	A	N	I		K	E	E	P	O	N
A	M	P	E	R	S	A	N	D		S	N	I	P	E
S	O	U	R			T	G	I	F			A	Y	E
S	C	R	E	E	C	H		S	E	A	S			
I	K	E		T	H	E	S	H	I	F	T	K	E	Y
S	E	E		N	E	M	O		G	R	E	E	N	E
I	D	S		A	W	A	Y		N	O	M	A	D	S

93

A	S	E	C		B	O	F	F	O		S	H	U	E
THE	L	M	A		S	M	OLD	E	R		H	E	R	MAN
N	A	I	R		I	N	E	R	T		R	I	G	A
S	P	L	E	N	D	I	D				B	I	N	E	T
		F	E	E	S		C	H	I	N	E	S	E	
A	Z	O	R	E	S		F	L	A	S	K			
H	O	W	E		C	L	A	R	O		S	S	W	
E	R	N	E	S	T	H	E	M	I	N	G	W	A	Y
M	A	S		T	I	E	U	P		I	A	M	S	
		S	I	T	A	R		C	H	U	T	E	S	
E	G	O	T	R	I	P		B	A	I	L			
R	I	L	E	S		E	G	G	T	I	M	E	R	
R	V	E	R		R	E	S	I	N		A	C	M	E
AND	E	A	N		E	A	THE	R	E		N	A	U	SEA
S	S	N	S		C	U	R	L	Y		I	N	S	T

94

A	M	S		S	W	A	M	I		B	O	O	Z	E
C	A	P	I	T	A	L	O	F	F	E	N	S	E	S
T	H	E	D	E	F	E	N	S	E	R	E	S	T	S
O	R	L	E				A	T	E		A	A	A	
R	E	L	A	P	S		A	Y	E	A	R			
			A	U	L	D				E	L	S	A	
A	D	M	I	S	S	I	O	N	T	O	B	A	I	L
C	O	U	R	T	A	P	P	E	A	R	A	N	C	E
M	O	T	I	O	N	S	T	O	S	T	R	I	K	E
E	R	E	S			E	S	S	E					
		H	I	R	E	D		E	A	S	T	L	A	
A	L	G		V	I	M				T	I	O	S	
J	U	R	Y	O	F	O	N	E	S	P	E	E	R	S
E	X	P	E	R	T	T	E	S	T	I	M	O	N	Y
T	E	S	T	Y		E	S	Q	U	E		N	E	R

95

S	C	O	T	S		I	M	A	C	S		A	S	H
C	O	U	R	T		M	A	R	I	S		N	E	A
U	N	T	I	E	D	F	R	O	N	T		T	A	J
B	A	B	B	L	E		C	D	E		S	O	L	I
A	N	Y		L	A	S	H		P	A	I	N		
		M	A	R	T	I	A	L	B	L	I	S	S	
D	A	T	A		E	N	D	E	A	V	O	R	S	
I	N	H	U	M	A	N		E	X	T	E	N	T	S
A	N	A	L	O	G	O	U	S		R	I	A	S	
L	A	N	D	I	N	G	S	T	I	E	S			
		K	I	L	O		H	E	L	D		R	I	M
G	W	Y	N		S	U	E		U	B	O	A	T	S
L	A	O		I	T	S	R	E	V	E	R	S	E	D
I	C	U		V	I	D	E	O		R	E	T	R	O
B	O	S		S	C	A	D	S		G	L	A	S	S

96

N	E	W	M	A	N		O	N	T	H	E	W	A	Y
E	X	H	U	M	E		P	I	R	A	N	H	A	S
W	H	E	R	E	T	H	E	B	O	Y	S	A	R	E
S	I	N	I	S	T	E	R		N	E	U	T	E	R
		L	I	A		V	E	A	L		S	R	I	
N	A	F	T	A		P	T	A	S		E	N	D	O
I	R	A	I	S	E		E	N	O	S		T	E	X
S	A	L	C	H	O	W		E	L	E	V	A	T	E
A	T	L		E	N	I	D		D	E	L	R	A	Y
N	E	I	L		S	P	E	C		D	A	N	C	E
		N	I	A		E	E	R	O		D	A	H	
A	R	L	E	N	E		P	E	R	M	I	T	M	E
W	H	O	N	E	E	D	S	E	N	E	M	I	E	S
L	I	V	E	A	L	I	E		O	N	I	O	N	S
S	N	E	E	R	S	A	T		T	U	R	N	T	O

97

B	O	U	L	D	E	R	■	■	B	A	R	R	E	D
O	N	S	E	C	O	N	D	■	A	P	I	E	C	E
L	E	G	A	L	E	S	E	■	R	E	V	S	U	P
D	I	R	K	■	■	■	S	O	D	S	■	T	A	R
E	R	A	■	B	A	S	E	D	■	■	B	O	D	E
R	O	N	■	A	L	E	X	E	I	■	O	R	O	S
■	N	T	E	S	T	S	■	■	S	E	W	E	R	S
■	■	I	T	E	S	■	B	A	L	E	■	■	■	■
B	O	R	D	E	R	■	A	B	I	D	E	S	■	■
O	B	O	E	■	S	O	V	I	E	T	■	N	I	S
A	S	T	R	■	■	V	I	L	L	E	■	T	N	T
R	C	A	■	B	E	A	T	■	■	■	B	E	A	R
D	U	T	I	E	S	■	A	L	A	C	A	R	T	E
E	R	O	D	E	S	■	L	A	B	O	R	E	R	S
R	E	R	A	T	E	■	P	O	S	E	D	A	S	■

98

R	A	I	S	E	■	E	N	Y	A	■	F	R	O	M
U	N	C	L	E	■	B	E	E	T	■	O	I	L	S
S	T	E	A	L	■	R	U	S	T	I	N	M	E	T
H	E	A	T	E	R	O	F	W	A	R	T	■	■	■
T	U	X	E	D	O	■	■	E	C	O	■	E	S	L
O	P	E	■	■	A	D	A	■	K	N	I	G	H	T
■	■	■	C	A	S	A	B	A	■	I	L	I	A	D
■	S	T	A	R	T	T	O	F	I	N	I	S	H	■
R	E	A	L	M	■	A	V	E	N	G	E	■	■	■
E	X	P	E	L	S	■	O	W	L	■	■	L	O	U
D	Y	E	■	O	K	S	■	A	C	T	O	U	T	■
■	■	■	R	A	I	L	W	A	Y	S	B	U	S	T
E	N	D	E	D	B	A	R	T	■	P	O	N	T	E
S	U	L	A	■	U	V	E	A	■	A	N	G	E	R
Q	T	I	P	■	M	E	N	D	■	N	E	E	D	S

99

Q	B	S	■	A	T	L	A	N	T	A	■	J	A	X
U	A	E	■	S	H	O	W	B	I	Z	■	A	L	F
E	R	R	■	P	A	G	E	A	N	T	■	R	P	I
S	T	E	V	E	N	■	■	S	E	A	G	A	L	■
T	O	N	E	R	■	A	S	H	■	C	R	O	C	E
S	K	A	T	■	I	M	P	E	L	■	U	N	A	S
■	■	■	E	A	S	T	E	R	E	G	G	■	■	■
C	H	A	R	L	E	S	D	E	G	A	U	L	L	E
R	E	B	A	T	E	■	■	O	I	L	I	E	R	■
A	M	I	N	O	■	P	I	C	■	T	A	B	O	O
M	I	T	■	S	A	S	H	A	■	■	E	N	S	■
■	■	■	M	A	R	C	C	H	A	G	A	L	L	■
F	O	U	L	O	U	T	■	S	I	M	I	L	A	R
E	N	C	L	O	S	E	■	E	L	E	V	A	T	E
B	A	H	A	M	E	N	■	R	E	N	E	W	E	D

100

M	A	V	E	N	■	I	N	F	R	A	■	G	U	T
E	D	I	N	A	■	M	O	R	O	N	■	O	N	E
G	E	T	T	H	E	P	B	O	U	T	■	F	T	D
A	S	A	R	U	L	E	■	S	T	E	R	O	I	D
■	■	■	E	M	I	R	A	T	E	■	O	R	L	Y
W	I	S	E	■	Z	I	G	S	■	R	U	T	■	■
I	B	N	■	S	A	A	B	■	A	S	H	E	S	■
L	A	P	S	E	■	L	E	W	■	S	E	E	T	O
D	R	A	W	N	■	■	L	A	S	H	■	A	A	A
■	■	N	E	T	■	F	L	I	P	■	T	U	S	K
U	R	A	L	■	G	O	S	T	A	L	E	■	■	■
P	I	L	L	A	R	S	■	S	C	O	F	F	A	T
P	A	L	■	C	A	S	T	F	E	■	A	L	I	B	I
E	T	E	■	E	I	E	I	O	■	M	O	V	I	E
R	A	Y	■	S	L	Y	E	R	■	S	N	E	E	R

101

O	N	E		G	H	O	S	T	S		N	O	T
R	A	N		R	A	N	T	E	D		A	L	S	O
O	U	T		E	M	C	E	E	S		T	E	S	T
S	T	O	R	Y		R	P	M		T	H	R	E	E
	I	S	L	E	S		I	O	R					
B	A	R	S		I	D	O		S	P	O	R	T	S
E	L	E	E		P	I	N		R	O	B	E	R	T
F	I	T		D	S	T		O	A	F		S	E	E
O	C	A	S	E	Y		A	P	E		S	E	A	N
G	E	R	M	A	N		R	E	L		W	E	S	T
		I	N	C		S	N	I	P	E				
A	P	P	L	E		P	E	A		A	D	A	M	S
N	O	S	E		H	E	N	R	Y	I		B	Y	A
O	K	A	Y		E	N	A	M	E	L		I	T	S
N	E	T		S	A	L	S	A	S		T	H	E	

102

C	U	R	B		U	F	O	S		P	A	S	T
A	S	E	A		N	I	V	E	A		O	P	I	E
B	E	D	S		S	L	U	E	S		E	P	E	E
	W	H	A	T		I	M	P	L	E	M	E	N	T
A	M	I		L	O	G		E	O	N		N	A	H
C	A	N	B	E	P	R	O	D	U	C	E	D		
E	G	G	Y		S	E	R		D	L	X			
R	I	S	E	S		E	F	S		S	I	B	Y	L
		A	H	S		E	E	R		T	R	O	Y	
	F	R	O	M	P	O	T	A	S	S	I	U	M	
A	L	I		N	I	L		A	D	S		A	R	E
N	I	C	K	E	L	A	N	D	I	R	O	N		
I	C	K	Y		E	N	I	A	C		F	E	A	R
T	I	L	L		D	E	L	T	A		I	N	R	E
A	T	E	E			R	E	E	L		T	O	T	E

103

A	D	A	G	E				B	R	O	O	M	S
R	E	P	L	A	N		F	A	U	X	P	A	S
R	E	P	O	S	E		S	I	D	E	L	I	N	E
	P	O	W	E	R	S	T	E	E	R	I	N	G	
I	F	I		D	U	O		S	P	I	E	L		
S	A	N	D	L		E	R	S	E		O	R	E	
O	T	T	O	I	V		M	A	X	E	R	N	S	T
		W	A	S	H	C	Y	C	L	E				
A	I	R	D	R	O	M	E		H	U	M	E	R	I
S	H	E		P	O	N	Y		L	O	C	O	S	
H	A	D	J	I		T	A	O			H	S	T	
	T	R	U	S	T	M	E	O	N	T	H	I	S	
M	E	E	I	T	H	E	R		C	R	E	D	I	T
D	I	S	C	O	R	D		D	I	A	N	N	E	
I	T	S	Y	O	U				B	R	A	I	N	

104

O	T	I	S		G	E	O	G		A	T	M	E
D	U	C	T		A	R	I	E	S		S	W	U	M
E	R	E	I		M	I	L	N	E		H	I	S	S
T	B	A	L	L	E	Q	U	I	P	M	E	N	T	
T	A	X	T	I	P		P	E	T	E		B	A	Y
A	N	E		E	L	I			T	B	O	N	E	
		S	T	A	T	O	R	S		E	R	G	S	
	T	B	O	O	N	E	P	I	C	K	E	N	S	
A	U	R	A		S	M	E	A	R	E	R			
T	B	A	R	S			L	A	Y		T	B	S	
H	E	M		A	D	A	B		P	T	B	O	A	T
	T	B	I	L	I	S	I	G	E	O	R	G	I	A
C	O	L	D		R	I	L	E	S		U	G	L	Y
E	P	E	E		K	A	B	O	B		S	L	O	E
E	S	S	O		N	O	S	Y		H	E	R	D	

105

```
S W E D E   A L F I E   S R I
M I X E D G R E E N S A L A D
O R A N G E M A R M A L A D E
G E M   E N O S   Y U P P I E
      T R E K   E S O S
A S T I R     R I D E S
G H A N A   I S O U R   A M I
R A I N B O W   S H E R B E T
A W L   B J O R K   C H U T E
      D I O N E   T O T E M
C R E W   T V A D
O U T E A T   E R A S   A D O
B L U E B E R R Y M U F F I N
R E D B E A N S A N D R I C E
A D E   D R A I N   S I T E S
```

106

```
B I T S   E W E R   V I S O R
A C H E   D O M E   E R O D E
C O R P   G O E S   N I X E D
K N O T T E D R O P E S
    S E E R   A L O E   M A O
      T A N G L E D R O O T S
A S P   M E A D     L O B O
F A U X P A S   B A D D E A L
A X L E     A E R O   D Y E
T O S S E D G R E E N S
E N E   L I A R   O U R S
      A D D L E D B R A I N S
I S S U E   L A I R   B L A H
Q U A D S   U R G E   L E G O
S P L I T   P S S T   E S S O
```

107

```
D A N C E   S P E A K   U F O
U S A I R   C A P R A   P O W
S T I N G S A L A R Y   T R E
T A L C   O R E   A S H E N
    H E O F D A R K N E S S
A R D E N T   R E S O R T
N O I S Y   S I M P   W I F E
T A N   A R T L E S S   V I M
E D N A   A U L D   A L E R T
  R E M A N D   S N O R E S
S U R P R I S E P I E S
A N D S O   V A L   E A R P
R N A   M I N I G L A S S E S
G E T   A G A T E   B I T E S
E R E   S O N A R   S T I L T
```

108

```
  B B L S   H E R A   C A N A
L E R O I   A L O T   A[LAM]O S
I D I N G   D O N T B[LAM]E M E
C[LAM]M I N G U P   N O I D E A
      P O P E S   S T A N
A S K F O R   T O N Y
I T A L S   C[LAM]O R   J A K E
M Y L I T T L E R U N A W A Y
S E E M   B O D Y   O N R Y E
    F R A T   G R E Y E D
  A F[LAM]E   H A R E M
A L U M N A   P I E A[LAM]O D E
S T R E E T[LAM]P S   R E M A P
S H O R   T A L E   A N I T A
T O R Y   Y S E R   E T T A
```

109

E	D	I	T		R	E	A	M		N	A	C	R	E
B	E	L	A		E	L	S	E		O	B	O	E	S
B	ARM	I	T	Z	V	A	H	S		B	L	E	E	P
S	E	E	T	O	I	T		A	L	LEG	E	D	L	Y
		L	O	V	E	D		E	A	R				
I	N	T	I	M	E		E	M	T	S		B	I	B
L	O	A	N		O	F	A	G	E		U	F	O	
I	T	S	G	O	N	N	A	C	O	S	T	Y	O	U
A	S	K		S	T	I	C	K		H	I	L	T	
D	O	S		C	E	N	T		S	P	E	N	D	S
	W	ARM	S		O	A	T	E	N					
T	A	X	R	A	T	E		P	A	G	O	D	A	S
O	H	B	O	Y		C	I	R	C	LEG	R	A	P	H
S	M	O	T	E		O	K	O	K		T	R	E	E
H	E	X	E	R		L	E	N	S		H	E	R	D

110

K	E	B	A	B		U	N	I		E	A	R	L	E
I	N	A	I	R		P	I	K	E	S	P	E	A	K
D	D	D	M	O	N	S	T	E	R	M	O	V	I	E
	S	K	I	E	R		T	E	K					
A	P	T		A	C	T	O	N	E		E	B	B	S
M	O	H	A	W	K		O	S	E		I	I	I	
P	O	W	S		E	T	A	T		N	I	K	O	N
H	H	H	C	L	U	B	M	E	E	T	I	N	G	
O	B	I	E	S		T	E	E	M		A	N	I	L
R	A	T		I	S	E			B	E	N	I	C	E
A	H	E	M		T	E	A	T	A	X		S	S	T
	C	S	A		S	O	R	T	S					
K	K	K	K	K	K	K	K	K	R	A	C	E	S	
L	A	F	A	Y	E	T	T	E		A	C	U	T	E
M	A	C	Y	S		S	O	N		S	K	E	E	T

111

W	A	S	N	T		P	I	T	A		L	A	P	P
A	L	L	A	H		A	B	O	U		O	S	L	O
S	I	A	M	E	SET	W	I	N	S		SET	S	I	N
H	E	T	E	R	O		D	E	P	O	R	T	E	D
		S	O	U	P		D	I	V	A				
A	D	V		S	T	A	B		C	A	C	K	L	E
D	E	I	C	E		P	A	C	E		K	E	E	L
E	C	R	U		P	E	SET	A	S		O	P	A	L
A	C	A	R		O	R	E	M		A	F	I	R	E
F	A	L	SET	T	O		N	E	R	D		S	Y	N
	H	A	R	P		L	O	A	M					
B	O	X	E	D	S	E	T		A	M	E	R	C	E
A	V	I	D		H	O	R	SET	R	A	D	E	R	S
N	I	N	A		O	N	I	T		N	I	P	A	T
E	D	G	Y		T	Y	P	O		T	A	S	T	E

112

R	E	H	A	B		O	N	K	P		K	E	E	P
A	V	I	L	A		P	E	A	R		N	A	P	E
T	E	N	A	D	D	E	D	T	O	S	E	V	E	N
E	N	D		G	U	N	S		P	E	W	E	E	S
		M	I	N	E		T	H	E	O				
H	U	N	D	R	E	D	O	V	E	R	F	O	U	R
A	T	O	L	L		L	A	S	S		D	R	E	
Y	E	T	I		D	A	D	D	Y		R	I	I	S
O	R	I		H	U	M	E		P	E	N	C	E	
F	I	F	T	Y	M	I	N	U	S	E	I	G	H	T
	H	A	M	S		N	U	N	N					
S	M	A	R	T	Y		M	I	R	A		E	V	A
F	I	V	E	T	I	M	E	S	E	L	E	V	E	N
P	L	E	A		N	O	G	O		T	R	E	N	T
D	O	S	T		G	M	A	N		Y	A	R	D	S

113

```
C H A D   A R L O     S T A B
H O P I   N E A R   S H O R E
A J A X   T A R A   I O N I A
P O L I T I C A L S C R I P T
    E A C H     H S T
C R O C U S   R E A   A C D C
R E D U G   S E L M A   H U H
O L D P H O N E S E R V I C E
W E E   T H O S E   C E L T S
N E R O   A W E   R A R E S T
    D A R   A U D I
H A V E W E M E T B E F O R E
I G E T A   I D O L   I N O N
P A R T Y   L I N E   E B A N
S R T A   E T E S   D Y N E
```

114

```
L O O K B E T T E R     B E T A
U N D E R S C O R E     U R A L
G E E Y A T H I N K     R I D E
E A R L I E R     I P E C A C
  S N I D E   V O N D A
    E M S   M I N D F U L L Y
A B I E   E A S E L S   I O U
C O S     A D A T E     V A R
D I S   U S A G E S   C E N T
C L E R G Y M E N   P R O
    C L A E S   J O I N T
T E T R I S     N O N S T O P
O A H U   A N T I C I P A T E
P R O M   B O O K K E E P E R
S N U B   C R O S S D R E S S
```

115

```
L I C E N S E F E E   O B I S
E T H N I C V O T E   L A D A
G O A T C H E E S E   D C L I
G O N E   O R S   W I N K E D
    R A T S   A I M A T
V I S I T O R S D U G O U T
D E T O X   S U I T S   B R O
A S S N   T O R A H   M A G S
U P A   O R R I N   R I C E S
B A L L P A R K F R A N K S
    L O U S Y   U E Y S
O H G O S H   U S D   T O A T
R O O K   B A S I C T R U T H
G L O M   A R T O O D E T O O
Y A D A   G R A N D S L A M S
```

116

```
Q A N D A   S T E E R S M A N
U S E A S   T R A D E N A M E
I P O D S   A U T O P I L O T
B E N E T   T A I   P A R T
B R A   S C E N T E D   G A L
L I T E   A F C   N O S A L E
E T A L   D A Y T O N A
S Y L L A B I   R U S T L E R
    E X U R B A N   B O N O
I R O N E R   A N C   Y O G A
N A N   S Y O S S E T   K I D
S I L T   A K A   A H I N T
I D I O M A T I C   R E N E E
S E N T I M E N T   P A T E S
T R E E R I N G S   S P O R T
```

117

	Y	O	U	O	K		S	T	E	M	L	E	S	S
B	E	R	N	I	E		C	O	R	S	E	L	E	T
L	A	D	I	D	A		U	N	I	Q	U	E	L	Y
A	H	E	M			A	D	I	E	U		M	A	X
S	I	R	P	A	U	L			S	A	W			
E	M	B	R	I	T	T	L	E		D	R	U	S	E
	F	L	E	S	H	I	E	S	T		O	N	E	A
B	I	A	S		E	M	O	T	E		N	L	A	T
I	N	N	S		R	A	N	R	A	G	G	E	D	
P	E	K	E	S		S	E	A	S	O	N	T	W	O
			D	T	S		D	E	P	U	T	E	S	
P	O	I		P	O	D	I	A			M	A	L	T
S	A	N	T	E	R	I	A		P	O	B	B	L	E
S	T	R	A	T	T	O	N		D	U	E	L	E	R
T	H	E	B	E	A	R	S		F	I	R	E	R	

118

F	A	T	S	W	A	L	L	E	R			W	E	B	S
I	G	E	T	A	R	O	U	N	D		A	Q	U	A
R	E	N	O	N	E	V	A	D	A		L	U	S	T
E	L	O	P	E		E	N	L	S		L	I	L	I
F	I	N	S		B	I	D	E			F	A	R	
O	N	E		D	Y	N	A	S	T		J	A	N	E
X	E	R	O	X	E	S		S	I	L	E	X	E	S
		W	I	N			L	O	S					
Z	I	L	L	I	O	N		A	T	A	T	I	M	E
H	M	O	S		W	E	E	D	E	D		N	O	N
I	E	S			P	R	O	D		L	U	N	G	
V	A	T	S		S	T	E	P		S	I	T	K	A
A	N	A	T		A	U	C	T	I	O	N	E	E	R
G	I	R	L		I	N	T	E	R	F	E	R	E	D
O	T	T	O		D	E	S	E	R	T	R	O	S	E

119

M	Y	S	P	A	C	E			G	O	S	S	I	P
I	O	M	O	T	H	S		R	E	D	W	I	N	E
S	K	I	P	O	U	T		O	N	E	F	L	A	T
S	O	T		P	G	A	T	O	U	R		E	P	I
T	O	T	O		S	T	A	T	S		S	N	I	T
E	N	E	M	Y		E	R	E		T	I	T	L	E
P	O	N	I	E	S		T	R	O	U	N	C	E	S
		G	A	L	L		S	A	N	A				
I	M	N	O	T	Y	O	U		T	I	T	H	E	S
D	R	E	S	S		V	C	R		C	R	E	P	T
E	S	T	H		B	E	L	O	W		A	R	I	D
A	L	F		H	A	S	A	C	O	W		E	T	E
M	A	L	A	I	S	E		K	R	A	T	I	O	N
E	T	I	C	K	E	T		O	R	I	G	A	M	I
N	E	X	T	E	L			N	Y	T	I	M	E	S

120

S	Q	U	E	E	G	E	E	S		O	H	W	O	W
A	U	S	T	R	A	L	I	A		D	U	A	N	E
N	O	N	E	A	T	A	L	L		I	N	I	T	S
E	T	A	S		E	Y	E	S		E	A	T	I	T
R	E	V			S	N	E	A	D		N	A	P	E
	D	Y	E	R		E	N	D	U	P		S	T	R
		N	O	S		S	I	M	O	L	E	O	N	
B	I	G	T	A	L	K		P	A	L	A	C	E	S
O	V	E	R	D	O	N	E		S	O	S			
R	E	T		S	P	A	M	S		S	T	I	R	
A	H	A	T		S	P	O	T	S			N	O	B
B	A	L	E	S		S	T	E	P		A	B	B	Y
O	D	I	S	T		A	I	R	I	N	G	O	U	T
R	I	F	L	E		C	O	N	C	O	U	R	S	E
A	T	E	A	M		K	N	E	E	P	A	N	T	S

121

I	N	A	S	P	O	T	■	■	C	A	N	T	B	E
C	A	R	A	L	A	R	M	■	R	C	C	O	L	A
I	B	E	F	O	R	E	E	■	I	C	A	R	U	S
C	O	N	E	Y	■	E	D	A	M	■	A	N	E	T
L	B	A	R	■	X	F	I	L	E	S	■	I	R	E
E	S	S	■	S	C	O	U	T	S	H	O	N	O	R
■	■	S	T	O	R	M	■	C	O	S	T	A	S	■
■	P	O	I	R	O	T	■	L	E	T	S	O	N	■
S	I	F	T	E	R	■	S	A	N	A	A	■	■	■
O	N	T	H	E	D	O	C	K	E	T	■	P	I	S
D	E	T	■	P	I	X	I	E	S	■	S	A	N	E
A	C	I	D	■	N	O	P	E	■	S	K	I	D	S
P	O	M	O	N	A	■	I	R	S	A	U	D	I	T
O	N	E	S	E	T	■	O	I	L	G	A	U	G	E
P	E	S	T	L	E	■	■	E	Y	E	S	P	O	T

122

D	E	N	S	E	F	O	G	■	A	P	L	O	M	B
E	X	I	T	L	A	N	E	■	P	R	E	M	I	E
B	E	N	E	D	I	C	T	■	T	E	N	A	N	T
S	C	O	R	E	L	E	S	S	■	S	T	R	U	T
■	■	■	O	S	S	■	C	E	L	S	■	S	T	E
S	P	L	I	T	■	S	A	D	I	E	■	H	E	R
L	E	A	D	■	S	P	R	A	T	S	■	A	M	I
E	A	T	S	■	H	A	R	T	E	■	B	R	A	D
E	S	E	■	D	O	R	I	E	S	■	E	I	R	E
P	H	I	■	E	A	R	E	D	■	K	A	F	K	A
T	E	N	■	C	L	O	D	■	M	A	S	■	■	■
I	L	L	E	R	■	W	A	T	E	R	P	I	P	E
G	L	I	D	E	R	■	W	A	R	Z	O	N	E	S
H	E	F	N	E	R	■	A	P	I	A	R	I	E	S
T	R	E	A	D	S	■	Y	A	T	I	T	T	L	E

123

L	E	A	V	E	S	A	B	A	D	T	A	S	T	E
A	R	T	A	P	P	R	E	C	I	A	T	I	O	N
B	Y	T	R	I	A	L	A	N	D	E	R	R	O	R
■	■	A	M	C	■	O	M	E	N	■	O	R	T	O
L	E	G	I	S	T	■	■	T	U	P	E	L	O	■
A	G	I	N	■	E	K	E	S	■	S	H	E	E	T
T	O	R	T	■	T	I	N	A	F	E	Y	■	■	■
E	S	L	■	F	O	N	D	L	E	D	■	A	L	A
■	■	G	O	N	D	O	L	A	■	I	R	I	S	■
F	R	E	R	E	■	A	W	E	S	■	M	M	E	S
R	A	R	E	S	T	■	■	T	O	E	O	U	T	■
I	M	I	N	■	R	I	C	E	■	M	A	R	■	■
E	S	C	A	P	E	M	E	C	H	A	N	I	S	M
D	E	A	D	A	S	A	D	O	O	R	N	A	I	L
A	S	S	E	S	S	M	E	N	T	R	O	L	L	S

124

A	S	B	A	D	A	S	B	A	D	C	A	N	B	E
T	H	E	R	E	Y	O	U	G	O	A	G	A	I	N
L	I	T	T	L	E	O	R	N	O	T	H	I	N	G
■	M	A	S	T	■	T	R	I	M	■	A	V	G	S
■	■	■	C	Y	S	■	■	I	S	E	E	■	■	■
F	A	J	I	T	A	■	■	P	I	C	■	■	■	■
O	V	E	R	A	N	D	D	O	N	E	W	I	T	H
A	I	R	A	M	E	R	I	C	A	R	A	D	I	O
M	A	K	E	A	R	E	S	O	L	U	T	I	O	N
■	■	L	S	D	■	■	I	N	T	O	N	E	■	■
■	P	L	I	E	■	■	E	K	E	■	■	■	■	■
B	A	I	N	■	K	A	N	E	■	J	O	A	D	■
L	I	B	E	R	A	L	D	E	M	O	C	R	A	T
A	N	Y	P	O	R	T	I	N	A	S	T	O	R	M
S	E	A	T	T	L	E	S	E	A	H	A	W	K	S

125

G	O	F	O	R	A	D	I	P			S	O	P	O	R
A	B	O	R	I	G	I	N	E			C	L	A	R	O
V	E	R	K	L	E	M	P	T			A	S	S	A	Y
A	R	T	I	E			M	R	T			L	O	T	T	A
G	O	W	N			Q	E	I	I			E	N	R	O	L
E	N	O			T	U	R	N	E	R			A	R	I	
			A	H	A			T	S	U	N	A	M	I	S
A	M	B	I	E	N	T			T	S	E	L	I	O	T
Q	U	I	X	O	T	I	C			H	A	L			
U	S	A			A	M	U	L	E	T			R	A	J
A	S	S	A	D			E	R	A	S			M	E	T	O
T	E	T	R	A			L	A	O			G	A	T	O	S
I	D	I	O	T			A	C	T	S	A	L	O	N	E
C	U	R	S	E			G	A	Z	A	S	T	R	I	P
S	P	E	E	D			S	O	U	L	P	A	T	C	H

126

S	T	O	P	S	I	N			Q	U	I	V	I	V	E
H	O	P	I	N	T	O			U	N	M	O	R	A	L
I	R	E	P	E	A	T			A	C	U	T	E	L	Y
A	N	N	E	E			A	F	R			S	E	L	E	S
T	O	S	S			B	R	U	T	E			D	A	R	E
S	U	E			F	R	I	Z	Z	L	E			N	I	E
U	T	A	H	J	A	Z	Z			E	L	U	D	E	S
				M	O	N	E	Y	B	A	G	S			
R	E	C	O	R	D			M	E	N	I	S	C	U	S
E	P	A			D	E	C	A	G	O	N			R	K	O
N	I	L	E			D	O	T	E	R			B	A	R	N
E	T	O	N	S			A	H	N			C	O	N	A	N
G	O	R	E	T	E	X			T	W	I	N	K	I	E
E	M	I	R	A	T	E			L	A	R	G	E	N	T
D	E	C	O	Y	E	D			E	N	C	O	D	E	S

127

A	C	T	F	O	R			P	R	I	C	E	T	A	G
M	A	H	A	L	O			R	I	G	H	T	A	R	M
O	P	E	N	E	R			E	C	L	E	C	T	I	C
R	I	C			G	Y	M	S	H	O	E	S			
A	T	R	A			A	U	T	O	S			S	H	H
L	A	U	G	H	A	T	M	E			E	A	P	O	E
		S	O	U	T	H	E	R	N	C	R	O	S	S	
C	H	A	R	G	E				D	A	N	T	E	S	
M	A	D	A	M	E	S	P	E	A	K	E	R			
D	I	E	S	E			P	I	C	K	E	T	E	R	S
R	R	S			T	O	U	G	H			T	M	E	N
			D	I	R	T	P	O	O	R			O	D	A
A	B	R	O	G	A	T	E			D	O	O	V	E	R
H	E	I	G	H	T	E	N			D	O	T	E	L	L
S	T	P	E	T	E	R	S			S	T	O	R	M	Y

128

C	B	S			C	O	L	T			U	T	A	H	A	N
O	R	A	T	O	R	I	O			N	O	S	A	L	E
A	U	T	O	M	A	T	E			C	O	S	S	E	T
S	N	A	P	P	L	E			C	O	L	I	N		
T	O	N	G	A			B	O	N			S	O	L	E
			U	N	I	V	E	R	S	I	T	I	E	S	
R	A	I	N	Y	S	E	A	S	O	N			D	A	S
E	D	S			M	A	R	S	A	L	A			E	R	A
T	I	O			E	A	S	T	G	E	R	M	A	N	Y
R	E	C	O	N	C	I	L	E	D	T	O				
Y	U	R	I			H	O	Y			I	D	E	S	T
			A	L	B	A	N			C	A	S	E	L	A	W
A	R	T	E	R	Y			D	O	C	T	R	I	N	E
C	H	E	R	I	E			N	O	M	I	N	A	T	E
T	O	S	S	E	S			A	L	E	C			S	A	D

129

	S	H	A	G	C	A	R	P	E	T	S		
	S	T	E	P	T	O	T	H	E	R	E	A	R
C	H	A	R	L	O	T	T	E	A	M	A	L	I	E
H	I	N	D	U	S		R	A	N	A	R	A	C	E
A	N	D	E	S		Z	A	S	U		I	D	O	L

SHAGCARPETS / STEPTOTHEREAR / CHARLOTTEAMALIE / HINDUS RANARACE / ANDES ZASU IDOL / IBID DOC TSE / TON UINTA ASMAD / ENGARDE MIXTAPE / AEONS DAMME LPS / TAE TAP WALK / HOPE XMEN HAYES / URICACID GYRATE / TELEVISIONPILOT / MEDITERRANEAN / DESERTSTORM

130

BANANASPLIT / MUSICALPIECES / BASKETBALLTEAMS / ATTICS SALTFREE / BRINE SKYS LORE / KONG PEAS MOUSY / ANG SOAP ARETHA / GALLERIES / CLERKS NERD JOB / HIRES MISS CARR / INRE GENT HOWIE / MEANDERS SORBET / PUTTINGUPAFRONT / PIERRELENFANT / CAKESANDALE

131

MAZELTOV ASTHMA / EMILIANO LUREIN / SANMATEO IDUNNO / STN READIES RID / ROIS SCORN MYMY / SLAPS TOA GAVIN / RIB EQUALIZE / FIBONACCISERIES / INNUENDO OLA / LSATS RNS SUBIC / LETS KOOKY XENA / ICU JAMMIES TER / NURSER ITSALIVE / GRAHAM COWHIDES / SELENA SWELTERS

132

CBS *OFFS SAW* / HIES URIAH OTIC / ETCH PENTA DADO / ETRE OSAKA BEV / CHEESES HORMONE / HECTOR TRIER / *YSPRINGFIELD / POLITIC / INTERSTELLAR* / CREED CELEBS / HITTUNE WHIPSUP / ADZ PENNE HOSE / LIES ADOBE ALTE / KURT LIVEN SEED / *MOP STAR* DRY

* = Dust

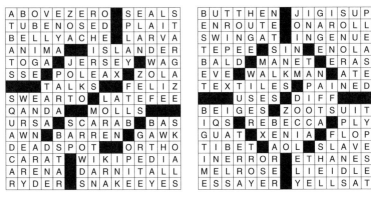

133

A	B	O	V	E	Z	E	R	O	█	S	E	A	L	S
T	U	B	E	N	O	S	E	D	█	P	L	A	I	T
B	E	L	L	Y	A	C	H	E	█	L	A	R	V	A
A	N	I	M	A	█	█	I	S	L	A	N	D	E	R
T	O	G	A	█	J	E	R	S	E	Y	█	W	A	G
S	S	E	█	P	O	L	E	A	X	█	Z	O	L	A
█	█	█	T	A	L	K	S	█	F	E	L	I	Z	█
S	W	E	A	R	T	O	█	L	A	T	E	F	E	E
Q	A	N	D	A	█	█	M	O	L	L	S	█	█	█
U	R	S	A	█	S	C	A	R	A	B	█	B	A	S
A	W	N	█	B	A	R	R	E	N	█	G	A	W	K
D	E	A	D	S	P	O	T	█	O	R	T	H	O	█
C	A	R	A	T	█	W	I	K	I	P	E	D	I	A
A	R	E	N	A	█	D	A	R	N	I	T	A	L	L
R	Y	D	E	R	█	S	N	A	K	E	E	Y	E	S

134

B	U	T	T	H	E	N	█	J	I	G	I	S	U	P
E	N	R	O	U	T	E	█	O	N	A	R	O	L	L
S	W	I	N	G	A	T	█	I	N	G	E	N	U	E
T	E	P	E	E	█	S	I	N	█	E	N	O	L	A
B	A	L	D	█	M	A	N	E	T	█	E	R	A	S
E	V	E	█	W	A	L	K	M	A	N	█	A	T	E
T	E	X	T	I	L	E	S	█	P	A	I	N	E	D
█	█	█	U	S	E	S	█	D	I	F	F	█	█	█
B	E	I	G	E	S	█	Z	O	O	T	S	U	I	T
I	Q	S	█	R	E	B	E	C	C	A	█	P	L	Y
G	U	A	T	█	X	E	N	I	A	█	F	L	O	P
T	I	B	E	T	█	A	O	L	█	S	L	A	V	E
I	N	E	R	R	O	R	█	E	T	H	A	N	E	S
M	E	L	R	O	S	E	█	L	I	E	I	D	L	E
E	S	S	A	Y	E	R	█	Y	E	L	L	S	A	T

135

A	B	E	V	I	G	O	D	A	█	I	D	T	A	G
N	I	N	E	L	I	V	E	S	█	N	A	I	V	E
G	O	D	S	A	V	E	T	H	E	Q	U	E	E	N
O	N	U	P	█	E	R	R	O	L	█	B	O	R	E
L	I	R	A	S	█	T	O	R	M	E	█	N	S	F
A	C	E	█	L	O	O	I	E	█	A	N	E	E	L
█	█	█	C	O	U	N	T	█	M	R	M	O	T	O
C	A	P	T	U	R	E	█	C	O	M	E	N	O	W
O	R	I	N	G	S	█	B	O	R	A	X	█	█	█
S	M	A	S	H	█	M	A	L	A	R	█	A	S	L
T	I	N	█	S	P	I	R	O	█	K	N	U	T	E
U	N	O	S	█	I	S	E	R	E	█	O	T	R	A
M	A	K	E	A	N	E	X	A	M	P	L	E	O	F
E	R	E	C	T	█	R	A	D	I	O	T	U	B	E
S	M	Y	T	H	█	S	M	O	L	D	E	R	E	D

136

T	H	E	F	O	N	Z	█	S	T	E	I	G	█	█
H	E	L	L	W	E	E	K	█	A	R	E	N	O	T
E	A	T	A	L	O	N	E	█	R	E	N	D	E	R
I	R	O	N	S	█	I	N	F	I	X	█	I	S	O
S	E	R	█	A	T	T	O	█	█	B	A	H	T	█
T	R	O	Y	█	C	H	U	R	N	█	R	I	O	T
█	█	█	A	P	T	█	C	A	L	L	O	N	M	E
A	N	A	K	I	N	S	K	Y	W	A	L	K	E	R
D	E	S	K	C	O	P	Y	█	E	M	I	█	█	█
J	O	S	E	█	W	A	D	E	S	█	N	A	S	L
O	N	E	D	█	T	E	X	T	█	F	L	U	█	█
I	L	S	█	Q	B	E	R	T	█	H	A	R	U	M
N	A	S	H	U	A	█	B	R	A	I	N	A	G	E
S	M	O	R	E	S	█	Y	A	R	D	S	I	G	N
█	P	R	E	S	S	█	█	S	P	E	E	D	O	S

137

E	Z	P	A	S	S			L	A	T	R	O	B	E
L	E	E	R	A	T		R	O	T	H	I	R	A	S
M	A	R	I	N	E	B	I	O	L	O	G	I	S	T
I	L	I	E	D		I	P	S	A		A	G	E	
R	O	S	S	I		B	L	E	S	S		I	P	O
A	T	H		E	U	L	E	R		L	A	N	A	I
			G	R	E	Y		N	O	B	A	I	L	
L	A	P	D	O	G	S		J	E	W	E	L	R	Y
S	N	E	E	Z	E		S	E	A	N				
A	S	K	T	O		T	I	T	L	E		S	I	S
T	W	O		O	P	E	N	S		W	H	I	N	E
	E	E	N		O	N	E	K		S	O	L	A	R
M	R	T	O	A	D	S	W	I	L	D	R	I	D	E
S	T	E	A	D	I	E	S		G	A	S	C	A	N
G	O	A	H	E	A	D			A	Y	E	A	Y	E

138

G	R	A	N	O	L	A	B	A	R		M	V	P	S
R	E	N	O	N	E	V	A	D	A		C	A	L	I
E	V	I	T	A	P	E	R	O	N		S	N	A	G
N	O	M	E		E	N	R	A	G	E		U	S	N
A	K	A		R	U	I	N		N	E	A	T	O	
D	E	L	T	S		E	O	N		V	O	T	E	R
E	S	S	A	Y	S		S	I	N	E	C	U	R	E
			T	R	A	P		E	R	L	E			
O	L	D	T	I	M	E	R		C	O	N	T	R	A
P	A	U	L	A		T	E	D		P	E	R	E	S
E	B	S	E	N		S	T	U	D		A	D	S	
N	E	T		S	A	T	I	R	E		B	I	D	E
B	L	U	E		H	O	R	O	S	C	O	P	E	R
A	L	P	S		E	R	E	C	T	O	R	S	E	T
R	E	S	T		M	E	S	S	E	N	G	E	R	S

139

M	R	B	O	J	A	N	G	L	E	S		B	B	S
A	I	R	F	O	R	C	E	O	N	E		A	R	T
P	L	A	Y	S	A	R	O	U	N	D		N	O	R
S	E	G	O			L	I	E	A	W	A	K	E	
		R	A	M	B	O	S		N	O	N	E	T	
S	P	E	E	D	B	A	G			M	A	R	C	
T	A	V		M	A	R	Y	J		H	A	R	S	H
A	R	I	D	E	S	T		E	M	A	N	A	T	E
T	A	L	O	N		H	A	D	I	T		M	I	R
E	M	I	L			W	I	N	E	S	A	P	S	
H	O	N	E	S		D	E	S	E	R	T			
O	U	T	D	A	T	E	S			U	F	O	S	
U	N	E		N	I	C	O	L	A	S	C	A	G	E
S	T	N		D	N	A	M	O	L	E	C	U	L	E
E	S	T		S	A	F	E	T	Y	Z	O	N	E	S

140

P	A	P	A	S	M	U	R	F		U	S	O	F	A
I	C	E	S	K	A	T	E	R		F	I	N	I	S
R	U	P	P	A	R	E	N	A		O	V	E	R	T
A	M	P	S		C	N	O	T	E		A	C	E	R
T	E	E		V	H	S		B	L	T		A	L	I
E	N	D		E	M	I		O	V	E	R	R	A	N
		H	E	A	L		Y	I	N	Y	A	N	G	
A	B	O	A	R	D			S	P	A	T	E	S	
C	Y	C	L	O	N	E		S	P	A	N			
I	G	O	O	F	E	D		I	R	S		B	B	B
D	E	T		F	S	U		G	E	T		R	E	L
R	O	I	L		S	C	A	N	S		B	A	M	A
A	R	L	E	S		A	P	O	L	L	O	V	I	I
I	G	L	O	O		T	I	R	E	I	R	O	N	S
N	E	O	N	S		E	A	S	Y	T	O	S	E	E

141

```
N E C E S S A R Y ■ C L A S H
O P O S I T I V E ■ L E N T O
M E L S D I N E R ■ E A G E R
O E D ■ E N G R ■ W A D E I N
■ S T O K E ■ T A V E R N S ■
C R O O N S ■ R O V E R ■ .
L A R U E ■ P O W E R B A S E
A G E R ■ S E L E S ■ O R E N
M U S I C H A L L ■ J A R E D
■ N A I L S ■ C A R O M S ■
O R I G I N S ■ A A N D W ■
H E L P M E ■ S L R S ■ H B O
A G O R A ■ G O T O S L E E P
R A N O N ■ I N E L E G A N T
A N A S S ■ S E R E N A D E S
```

142

```
C A M P H O R O I L ■ M I T A
U N I T A R I A N S ■ A P I N
R A T A T A T T A T ■ R O E G
A C T ■ S N A C K ■ M I D G E
T I E R ■ G R A N D C A N A L
E N N E ■ E D K O C H ■ A M P
■ F L Y ■ E T L A ■ N E I
O L D I E ■ ■ L O O S E
N Y U ■ D E B T ■ T E R ■
E N T ■ G O U R D E ■ D E C O
O X Y G E N B A R S ■ O D O R
R E F E R ■ B L A T S ■ I L E
T Y R E ■ P L A Z A H O T E L
W E E K ■ F E L I C I T O U S
O D E S ■ C R A Z Y H O R S E
```

143

```
E S T E R ■ E C O N ■ D A Z E
A H E A D ■ A H S O ■ E X I T
G R A S S S T A I N ■ B I T E
L E S T ■ M E T R O P O L I S
E D E L ■ A R T I S A N ■
■ D A I S I E S ■ R A J A H
S C H ■ S H E D ■ P R I O R I
T O A D I E S ■ Q U O R U M S
I D I O T S ■ C U L T ■ R S T
R E R U N ■ C A I S S O N ■
■ B O N A N Z A ■ N A P E
N E X T T O L A S T ■ A L L A
A C M E ■ M A S H E D P E A S
C H A R ■ A S T O ■ C A S T E
L O S S ■ S H A W ■ C R E E L
```

144

```
F L A S H L I G H T ■ A B C S
A U C T I O N E E R ■ B A H T
V I R A L V I D E O ■ S T A R
A S E ■ L E G S ■ T S E T S E
■ L A L O ■ S T A N L E E
P A S T R Y ■ S K I N T E S T
E N T R Y ■ T W E E D ■ M C C
P D A S ■ T R I E R ■ D E E R
E S T ■ A R E N T ■ P E N N E
L O I S L A N E ■ L A S T E D
E T C H A N T ■ W O R K ■
M O L A R S ■ G O A T ■ C P O
O B I S ■ E U R O D I S N E Y
K E N T ■ P R I Z E T A B L E
O D E A ■ T I N Y D A N C E R
```

145

M	A	R	K	C	U	B	A	N		E	L	F	I	N
A	T	A	N	Y	T	I	M	E		R	O	L	L	S
C	A	M	E	R	A	B	A	G		R	O	I	L	Y
A	R	E	A			N	E	V		S	P	A	N	
W	I	N	D	S		D	A	V	E	S		F	T	C
		H	A	I			H	A	I	L	E			
R	E	A	D	I	N	G	R	A	I	L	R	O	A	D
E	X	Q	U	I	S	I	T	E	C	O	R	P	S	E
C	O	U	N	T	O	N	E	S	L	O	S	S	E	S
	T	A	K	E	N			O	E	N				
C	I	V		S	I	G	E	P		S	A	L	E	M
A	C	E	D		A	O	L			S	U	M	O	
P	I	L	E	S		D	O	N	T	I	K	N	O	W
R	S	V	P	D		O	R	I	E	N	T	A	T	E
A	M	A	T	I		T	O	M	A	T	O	R	E	D

146

S	P	E	E	D	O			S	A	P	S	A	G	O
H	I	N	T	O	N		S	T	R	E	A	M	E	R
O	N	C	A	L	L		T	R	I	P	L	A	N	E
W	H	O	L	L	Y		R	O	S	S	E	T	T	I
M	O	M		A	C	T	I	V	E		P	E	E	L
A	L	I		R	H	O	D	E		G	R	U	E	L
N	E	A	P	T	I	D	E		F	A	I	R	L	Y
		A	R	L	O		M	A	R	C				
H	A	T	R	E	D		R	O	N	D	E	L	E	T
I	R	A	T	E		F	I	L	L	E		E	X	E
T	C	B	Y		V	E	B	L	E	N		S	H	E
H	A	L	F	M	I	L	E		T	H	R	O	A	T
O	D	I	O	U	S	L	Y		T	O	O	T	L	E
M	I	N	U	T	I	A	E		E	S	T	H	E	R
E	A	G	L	E	T	S			R	E	S	O	D	S

147

T	F	O	R	M	A	T	I	O	N		P	R	O	S
R	E	P	U	G	N	A	N	C	E		R	A	I	N
A	M	E	N	T	O	T	H	A	T		O	G	L	E
N	I	N	E		S	T	I	N	T		M	O	L	E
S	N	A			E	B	A	Y		Q	U	I	Z	
F	I	R	S		G	R	I	D		B	U	T	T	E
A	N	E	T		A	S	T	A	I	R	E			
T	E	A	A	C	T				P	R	E	V	I	N
		G	U	E	S	S	S	O		N	I	C	O	
J	U	D	G	E		C	A	W	S		S	T	E	T
E	R	I	E		G	A	Y	E				A	D	A
T	S	A	R		U	N	H	A	T		A	M	O	K
L	U	L	L		I	N	I	T	I	A	T	I	V	E
A	L	O	E		D	E	T	E	R	M	I	N	E	R
G	A	G	E		O	D	O	R	E	A	T	E	R	S

148

N	E	T	F	L	I	X		P	V	C	P	I	P	E
F	A	I	R	E	S	T		A	E	R	O	S	O	L
L	U	M	I	E	R	E		C	R	U	S	A	D	E
D	D	E		S	E	R	I	E	S	E		B	U	N
R	E	Z	A		D	R	A	C	O		J	E	N	A
A	V	O	W	S		A	M	A		B	A	L	K	S
F	I	N	A	L	S		B	R	A	U	N			
T	E	E	S	O	F	F		S	C	R	E	W	I	T
			H	O	O	E	Y		E	N	D	A	S	H
S	C	R	I	P		V	A	C		T	O	R	T	E
C	L	A	N		D	E	L	O	S		E	C	H	O
H	O	I		O	A	R	L	O	C	K		R	A	N
W	A	L	D	O	R	F		K	U	W	A	I	T	I
A	C	O	U	P	L	E		E	S	O	B	E	S	O
B	A	N	D	S	A	W		D	I	N	E	S	O	N

149

```
A S S O O N A S ■ B L E E P S
M A T A H A R I ■ B A L B O A
T H A T S R I D I C U L O U S
S L R ■ C L E M ■ R E A R S
■ S O L O S ■ T E E N T S Y
E R I C A ■ ■ D I L L S ■
L I G H T A F I R E ■ N E W
S E N S I T I V E N A T U R E
E N S ■ I N A D I L E M M A
■ ■ T I L E S ■ B A B A R
P O L E N T A ■ F R A M E ■
S P A N S ■ R O L E ■ R I P
H E Y D O N T L O O K A T M E
A R E O L E ■ D R I L L E R S
W A R N E D ■ S A L M I N E O
```

150

```
S P Y V S S P Y ■ C O C C I
T H E N A T I O N ■ B A R O N
P A M E L A S U E ■ S H A N T
E L E C T S ■ O W N S U P T O
T A N K S ■ O N T A P ■ P A N
E N I S ■ S A L ■ P O L I C E
R X S ■ C I T Y S T R E E T S
■ S A T E L L I T E ■
S A N A T O R I U M S ■ E L F
O N E M A N ■ V E E ■ C L E O
Y O W ■ T I R E D ■ C A N A L
B I S C O T T O ■ D A R I N G
E N D O N ■ E N D U R A N C E
A T A R I ■ S C E N E F O U R
N S Y N C ■ E Y E T E S T S
```

151

```
C L E W ■ H E A T D A M A G E
L A S H ■ E R R O R R A T E S
E S P Y ■ F R O N T A X L E S
O E R ■ E T O N ■ B A N A
P R E T Z E L ■ C A R A W A Y
A B S U R D ■ C H L O E ■
T E S T A ■ D E A D W R O N G
R A O ■ P O D I A ■ R O I
A M S T E R D A M ■ C H A S M
■ O N A I R ■ B O A T E L
R E C L A M E ■ L A P R O B E
I D O L ■ S E I S ■ R A T
C U R B A P P E A L ■ M I N E
O C E A N B O R N E ■ B O D Y
H E A R T S E A S E ■ E S S E
```

152

```
E N T E B B E ■ W H A T A M I
S I E R R A S ■ N O W I S E R
T E N N E S S E E W A L K E R
A C T I V E I N T E R E S T S
R E S E E D E D ■
■ Z A N I N E S S
S P A N I S H O M E L E T T E
E U R O P E A N T H E A T E R
C R E A S E R E S I S T A N T
O L D H A N D S ■
■ E A R H O L E S
R E A L E S T A T E A G E N T
I S E A G E R T O P L E A S E
S A O T O M E ■ M O V E S U P
K I N E S I S ■ S T A S H E S
```

153

```
P L A N B   T O T S     C C U P
E O L I A N H A R P     O R N E
P O I N D E X T E R     T E D S
E N T E R S   H O U S E P E T
      R A C E S   C A D E T
R A M   P A X   S E R A P E S
A V I S   F I J I   O Z A R K
J A C Q U E L I N E D U P R E
A S K U P   E M I R   R E E D
S T E A D E D   S A S   R D S
  M Y R O N   H E S H E
S A F E S I D E   M A L O N E
A T I C   G A S G U Z Z L E R
R E N U   M I S S S A I G O N
G Y N T   A S E A   M E A N S
```

154

```
T H E T H I N G I S     E N O W
S O C I A L C A L L     L O R I
A N O T H E R D A Y     I W O N
R E L O A N     E L A Y N E
      S E W E R     A H O O T
C A S E   S E R U M S   U M A
E L M S T   B A B U S H K A S
A L A M O D E   I M E A N I T
S A L E M S L O T   S T O N E
E N L   C L O R I S   E W E R
F A T H A   S E N O R
I D I O T S     R E G A L E
R A M S   U T N E R E A D E R
E L E E   R A G G E D Y A N N
S E R A   G O O G L Y E Y E S
```

155

```
  A S P C A     C A M P E D
I N T E R N S   R E C A R V E
C O R R U G A T E D S T E E L
E D I T S   M I C E   A C R E
R E V E T   I N T   H O Y T
  S E R A   S T O A   A L O E
    C R E E   B O R O N S
  C O M E U N D E R F I R E
H A B E A S   G R A F
E L S A   E L L O   C O D S
P L O T   E A T   A W A C S
T A L C   S I S I   M E N A T
A H E A D O F S C H E D U L E
D A T S U N S   A E R O B A T
S N E E Z Y     S A N E R
```

156

```
S H E B A N G   S T J A M E S
R O T A T O R   Y A R D A G E
T R U S T M E   M T S I N A I
A D D I S A B A B A   D I N S
S E E N   D E L I   V A C
    G D S   J O E I S U Z U
C O W E R   E A S Y A   R A P
F L O R E N Z Z I E G F E L D
O I L   S T I E S   R O D E O
S O F T S H O E   T A L
  S H Y   P R E S   D I E M
R E B A   G I A N T P A N D A
O V A T I O N   G R A B B A G
B E N I T E Z   R A N L A T E
O L E S T R A   S P E E D E E
```

157

B	E	F	O	R	E	T	H	E	O	T	H	E	R	S
I	T	A	L	I	A	N	A	L	P	H	A	B	E	T
G	I	R	L	F	R	O	M	I	P	A	N	E	M	A
D	E	M	I	T	■	T	A	C	■	D	O	R	A	G
O	N	C	E	■	B	E	N	I	N	■	I	L	I	E
S	N	L	■	B	U	S	■	T	U	G	■	E	N	D
■	E	U	L	E	R	■	D	E	C	R	Y	■	■	■
■	■	B	E	A	R	D	E	D	L	A	D	Y	■	■
■	■	■	O	D	I	U	M	■	E	P	S	O	M	■
U	N	A	■	S	T	N	■	H	U	E	■	D	O	L
S	O	P	S	■	O	K	R	A	S	■	B	E	N	E
B	R	I	T	T	■	T	A	S	■	S	A	L	T	S
A	M	E	R	I	C	A	N	S	T	U	D	I	E	S
N	I	C	O	T	I	N	E	L	O	Z	E	N	G	E
K	E	E	P	O	N	K	E	E	P	I	N	G	O	N

158

H	A	D	D	■	I	B	S	■	S	T	A	P	L	E	R
O	N	E	O	C	A	T	■	P	A	L	E	A	L	E
T	A	T	T	E	R	Y	■	A	R	B	O	R	E	D
T	H	E	E	D	G	E	■	S	T	E	P	D	A	D
E	E	N	S	I	E	■	■	A	R	L	E	N	E
S	I	T	O	N	I	T	■	E	N	T	E	R	O	N
T	M	E	N	■	N	A	I	L	S	■	S	S	R	S
■	■	■	B	O	G	■	■	■
N	I	L	S	■	E	O	S	I	N	■	M	O	S	H
O	N	A	T	E	A	R	■	N	O	T	A	L	I	E
W	A	G	I	N	G	■	■	N	I	K	O	L	A
W	R	A	N	G	L	E	■	C	H	E	E	R	E	D
H	U	S	K	I	E	R	■	L	E	S	S	O	N	S
A	S	S	E	N	T	S	■	A	R	T	I	S	T	E
T	H	E	R	E	S	T	■	R	O	O	T	O	U	T

159

S	T	E	P	F	A	T	H	E	R	■	M	A	N	S
N	I	N	E	O	N	E	O	N	E	■	A	M	O	I
A	T	T	E	N	D	A	N	T	S	■	N	O	T	E
P	L	E	N	T	Y	M	O	R	E	■	I	R	A	S
P	I	N	S	■	■	E	R	O	T	I	C	I	S	T
E	N	T	■	S	T	R	E	P	■	C	O	S	T	A
A	G	E	L	E	S	S	■	Y	V	E	T	T	E	S
■	■	A	A	A	■	L	A	T	■
A	N	T	W	E	R	P	■	T	A	X	I	C	A	B
S	E	A	L	A	■	R	I	O	D	E	■	L	T	R
S	U	P	E	R	H	E	R	O	■	S	O	T	O
I	T	I	S	■	O	P	E	R	A	M	U	S	I	C
G	R	O	S	■	H	A	N	D	C	A	M	E	R	A
N	A	C	L	■	O	R	I	E	N	T	A	T	E	D
S	L	A	Y	■	S	E	C	R	E	T	C	O	D	E

160

B	R	A	D	S	H	A	W	■	P	R	I	S	M	S
D	E	V	I	L	I	S	H	■	A	D	R	I	A	N
A	V	E	M	A	R	I	A	■	C	A	S	T	R	O
L	E	N	■	B	E	A	T	L	E	S	■	U	A	R
T	N	U	T	■	E	N	S	O	R	■	H	A	N	K
O	G	E	E	S	■	S	T	Y	■	B	I	T	T	E
N	E	S	T	L	E	■	H	A	D	A	M	E	A	L
■	■	H	O	R	S	E	L	E	S	S	■	■
F	I	R	E	B	O	M	B	■	L	I	E	S	T	O
O	M	A	R	S	■	E	I	N	■	E	L	L	E	R
R	P	M	S	■	M	A	G	I	C	■	F	O	R	D
G	A	P	■	M	A	R	I	N	E	R	■	G	R	E
I	N	A	B	I	T	■	D	O	R	A	M	A	A	R
V	E	N	I	C	E	■	E	N	T	R	A	N	C	E
E	L	T	O	R	O	■	A	S	S	E	S	S	E	D

161

S	P	A	C	E	C	R	A	F	T	■	A	M	O	S
H	E	L	L	O	H	E	L	L	O	■	M	O	L	T
I	N	S	I	N	U	A	T	E	S	■	O	N	M	E
A	T	O	M	I	C	■	■	W	I	R	E	T	A	P
■	■	B	A	K	E	D	■	R	U	B	E	N	S	■
A	R	S	O	N	■	X	I	S	■	B	A	S	R	A
D	O	W	N	■	P	A	S	T	E	L	■	S	I	S
I	L	E	■	J	A	C	C	U	S	E	■	O	V	I
O	L	E	■	U	N	T	A	C	K	■	M	R	E	D
S	E	T	O	N	■	A	R	C	■	Z	A	I	R	E
A	D	E	P	T	S	■	D	O	T	E	R	■	■	■
M	O	N	T	A	N	A	■	■	R	A	S	S	L	E
I	V	E	S	■	I	N	O	C	U	L	A	T	O	R
G	E	R	T	■	P	I	N	A	C	O	L	A	D	A
O	R	S	O	■	S	T	A	T	E	T	A	X	E	S

162

P	A	L	M	■	G	I	F	T	E	D	K	I	D	S
O	M	O	O	■	I	N	S	I	D	E	I	N	F	O
L	A	C	E	■	G	U	T	T	E	R	B	A	L	L
E	R	A	S	■	G	R	A	I	N	■	O	L	A	V
M	I	L	■	A	L	E	R	■	■	S	I	T	E	■
I	L	L	B	R	E	D	■	D	U	C	H	E	S	S
C	L	A	R	E	T	■	H	U	G	O	■	■	■	■
S	O	W	O	N	E	S	W	I	L	D	O	A	T	S
■	■	A	S	H	Y	■	Y	E	O	M	A	N	■	■
I	L	P	O	S	T	O	■	U	S	R	O	U	T	E
N	E	A	T	■	■	U	P	C	S	■	D	E	A	■
P	E	S	O	■	P	A	R	L	E	■	D	A	R	K
A	L	C	O	H	O	L	B	A	N	■	A	R	T	S
R	E	A	L	E	S	T	A	T	E	■	B	Y	O	B
T	E	L	E	P	H	O	N	E	S	■	O	A	T	Y

163

S	H	E	A	R	S	■	S	A	W	H	O	R	S	E
N	E	X	T	U	P	■	I	C	E	Q	U	E	E	N
O	R	T	E	G	A	■	T	H	E	S	T	A	N	D
W	O	R	M	S	■	C	U	E	S	■	E	M	T	S
S	N	A	P	■	G	O	A	F	T	E	R	■	■	■
■	L	O	S	E	S	T	O	■	L	E	A	P	T	■
D	N	A	■	C	A	T	E	R	■	P	A	T	I	O
E	A	R	N	E	R	■	■	F	A	R	I	N	A	■
L	T	G	E	N	■	A	P	L	U	S	■	M	E	T
L	O	E	W	E	■	I	R	O	N	O	R	E	■	■
■	D	I	A	M	O	N	D	■	A	T	O	B	■	■
A	R	T	E	■	L	E	V	I	■	C	R	O	N	E
P	O	O	L	S	I	D	E	■	L	I	E	D	E	R
S	U	S	H	I	B	A	R	■	E	N	S	I	L	E
E	X	H	I	B	I	T	B	■	I	Q	T	E	S	T

164

G	L	E	E	C	L	U	B	■	A	L	B	E	D	O
F	O	X	G	L	O	V	E	■	B	E	A	R	U	P
O	R	I	G	I	N	A	L	■	D	A	T	I	V	E
R	E	S	H	O	E	■	I	S	U	R	E	C	A	N
C	A	T	E	S	■	J	E	L	L	■	A	I	L	S
E	L	S	A	■	L	E	V	I	■	A	U	D	I	E
■	■	D	I	A	Z	E	P	A	M	■	L	E	A	■
G	E	T	S	O	R	E	■	S	U	F	F	E	R	S
U	G	O	■	L	A	B	O	H	E	M	E	■	■	■
N	O	L	T	E	■	E	C	O	L	■	A	H	A	B
S	M	E	W	■	F	L	E	D	■	P	R	I	M	E
M	A	R	I	P	O	S	A	■	M	E	S	S	R	S
I	N	A	N	E	R	■	N	E	U	R	O	S	I	S
T	I	N	G	E	D	■	U	L	T	I	M	A	T	E
H	A	T	E	R	S	■	S	K	E	L	E	T	A	L

165

S	C	R	A	P	E	■	P	O	S	T	C	A	R	D
T	I	E	D	I	N	■	L	I	M	A	O	H	I	O
E	V	A	D	E	D	■	A	L	A	N	L	A	D	D
P	I	N	■	R	E	I	N	■	R	O	T	T	E	D
C	L	I	■	C	A	N	T	A	T	A	S	■	■	■
H	U	M	P	E	R	D	I	N	C	K	■	D	E	S
A	N	A	I	S	■	I	N	G	A	■	G	R	I	T
N	I	T	E	■	W	A	G	E	R	■	R	A	G	A
G	O	E	S	■	I	N	T	L	■	T	I	G	H	T
E	N	D	■	O	N	A	H	I	G	H	N	O	T	E
■	■	E	M	I	N	E	N	C	E	■	N	O	T	■
O	M	E	L	E	T	■	S	A	L	T	■	F	U	R
B	I	G	A	R	A	D	E	■	E	R	M	I	N	E
I	C	A	N	T	L	I	E	■	F	I	E	R	C	E
S	A	N	D	A	L	E	D	■	S	P	R	E	E	S

The New York Times

Crossword Puzzles

The #1 Name in Crosswords

Available at your local bookstore or online at nytimes.com/nytstore

New This Season!

Little Luxe Book of Crosswords	0-312-38622-2
The Crossword Connoisseur	0-312-38627-3
Ready, Set, Solve! Crosswords	0-312-38623-0
Tension-Taming Crosswords	0-312-38624-9
Crosswords 101	0-312-38619-2
Large-Print Crossword Omnibus Vol. 9	0-312-38620-6
Sunday Crossword Puzzles Vol. 34	0-312-38635-4
Double Flip Book of the New York Times Crosswords and Sudoku	0-312-38635-4
Sunday Delight Crosswords	0-312-38626-5

Special Editions

1,001 Crossword Puzzles to Do Right Now	0-312-38253-7
Crosswords to Keep Your Brain Young	0-312-37658-8
Little Black (and White) Book of Crosswords	0-312-36105-X
The Joy of Crosswords	0-312-37510-7
Little Red and Green Book of Crosswords	0-312-37661-8
Little Flip Book of Crosswords	0-312-37043-1
How to Conquer the New York Times Crossword Puzzle	0-312-36554-3
Will Shortz's Favorite Crossword Puzzles	0-312-30613-X
Will Shortz's Favorite Sunday Crossword Puzzles	0-312-32488-X
Will Shortz's Greatest Hits	0-312-34242-X
Will Shortz Presents Crosswords for 365 Days	0-312-36121-1
Will Shortz's Funniest Crossword Puzzles	0-312-32489-8
Will Shortz's Funniest Crossword Puzzles Vol. 2	0-312-33960-7
Will Shortz's Xtreme Xwords	0-312-35203-4
Vocabulary Power Crosswords	0-312-35199-2

Daily Crosswords

Fitness for the Mind Crosswords Vol. 2	0-312-35278-6
Fitness for the Mind Crosswords Vol. 1	0-312-34955-6
Crosswords for the Weekend	0-312-34332-9
Daily Crossword Puzzles Vol. 72	0-312-35260-3
Daily Crossword Puzzles Vol. 71	0-312-34858-4

Daily Crossword Puzzles Volumes 57–70 also available.

Easy Crosswords

Easy Crossword Puzzles Vol. 9	0-312-37831-9
Easy Crossword Puzzles Vol. 8	0-312-36558-6
Easy Crossword Puzzles Vol. 7	0-312-35261-1

Easy Crossword Puzzles Volumes 2–6 also available.

Tough Crosswords

Tough Crossword Puzzles Vol. 13	0-312-34240-3
Tough Crossword Puzzles Vol. 12	0-312-32442-1
Tough Crossword Puzzles Vol. 11	0-312-31456-6

Tough Crossword Puzzles Volumes 9–10 also available.

Sunday Crosswords

Sunday in the Sand Crosswords	0-312-38269-3
Simply Sunday Crosswords	0-312-34243-8
Sunday in the Park Crosswords	0-312-35197-6
Sunday Morning Crossword Puzzles	0-312-35672-2
Everyday Sunday Crossword Puzzles	0-312-36106-8
Sunday Brunch Crosswords	0-312-36557-8
Sunday at the Seashore Crosswords	0-312-37070-9
Sleepy Sunday Crossword Puzzles	0-312-37508-5
Sunday's Best	0-312-37637-5
Sunday at Home Crosswords	0-312-37834-3
Sunday Crossword Puzzles Vol. 33	0-312-37507-7
Sunday Crossword Puzzles Vol. 32	0-312-36066-5
Sunday Crossword Puzzles Vol. 31	0-312-34862-2

Large-Print Crosswords

Large-Print Big Book of Holiday Crosswords	0-312-33092-8
Large-Print Crosswords for a Brain Workout	0-312-32612-2
Large-Print Crosswords for Your Coffee Break	0-312-33109-6
Large-Print Will Shortz's Favorite Crossword Puzzles	0-312-33959-3
Large-Print Crosswords to Boost Your Brainpower	0-312-32037-X
Large-Print Daily Crossword Puzzles Vol. 2	0-312-33111-8
Large-Print Daily Crossword Puzzles	0-312-31457-4
Large-Print Crosswords for Your Bedside	0-312-34245-4
Large-Print Big Book of Easy Crosswords	0-312-33958-5
Large-Print Easy Crossword Omnibus Vol. 1	0-312-32439-1
Large-Print Crossword Puzzle Omnibus Vol. 8	0-312-37514-X
Large-Print Crossword Puzzle Omnibus Vol. 7	0-312-36125-4
Large-Print Crossword Puzzle Omnibus Vol. 6	0-312-34861-4

Omnibus

Weekend in the Country	0-312-38270-7
Crosswords for Two	0-312-37830-0
Crosswords for a Relaxing Weekend	0-312-37829-7
Easy to Not-So-Easy Crossword Puzzle Omnibus Vol. 2	0-312-37832-7
Easy to Not-So-Easy Crossword Omnibus Vol. 1	0-312-37516-6
Crosswords for a Lazy Afternoon	0-312-34247-0
Lazy Weekend Crossword Puzzle Omnibus	0-312-35279-4
Lazy Sunday Crossword Puzzle Omnibus	0-312-33533-4
Big Book of Holiday Crosswords	0-312-34927-0
Giant Book of Holiday Crosswords	0-312-31622-4
Ultimate Crossword Omnibus	

Tough Crossword Puzzle Omnibus Vol. 1	0-312-32441-3
Crossword Challenge	0-312-33951-8
Crosswords for a Weekend Getaway	0-312-35198-4
Biggest Beach Crossword Omnibus	0-312-35667-6
Weekend Away Crossword Puzzle Omnibus	0-312-35669-2
Weekend at Home Crossword Puzzle Omnibus	0-312-35670-6
Holiday Cheer Crossword Puzzles	0-312-36126-2
Crosswords for a Long Weekend	0-312-36560-8
Crosswords for a Relaxing Vacation	0-312-36694-9
Will Shortz Presents Fun in the Sun Crossword Puzzle Omnibus	0-312-37041-5
Sunday Crossword Omnibus Vol. 9	0-312-35666-8
Sunday Crossword Omnibus Vol. 8	0-312-32440-5
Sunday Crossword Omnibus Vol. 7	0-312-30950-3
Easy Crossword Puzzle Omnibus Vol. 6	0-312-38287-1
Easy Crossword Puzzle Omnibus Vol. 5	0-312-36123-8
Easy Crossword Puzzle Omnibus Vol. 4	0-312-34859-2
Crossword Puzzle Omnibus Vol. 16	0-312-36104-1
Crossword Puzzle Omnibus Vol. 15	0-312-34856-8
Crossword Puzzle Omnibus Vol. 14	0-312-33534-2
Supersized Book of Easy Crosswords	0-312-35277-8
Supersized Book of Sunday Crosswords	0-312-36122-X

Previous volumes also available.

Variety Puzzles

Acrostic Puzzles Vol. 10	0-312-34853-3
Acrostic Puzzles Vol. 9	0-312-30949-X
Sunday Variety Puzzles	0-312-30059-X

Portable Size Format

The Puzzlemaster's Choice	0-312-38271-5
In the Kitchen Crosswords	0-312-38259-6
Think Outside the Box Crosswords	0-312-38261-8
Big Book of Easy Crosswords	0-312-38268-5
Real Simple Crosswords	0-312-38254-5
Crosswords by the Bay	0-312-38267-7
Crosswords for Your Coffee Break	0-312-28830-1
Sun, Sand and Crosswords	0-312-30076-X
Weekend Challenge	0-312-30079-4
Crosswords for the Holidays	0-312-30603-2
Crosswords for the Work Week	0-312-30952-X
Crosswords for Your Beach Bag	0-312-31455-8
Crosswords to Boost Your Brainpower	0-312-32033-7
Cuddle Up with Crosswords	0-312-37636-7
C Is for Crosswords	0-312-37509-3
Crazy for Crosswords	0-312-37513-1
Crosswords for a Mental Edge	0-312-37069-5
Favorite Day Crosswords: Tuesday	0-312-37072-5
Afternoon Delight Crosswords	0-312-37071-7
Crosswords Under the Covers	0-312-37044-X
Crosswords for the Beach	0-312-37073-3
Will Shortz Presents I Love Crosswords	0-312-37040-7
Will Shortz Presents Crosswords to Go	0-312-36695-7
Favorite Day Crosswords: Monday	0-312-36556-X
Crosswords in the Sun	0-312-36555-1
Expand Your Mind Crosswords	0-312-36553-5
After Dinner Crosswords	0-312-36559-4
Groovy Crossword Puzzles from the '60s	0-312-36103-3
Piece of Cake Crosswords	0-312-36124-6
Carefree Crosswords	0-312-36102-5
Fast and Easy Crossword Puzzles	0-312-35629-3
Backyard Crossword Puzzles	0-312-35668-4
Easy Crossword Puzzles for Lazy Hazy Crazy Days	0-312-35267-4
Brainbuilder Crosswords	0-312-35276-X
Stress-Buster Crosswords	0-312-35196-8
Super Saturday Crosswords	0-312-30604-0
Café Crosswords	0-312-34854-1
Crosswords for Your Lunch Hour	0-312-34857-6
Easy as Pie Crossword Puzzles	0-312-34331-0
Crosswords to Soothe Your Soul	0-312-34244-6
More Quick Crosswords	0-312-34246-2
Beach Blanket Crosswords	0-312-34250-0
Crosswords to Beat the Clock	0-312-35954-2
Crosswords for a Rainy Day	0-312-33952-6
Crosswords for Stress Relief	0-312-33953-4
Cup of Crosswords	0-312-33955-0
Crosswords to Exercise Your Brain	0-312-33536-9
Crosswords for Your Breakfast Table	0-312-33535-0
More Crosswords for Your Bedside	0-312-33612-8
T.G.I.F. Crosswords	0-312-33116-9
Quick Crosswords	0-312-33114-2
Planes, Trains and Crosswords	0-312-33113-4
More Sun, Sand and Crosswords	0-312-33112-6
Crosswords for a Brain Workout	0-312-32610-6
A Cup of Tea Crosswords	0-312-32435-9
Crosswords for Your Bedside	0-312-32032-0
Coffee Break Crosswords	0-312-37515-9
Rise and Shine Crossword Puzzles	0-312-37833-5
Coffee, Tea or Crosswords	0-312-37828-9
Will Shortz Presents I Love Crosswords Vol. 2	0-312-37837-8
Sweet Dreams Crosswords	0-312-37836-X

Other volumes also available.

St. Martin's Griffin